Mariam Daud has built a devoted social media following by sharing beautifully prepared, comforting meals that feel both timeless and entirely her own—from cherished classics like her mother's irresistible **Cheese Fatayer,** a traditional, savory cheese-stuffed pastry to her takes on everyday favorites like **Triple-Stack Smash Burgers** or tender, pull-apart **Cinnamon Rolls.**

And here, in *I Sleep in My Kitchen,* Mariam shares the flavors she grew up with in her Palestinian American home, including celebratory dishes like **Msakhan,** the national dish of Palestine made with soft flatbread, caramelized onions, tender stewed chicken, and toasted pine nuts, alongside playful recipes infused with Middle Eastern flavors, like her **Tahini and Browned Butter Banana Bread**.

Spanning breakfasts, small plates, salads, soups, mains, and her signature sweet and savory baked goods, this collection is an invitation to cook with generosity and curiosity, to explore the food that connects us to memory, place, and one another.

I Sleep in My Kitchen

I Sleep in My Kitchen

COMFORT FOOD RECIPES FROM MY PALESTINIAN AMERICAN HOME

Mariam Daud

with Emily Timberlake

PHOTOGRAPHS BY JIM HENKENS

CLARKSON POTTER/PUBLISHERS
New York

TO THE PEOPLE OF GAZA:

I hope I make you proud.

To the martyrs:

إِنَّا لِلَّهِ وَإِنَّا إِلَيْهِ رَاجِعونَ

Indeed, to God we belong and to God we shall return.

Contents

Introduction 9

Ingredients & Equipment 13

Breakfast & Brunch

Buttermilk Pancakes 18

Kishta and Pistachio-Stuffed French Toast 21

Sweet Banana Cream Pudding Crepes 23

French Toast Bake with Walnut Filling 27

Croissant Breakfast Sandwiches 28

Batata o Baid *(Eggs with Curry-Spiced Potatoes)* 31

Shakshuka 32

Smoked Salmon and Pepper Jelly Pastry 34

Tomato Galette with Za'atar 37

Caramelized Onion Ratatouille Tart 39

Small Plates

Mama's Homemade Hummus 45

Ful Medames with Tatbila *(Favas with Jalapeño Sauce)* 46

Khiyar bi Laban *(Cucumber Yogurt Dip)* 49

Baba Ghanoush-Stuffed Eggplant 50

Falafel 53

Sambosas 54

Kibbeh *(Beef and Bulgur-Stuffed Shells)* 57

The Middle Eastern Charcuterie Board 60

Salads & Sides

Crispy Potato Salad with Greens 65

Fattoush *(Fried Bread Salad)* 66

Mediterranean Pasta Salad with Sumac Vinaigrette 69

Roasted Squash with Pine Nuts and Tahini 70

Loaded Chickpea Salad with Lemon-Garlic Shrimp 73

Burrata Salad with Steak and Labneh Chimichurri 74

Soups & Stews

Addas *(Creamy Lentil Soup)* 79

Spiced Butternut Squash Soup 80

French Onion Soup 83

Clam Chowder 84

Chicken Noodle Soup 87

Creamy Chicken Gnocchi Soup 88

Tomato Soup with Garlic-Bread Grilled Cheese 91

Shishbarak *(Beef Dumplings in Yogurt Sauce)* 93

Molokhia *(Mallow Stew with Chicken)* 97

Bamia *(Okra Stewed in Tomato Sauce with Lamb)* 99

Pasta & Rice

Three-Cheese Creamy Baked Mac and Cheese 102

Roasted Yellow Pepper Pasta 105

Macarona Béchamel *(Egyptian-Style Pasta Bake)* 106

Pasta with Mussels and Shrimp 109

Vermicelli Rice 110

Oozi *(Spiced Rice with Beef, Peas, and Carrots)* 113

Maklouba *(Upside-Down Rice with Chicken Legs)* 114

Mansaf *(Rice with Lamb and Fermented Yogurt Sauce)* 117

Warak Dawali *(Stuffed Grape Leaves with Beef Ribs)* 122

Seafood, Poultry & Meat

Bang Bang Shrimp Tacos with Cabbage Slaw 127

Spiced Jumbo Crab Cakes with Lemon Aioli 128

Teriyaki Salmon with Mango Salsa and Quinoa 131

Slow-Roasted Jalapeño Salmon with Citrus Chimichurri 132

Pan-Seared Lemon-Caper Sea Bass 135

Chicken Shawarma Wraps 136

Msakhan *(Flatbread with Chicken, Sumac, and Caramelized Onions)* 139

Garlic-Parmesan Fried Chicken Sandwiches 142
Buttermilk-Brined Chicken and Waffle Sliders 144
Mini Chicken Alfredo Pizzas (fan fave) 148
Sumac and Lemon Roast Chicken with Tahini Salad 151
Cast-Iron Chicken with Tarragon, Olives, and Charred Lemon 153
Lamb Shoulder with Labneh and Fennel-Orange Glaze 155
Surf and Turf with Filet Mignon and Crab-Stuffed Lobster 157
Saniyeh Kofta *(Beef Patties in Tomato Sauce)* 161
Triple-Stack Smash Burgers (fan fave) 162
Marinated Brisket with Olive and Fig Tapenade 165

Breads & Savory Baked Goods

Pita Bread (fan fave) 168
Khubiz Taboon *(Traditional Palestinian Flatbread)* (fan fave) 172
Cast-Iron Sourdough Focaccia 176
Ka'ak al-Quds *(Jerusalem Bread)* (fan fave) 179
Fluffy Japanese Milk Bread 181
Sourdough Loaf 184
Brioche Buns 191
Fluffy Browned Butter Rolls with Flaky Sea Salt 193
Honey-Butter Cast-Iron Cornbread 197
Feta-Chive Buttermilk Biscuits with Roasted Garlic Butter 198
Homemade Garlic Knots 201
Mozzarella-Stuffed Pull-Apart Bread (fan fave) 202
Everything Bagels (fan fave) 205
Za'atar Soft Pretzels 207
Za'atar Manakeesh *(Za'atar Flatbread)* (fan fave) 211
Sfeeha *(Open-Faced Meat and Pine Nut Pies)* 213
Cheese Fatayer (fan fave) 217

Sweets & Desserts

Tahini and Browned Butter Banana Bread 220
Cinnamon Rolls (fan fave) 223
Old-Fashioned Sour Cream Donuts 225
Choose-Your-Own-Adventure Brioche Donuts 229
Apple Fritters 230
"Generational" Chocolate Chip Cookies 233
Ma'amoul *(Date-Stuffed Butter Cookies)* 234
Katayef *(Fried Stuffed "Pancakes")* 237
Perfect Fudge Brownies (fan fave) 240
Knafeh Kishna *(Sweet Cheese Pie)* 243
Awamah *(Fried Dough Balls in Orange Blossom Simple Syrup)* 245
Riz bi Haleeb *(Rich and Creamy Rice Pudding)* 246
Apple and Apricot Galette with Maple Crème Fraîche 249
Mtabouk *(Sweet Layered Pastry)* 250
Carrot Cake Loaf with Cream Cheese Frosting (fan fave) 253
Blueberry, Basil, and Lemon Olive Oil Loaf Cake 256
Chocolatey Tiramisu Cake 259
Raspberry Cheesecake (fan fave) 261
Chocoflan (fan fave) 263

Acknowledgments 266

Index 267

Introduction

If you lived in the Cleveland area in the early 2000s and happened to visit a restaurant called the Pyramid, then there's a very good chance you've been in a room with me and my family. My parents owned and operated the restaurant from 1996 to 2004, but that's really underselling their roles . . . they *were* the restaurant. They had a small handful of employees—a dishwasher, an occasional prep cook, and a couple of servers—but apart from that, they did all the cooking and hosting themselves.

While you were there, did you notice several babies napping in their car seats in the corner of the back room? Or teens and preteens folding napkins and drying silverware? Was there a handful of rambunctious five- to seven-year-olds running around your table or a toddler on the hip of the woman bringing you delicious Middle Eastern food? That woman was my mother, and the kids were me and my nine (yes, you read that right—nine!) siblings. In case you were wondering, I was the five-year-old scampering about, pretending to be helpful.

I'm the third-youngest in my family, so my memory of the Pyramid is quite faded compared to that of my older siblings. But I can still say that I'm proud to have grown up in a restaurant family, and I know that the experience shaped who I am today. My earliest memories are of my parents working so hard to feed my family and our community. When they had to sell the restaurant, there was even a time when my dad had to move away, to Pittsburgh, to earn a living. While he saved up enough money to move us all to join him, my mom was essentially a single mom, raising and feeding us all while my dad supported us from afar.

You may have heard that professional chefs do not like to cook at home, preferring instead to eat frozen dinners or delivery pizza. Well, that never applied to my mama. At home, she made *everything* from scratch. I don't think she touched a canned chickpea during my entire childhood. She always boiled big pots of dried chickpeas that she had soaked overnight, then stored leftovers in the freezer.

To this day, Mama is an incredible cook; she set the bar very high for me. But when I think about the most important lessons she taught me, I don't necessarily think about recipes. Instead, I think about her entire approach to cooking and hospitality—for her, the *spirit* in which food is shared is as important as the food itself. For example, if you walked up to my mom and asked her for the recipe for one of the dishes you'd enjoyed, she'd burst into a big smile and immediately write it down for you. I cannot imagine her *not* giving away a recipe to someone who asked. She loves teaching people about her food and her culture; that is why there are no "secret recipes" in our family.

At home, Mom was always the head chef, but from the time we were very young, we were her enthusiastic (but also not-so-enthusiastic) sous-chefs. It took a lot of work to feed a family of twelve, so we all pitched in where we could. Many of my favorite childhood memories involve me and my sisters standing around our kitchen island, arranged like a factory assembly line. Mom would prepare a big bowl of kibbeh filling (see page 57), and it was our job to press out and stuff the shells, then arrange them neatly on a tray for her to finish frying. I'd be lying if I said I was an expert from the very start—my mom definitely circled back to the kibbeh I shaped and filled on the sheet and "adjusted" them a bit to meet her standards. (Let's be real, they most definitely needed the help.) Other days, Mom would set out a bowl of sweet walnut- and coconut-studded katayef filling (see page 237), then she'd cook pancakes on a griddle and toss them onto a big tablecloth. From there, we'd spoon the filling into the pancakes, press them closed, and arrange them on a sheet pan so she could fry or bake them later.

I am the proud daughter of Palestinian immigrants, and sharing recipes that were passed down to me by my Palestinian mother is my life's greatest honor. This work feels especially important now, as my people have been the victims of horrific, genocidal violence. As you are reading this, there are men, women, and children in Gaza who are struggling not only to put food on their tables but also to find basic necessities like clothing and clean water. Entire families—entire communities—have been killed, with generations of their history eradicated in a single moment.

My mother has always encouraged me to share family recipes, because it plays a vital role in preserving our culture—a culture that is very much at risk of being lost forever. For me, sharing recipes is a way to give Palestine a voice, to honor our heritage and traditions. I am sharing this deeply personal part of my life with you because I hope that as you cook through the recipes in this book, as you share them with your friends and family, you hold the Palestinian people in your heart. I believe that celebrating Palestinian cooking and culture is a form of resistance—a way to announce to the world that we are still here, that our lives and stories matter, and that we will not be silenced.

About This Book

One of the hardest things about writing this cookbook was narrowing down the recipe list to just one hundred dishes. I felt like I could write an entire cookbook *just* about savory baking, or desserts, or the traditional Palestinian dishes I grew up with. In the end, I decided to combine all of my passions. So you'll find very traditional Arab desserts like knafeh, a pie that is popular across the Levant and known for its crunchy, flaky crust topped with decadent melty cheese and sweet sugar syrup (see page 243), alongside American classics like chocolate chip cookies.

This book also has lots of "back-pocket" recipes—by that I mean the type of recipe you should always have on hand (or in your back pocket), for those days when you need the comfort of a classic chicken noodle soup or clam chowder. But these back-pocket recipes are far from boring. They are the product of me obsessively testing and retesting different versions to find the absolute best. My goal is you should never have to Google "chicken noodle soup recipe" and take your chances on some random recipe ever again!

I titled this book *I Sleep in My Kitchen* because when I first launched my social media pages, I was developing recipes around the clock. I was twenty years old, and I was more than just passionate about cooking—I was obsessed! And I could never predict when inspiration would strike. One night, I might be watching a Studio Ghibli movie, then I'd decide that I *had* to bake a cake, even though it was 12:00 a.m. If a recipe I'd been working on didn't turn out well, I might jump out of bed at 2:00 a.m.

and try to fix it right then and there. I know, I need to learn how to stop being so ridiculous.

But my ridiculousness has its advantages . . . because now I have a book of one hundred tested (dare I say perfected?) recipes to share with all of you. And I promise, they taste just as good at regular mealtimes as they do in the middle of the night!

"Things Happen"

If you've read up until this point, you're probably thinking, "With a mother and family upbringing like that, Mariam was *destined* to be a good cook!" Well, I want to set the record straight right away: Once, when I was seventeen and trying to make french fries for my brother, I burned down my mom's kitchen. (I am crying and cringing as I type this.)

Honestly, the trauma makes the details a little hazy, but what I can tell you is this: I was in the kitchen when I heard one of my brothers come through the door—he had a new car, and he called everyone outside to check it out. I eagerly ran outside, as anyone would do.

My little sister came outside to meet us, and as soon as I saw the expression on her face, I knew it was bad. I ran inside and saw my mom in her nightgown with a huge box of baking soda. Baking soda was flying everywhere. (People with kitchen wisdom know that the best way to put out a cooking fire is *not* with water but with flour or baking soda.)

I couldn't hold back my tears. My mama's kitchen was her pride and joy, and I had destroyed it. She ran over to me and wrapped me in her arms. She said, "All I could imagine was *you* catching on fire!" I had long hair at the time, which was in pigtails. She stroked my hair, and I knew she was imagining it in flames.

Both the hood and the microwave above our oven were completely burned. When she thought I was out of earshot, I heard my mom sobbing as she hugged my big sister. I hid in the fancy room— that's what we called the living room off the kitchen—and bawled my eyes out.

A few moments later, my dad walked in; he had just arrived home from work. He walked straight past the kitchen and didn't notice a thing! My mom looked at him, disbelieving, and told him to walk back. He did—and slowly turned around the kitchen. Then, he walked into the fancy room and looked at me. I held my breath, wondering if he would be angry. He looked at me, shrugged, and said, "Things happen."

Things happen!

Every day since then—so, for the entirety of my career as a recipe developer and writer—I have carried my mom and dad's words with me. The fact that they were so calm and kind when I was at my lowest meant that I didn't have to be afraid of making mistakes in the kitchen. And I did make more mistakes! Never anything on the scale of burning down a kitchen . . . but sometimes, a cake doesn't rise, a sourdough loaf is overproofed, or an expensive piece of seafood is a bit more rubbery than I'd like. But I know in my heart that these little mistakes help me learn and make me a better cook. On the bright side, by burning down her kitchen, I gave my mom an excuse to finally start her dream renovation project. She got the kitchen island she'd always wanted and some really nice cabinets.

Obviously, my job here is to create recipes that are clear, thorough, and as foolproof as possible. I test and retest each recipe. My greatest hope is that each time you make a recipe from this book, you will end up with a beautiful, comforting, and delicious result, too. But the truth is, you may encounter a hiccup or two along the way. To quote my dad, "Things happen."

So my advice to all of you is to keep smiling and take the bumps in stride. Each time you even *attempt* to cook a new recipe, you are taking a step toward becoming a better cook—regardless of how the finished dish turns out. And who knows? If you *really* mess up, maybe you'll end up getting a new kitchen out of the ordeal.

Ingredients & Equipment

Ingredients

Most of the ingredients featured in this book are widely available at American grocery stores. However, a few might require you to pay a visit to your local Middle Eastern market or place an online order. When possible, please support local grocers and specialty markets! If this book inspires you to strike up a conversation with the people who work in the Arab grocery store near you, I will be so, so happy. There is nothing more wonderful than bonding over new ingredients and recipes.

Oils

Olive oil: Olive oil is a birthright for my people. Olive trees are one of the most culturally and economically important crops in Palestine. In addition to pickling olives whole, we press them to make some of the most beautiful olive oil available anywhere in the world.

My mom always had huge tin cans of Palestinian olive oil that she'd buy from our friends or neighbors—there was always someone with an overseas connection who would either carry back or ship large quantities of olive oil from Palestine to distribute to the expat community. The good news is today you can buy Palestinian olive oil online: Mount of Green Olives is a Palestinian company that collaborates with Palestinian farmers using fair trade principles. You can buy their olive oil at shoppalestine.org, a market run by the nonprofit Middle East Children's Alliance (MECA). Ya Albi is another Palestinian brand available online at ya-albi.com; I love their striking pink packaging and beautiful branding.

Neutral oil: Olive oil has a relatively low smoke point, so I often call for frying in a neutral oil. Vegetable oil, avocado oil, and canola oil are all good choices.

Dairy

Laban: In my family, we refer to Arab yogurt as laban. So when I call for laban in this book, look for an Arab-style yogurt or thick, plain, Greek-style yogurt.

Labneh: More often, I call for labneh, which is tarter, more acidic, and creamier than laban; it's more akin to French crème fraîche. Labneh is widely available at most US grocery stores.

Kishta: Sometimes called ashta, kishta is essentially Arab clotted cream. Try it alongside fruit or on toast for breakfast. You can make your own (page 22), buy it at an Arab grocery, or in some cases (for example, the French toast on page 21), you can substitute mascarpone.

Jameed: Jameed is essentially dried fermented laban (see above) that is shaped into balls. It was developed as a way to extend the life of dairy, before the days of refrigeration. The idea was that you could travel with your jameed balls and reconstitute them with water when needed.

Jameed is salty, sour, and tangy. Today, it is often sold in Arab markets and labeled Jameed Soup Starter. It typically comes in boxes with two packets of thick jameed inside.

Powdered milk: Also called dry or dehydrated milk, I use it in Katayef (page 237) and some of my other dough recipes. The advantage of milk powder is you can add it where you'd otherwise have to add hot milk—which is always risky, since heat can kill your yeast. Lukewarm water plus milk powder is a safer bet. It's sold in boxes, bags, and tins and is typically found in the baking aisle of most grocery stores.

Salt

Fine sea salt: This is my go-to salt for cooking because it distributes evenly in both cooking and baking.

Kosher salt: I also sometimes call for kosher salt. When I do, I'm referring to Diamond Crystal, my preferred brand.

Flaky sea salt: Occasionally, I suggest finishing a dish with a flaky sea salt, such as Maldon.

Spices

Seven spice: Seven spice, called *sabaa baharat* in Arabic, typically consists of cardamom, cinnamon, cloves, coriander, cumin, nutmeg, and black pepper and is an all-purpose seasoning for proteins. Look for it in Arab markets and online.

Spice blends: Often in Arab cooking, you'll find spice blends that are designed for specialized dishes. For example, there is **falafel spice, kibbeh spice,** and **ma'amoul spice.** I call for these spice blends in their namesake recipes, because they're a great way to take the flavor of these dishes to the next level.

Garlic powder/onion powder: Typically, I use these spices in concert with fresh garlic and fresh onion; this begs the question, "Why?" The answer is simple: I love garlic and onions, and garlic and onion powders enhance those flavors even more.

Za'atar: This herb and spice blend is a staple throughout the Levant. Typically made with sun-dried wild thyme, sumac, and sesame seeds, it's nutty, a bit sour, and very herbal. When it's toasted in olive oil, the flavor and aroma really start to sing.

Rice, Pasta, Grains, and Dried Legumes

Most of the **rice** in this book is standard enriched long-grain white rice. You can use whatever is available near you.

For the Vermicelli Rice (page 110), you can buy **fine-cut vermicelli noodles** that come already broken up into pieces at your local Arab grocer.

Bulgur is widely available in US grocery stores and is a grain made from cracked wheat. As such, it is not suitable for people with gluten sensitivities (even though it kinda looks like rice!).

Look for **dried chickpeas** and **dried favas** at an Arab or Middle Eastern market. I cannot tell you why, but I swear they cook differently (and so much better, in my experience) than the dried legumes I find in other grocery stores.

Other Miscellaneous Ingredients

Bouillon cubes: My mom often cooks with chicken bouillon cubes, so that ingredient shows up in a lot of my cooking, too. I find it's a great way to add depth to recipes that are missing that certain something. It also packs a wonderful umami flavor! My mom has always used Maggi brand, but whatever you find at your market works. Some of my recipes call for chicken bouillon powder, which you can buy in packets—or you can use a Microplane grater to finely grate the cubes.

Grape leaves: You'll need to buy grape leaves for the Warak Dawali (page 122). They are sold jarred in brine.

Orange blossom water: This is made from the flowers of the bitter orange tree, a species that isn't really grown in the United States. A little goes a long way. Some well-stocked grocery stores carry orange blossom water (in the baking or international aisles), or you can buy it from an Arab grocery or online.

INGREDIENTS & EQUIPMENT

Equipment

Essentials

- **Chef's knife.** Wash it by hand, never in the dishwasher, to keep it sharp!
- **Wood cutting board**
- **Dutch oven for braises.** I recommend 5½-quart size or larger.
- **Deep heavy-bottomed pot or Dutch oven for deep-frying.** The pot should be deep enough to have at least 4 inches of clearance above the oil.
- **Cast-iron, nonstick, and stainless steel skillets.** Anywhere from 10 to 12 inches is a versatile size for home use.
- **1-quart stainless steel saucepan**
- **Sheet pans.** 18 × 13 inches is standard, and they are great for baking and roasting.
- **Large soup pot**
- **Loaf pan.** A standard 1-pound loaf pan is about 9 × 5 inches. For the carrot cake recipe on page 253, I ask you to use a 1½-pound pan, which is 10 × 5 inches.
- **Rolling pin**
- **Mixing bowls**
- **Measuring cups and spoons**
- **Instant-read thermometer**
- **Large wooden spoon**
- **Whisk**
- **Heatproof silicone spatula**
- **Long tongs**
- **9 × 13-inch baking dish** (glass or ceramic preferred)
- **Pie dish**
- **Round cake pans** (8- or 9-inch)
- **Wire racks for cooling**
- **Blender or immersion blender**
- **Fine-mesh sieve**
- **Stand mixer or hand mixer.** You *can* mix doughs by hand, but if you love baking as much as I do, a mixer is such a good investment.

Extra Credit

- **A round pan** to store rocks for baking Khubiz Taboon (page 172)
- **The rocks** for baking Khubiz Taboon
- **Food processor or mini food processor**
- **Digital scale,** for measuring baking ingredients by weight
- **Microplane grater**
- **Pastry brush**
- **Mandoline** for thinly slicing fruits and vegetables

INGREDIENTS & EQUIPMENT

breakfast & brunch

buttermilk pancakes

Makes about 10 pancakes

- 2½ cups / 315g all-purpose flour
- ¾ teaspoon Diamond Crystal kosher salt
- 1 tablespoon baking powder
- ½ teaspoon baking soda
- 2 cups / 450g buttermilk
- ¼ cup unsalted butter, melted, plus more for the griddle
- 2 large eggs, whisked
- ¼ cup / 50g granulated sugar
- 1½ teaspoons vanilla extract

For Serving
- Salted butter
- Maple syrup
- Sliced strawberries, bananas, or other fresh fruit
- Whipped Cream (recipe follows)
- Confectioners' sugar

When it comes to pancakes, everyone has their preferred texture. I'm big on fluffy, perfectly round pancakes with a golden sheen. Picture the pancakes you'd see in a cartoon, topped with a knob of melting butter and syrup flowing down the sides. That's what this recipe is—just the ideal stack of pancakes.

In a large bowl, whisk together the flour, salt, baking powder, and baking soda.

In a medium bowl, whisk together the buttermilk, melted unsalted butter, eggs, granulated sugar, and vanilla.

Using a spatula or spoon, fold the wet ingredients into the flour mixture, being careful not to overmix to avoid dense and flat pancakes (it's okay if there are still a few lumps in the batter). Let the batter rest for a few minutes.

Preheat an electric griddle to 400°F or preheat a skillet over medium-low heat.

Add butter to the griddle and, working in batches, ladle on about ½ cup batter per pancake. Wait until most of the small bubbles that form pop, creating little holes in the pancake, and the edges start to look set and slightly golden, 3 to 4 minutes. The pancake should easily lift off the pan. If it sticks, give it a bit more time. Flip the pancake and cook the other side until it's golden and unsticks easily from the pan, about 2 minutes more. Stack the finished pancakes on a plate and cover loosely with a kitchen towel while you make the rest.

To serve: Divide the pancakes among serving plates and top with salted butter, syrup, and any of your go-to favorite toppings!

whipped cream

Makes about 5 cups

- 2 cups heavy cream, cold
- ¼ cup crème fraîche (optional but highly recommended)
- ¼ cup confectioners' sugar
- ¼ teaspoon Diamond Crystal kosher salt

In a stand mixer fitted with the whisk attachment (or in a medium bowl using a hand mixer), combine the cream, crème fraîche (if using), sugar, and salt. Whip on medium-high speed until stiff peaks form, 3 to 5 minutes (up to 8 minutes with a hand mixer). The mixture will increase in volume, and when you raise your whisk out of it, the peaks will hold firmly to the tip of the whisk but still have slightly soft tips.

Keep refrigerated for up to 8 hours, but it is best made right before you plan to use it.

kishta and pistachio-stuffed french toast

Serves 4

- 1 cup raw pistachios
- 1 cup kishta, homemade (recipe follows) or store-bought, or mascarpone
- 1½ teaspoons tahini
- 4 thick slices brioche loaf, homemade (page 192) or store-bought
- 2 large eggs
- ½ cup heavy cream
- 1 tablespoon granulated sugar
- 2 teaspoons ground cinnamon
- 1 teaspoon vanilla extract
- ½ teaspoon ground cardamom (optional)
- 1 tablespoon butter, salted or unsalted, for frying

For Serving
- Whipped Cream (page 18)
- Orange Blossom Simple Syrup (recipe follows), at room temperature
- Chopped salted or unsalted pistachios
- Edible dried rose buds (optional)
- Confectioners' sugar
- Fresh berries (optional)

This delicious morning treat pairs two of my favorite things: French toast and knafeh (see page 243), a traditional Arab dessert made from pastry layered with syrup, pistachios, and cheese or kishta (our version of clotted cream). In this recipe, you cut a pocket into a slice of bread and then stuff it with an amazing tahini, kishta, and pistachio filling. I encourage you to fill the bread with every last bit of this filling because it really is magical, and there's something so delightful about cutting into what appears to be regular French toast and finding a rich, decadent surprise inside.

tip If you don't have a pastry bag for filling the bread slices, transfer the filling to a resealable plastic bag, then twist the bag closed to seal the filling inside. Use a pair of scissors to snip off a tiny corner of the bag—you then have your own DIY pastry bag.

In a food processor, blitz the pistachios to small crumbly pieces, then keep blitzing to a paste, 5 to 10 minutes. Transfer to a small bowl and fold in the kishta and tahini.

Cut a horizontal slit into each bread slice to make a pocket, stopping about ½ inch from the edge of the bread. Use your hands or a knife to really open up the pocket so you get as much space as possible. Use a spoon or piping bag (see Tip) to fill each pocket with the pistachio filling. Set aside.

In a shallow bowl, whisk together the eggs, cream, granulated sugar, cinnamon, vanilla, and cardamom (if using) until smooth.

Preheat a large skillet over medium heat and add the butter. Dip each stuffed bread slice into the egg mixture, coating both sides and allowing the excess to drip off. Fry until golden brown and crispy, 3 to 4 minutes per side.

To serve: Arrange the French toast on plates and top with a dollop of whipped cream. Drizzle with orange blossom syrup, sprinkle with pistachios and dried rose buds (if using), and dust with confectioners' sugar. If desired, serve with your favorite berries.

recipe continues →

kishta and pistachio–stuffed french toast, *continued*

kishta

Makes about 4½ cups

2¼ cups whole milk, cold
2 cups heavy cream
2 tablespoons sugar
¼ cup cornstarch
1 tablespoon orange blossom water

In a medium saucepan, combine 2 cups of the milk, the cream, and sugar. Bring to a gentle simmer over medium heat, stirring occasionally. Simmer until slightly reduced, about 15 minutes.

Meanwhile, in a small bowl, whisk together the cornstarch and the remaining ¼ cup milk to create a smooth slurry with no lumps.

Slowly pour the cornstarch slurry into the simmering milk mixture, stirring constantly to prevent lumps from forming. Continue to simmer, stirring frequently, until the mixture thickens to a creamy consistency, about 5 minutes.

Just before removing the saucepan from the heat, stir in the orange blossom water for a fragrant finish.

Transfer the kishta to a bowl and cover with plastic wrap, pressing the wrap directly onto the surface to prevent a skin from forming. Let cool completely, then refrigerate overnight. Now you're ready to use it for all your favorite Middle Eastern sweets! Keep refrigerated for up to 5 days.

orange blossom simple syrup

Makes about 2½ cups

3 cups sugar
1 teaspoon fresh lemon juice
1½ teaspoons orange blossom water

In a saucepan, combine the sugar and 1½ cups water. Bring to a boil over high heat. Once boiling, add the lemon juice and reduce the heat to low. Let simmer for 10 minutes, then add the orange blossom water. Remove the pan from the heat and let the syrup cool completely. Store in an airtight container in the fridge indefinitely.

I SLEEP IN MY KITCHEN

sweet banana cream pudding crepes

Makes 12 crepes

Crepe Batter
- 1½ cups / 190g all-purpose flour
- ¼ cup / 50g granulated sugar
- 3 large eggs, whisked
- 1½ cups / 360g whole milk
- 2 tablespoons unsalted butter, melted
- 1½ teaspoons vanilla extract
- ¼ teaspoon Diamond Crystal kosher salt

Banana Pastry Cream
- 1 cup whole milk
- ½ cup heavy cream
- 4 large egg yolks
- ¼ cup granulated sugar
- 2 tablespoons cornstarch
- 1½ teaspoons vanilla extract
- Pinch of fine sea salt
- 1 tablespoon unsalted butter
- 2 ripe bananas, mashed

To Finish
- Butter or neutral oil, for the pan
- Sliced bananas or, if you're feeling fancy, Caramelized Bananas (recipe follows)
- Confectioners' sugar
- Whipped Cream (page 18)
- Crushed Nilla wafers
- Banana chips

My older sister didn't spend much time in the kitchen when we were younger—she was a good cook and baker, but it just wasn't her passion. That made it all the more special when I came downstairs one morning to find her making crepes. On the counter, a tall stack of thin golden crepes, bowls of fresh fruit, Cool Whip, jam, confectioners' sugar, and every other topping I could dream of had been set out by her. I don't know what inspired her to build a crepe bar that day, but my siblings and I were obsessed. What started as her spontaneous idea quickly became a weekend tradition. Crepes might seem intimidating at first (they do involve a bit of technique; see Perfecting Crepes, opposite), but once you get the hang of it, you may never stop!

Make the crepe batter: In a large bowl, whisk together the flour, granulated sugar, eggs, milk, butter, vanilla, and salt until smooth and free of lumps. Cover the bowl with plastic wrap and let the dough rest in the refrigerator for 30 minutes to allow the flour to fully hydrate (this will yield more tender crepes).

Make the banana pastry cream: In a medium saucepan, heat the milk and cream over medium heat until small bubbles form around the edges; do not let it boil.

Meanwhile, in a medium bowl, whisk together the egg yolks, granulated sugar, and cornstarch until pale and thick, about 2 minutes.

Whisking constantly, gradually pour the heated milk mixture into the egg yolks to temper the eggs. Return the mixture to the saucepan and, whisking constantly, cook over medium heat until it thickens into a smooth pastry cream, 3 to 5 minutes.

Remove the pan from the heat and stir in the vanilla, salt, butter, and bananas. Transfer the pastry cream to a bowl, cover with plastic wrap, and press the plastic directly onto the surface to prevent a skin from forming. Refrigerate until completely chilled.

To finish: Heat a nonstick skillet or crepe pan over medium heat and lightly grease it with butter or oil. Pour about ¼ cup batter into the center of the pan and swirl to evenly coat the bottom with a nice thin layer. Cook until the edges of the crepe begin to lift and the bottom is lightly golden but not browned, 1 to 2 minutes. Flip the crepe and cook until the other side is set,

recipe continues →

sweet banana cream pudding crepes, *continued*

30 to 60 seconds. Transfer the crepe to a plate and repeat with the remaining batter, stacking the crepes as you go.

To serve, lay a crepe flat on a serving plate. Spoon about ¼ cup of the chilled banana pastry cream onto the center of the crepe, then add the banana slices. Fold the crepe into quarters or roll it up.

Dust the crepes with confectioners' sugar, add a dollop of whipped cream on the side or on top, and sprinkle crushed Nilla wafers and banana chips to complete your crepes!

Perfecting Crepes

1. A good nonstick skillet or crepe pan is, of course, a must.

2. Then, you want to keep the heat level at medium so the skillet grabs the batter but doesn't cook it too quickly.

3. Once you add the batter, tilt and rotate the pan in a circular pattern until the surface is coated with a thin, even layer—not transparent but not thick like a pancake either.

4. I personally don't like my crepes browned on the bottom; I prefer a pale golden color. As soon as I achieve that, I use a nonstick spatula to lift the edges from the pan, then I carefully use my fingers to gently peel the crepe away from the pan to flip it over. (Pros can do this just with a special crepe spatula, but that's quite challenging, and you risk tearing it.)

5. Once both sides are cooked, use your spatula to loosen it from the pan and slide it onto the plate. Before you know it, you'll have a stack of perfect Saturday morning treats.

caramelized bananas

If you want to take your crepes to the next level, you can caramelize the bananas used for serving.

Cooking spray, for the plate
3 tablespoons unsalted butter
¼ cup (packed) brown sugar
2 ripe but firm bananas, sliced
Pinch of ground cinnamon

Spray a plate with cooking spray and set aside.

In a medium skillet, melt the butter over medium heat. Stir in the sugar until combined and slightly bubbling. Add the banana slices in a single layer. Sprinkle with cinnamon and cook until each side is caramelized and golden, 2 minutes per side. Transfer to the prepared plate until ready to use.

I SLEEP IN MY KITCHEN

french toast bake *with* walnut filling

Serves 6 to 8

Walnut Filling
1 cup walnuts, finely chopped
¼ cup (packed) brown sugar
3 tablespoons unsalted butter, melted
1 teaspoon ground cinnamon
¼ teaspoon ground cloves (optional)

French Toast and Custard
Butter, for the baking dish
8 cups sliced or cubed brioche (about 1 loaf brioche, homemade, page 192, or store-bought), or 6 to 8 day-old croissants
5 large eggs
2 cups whole milk
½ cup heavy cream
½ cup granulated sugar
1 tablespoon vanilla extract
2½ teaspoons ground cinnamon
¼ teaspoon ground nutmeg
¼ teaspoon ground cloves
½ teaspoon fine sea salt

For Serving
Confectioners' sugar
Maple syrup
Favorite berries (optional)

I love hosting brunch but don't love the stress of having to wake up early to make sure everything's ready by the time my guests arrive. That's where this French toast bake comes in! You can prepare everything the day before, refrigerate it, and then pop it in the oven in the morning. When your friends and family walk through the door, they'll be greeted with the aroma of cinnamon, nutmeg, and cloves. Hand them a glass of orange juice, invite them to the table, and set this dish of custardy French toast with a walnut crunch in front of them—they'll assume you've been baking all morning.

Oh, one more tip—this is a perfect way to use up any stale bread that's lying around. Even old croissants work great!

Make the walnut filling: In a small bowl, mix together the walnuts, brown sugar, butter, cinnamon, and cloves (if using).

Make the French toast and custard: Butter a 9 × 13-inch baking dish. Spread the bread cubes in the dish and sprinkle on the walnut filling.

In a large bowl, whisk together the eggs, milk, cream, granulated sugar, vanilla, cinnamon, nutmeg, cloves, and salt until smooth. Pour the custard over the bread, pressing down gently to ensure the bread is soaked.

Cover the dish with plastic wrap and refrigerate for at least 1 hour or overnight.

Preheat the oven to 350°F. Let the dish sit at room temperature for 10 minutes (this helps it bake evenly, since it was in the fridge for a while). Bake, uncovered, until golden and set, 35 to 45 minutes.

To serve: Dust with confectioners' sugar and drizzle with maple syrup, then serve warm with your favorite berries, if desired.

croissant breakfast sandwiches

Makes 2 sandwiches

2 croissants
Mayonnaise
6 large eggs
2 tablespoons whole milk or water
1 tablespoon extra-virgin olive oil
6 to 8 slices beef bacon
4 slices provolone cheese
1 large tomato, sliced
Fine sea salt and black pepper
¼ red onion, thinly sliced
1 avocado, sliced (optional)
2 ounces microgreens

This recipe is what I like to call basic gourmet. It's simple to make but a bit more considered than some one-minute sandwiches you might throw together without thinking. *And* it has a croissant base. A croissant immediately elevates any recipe in my eyes.

Preheat the oven to 350°F.

Slice the croissants in half horizontally but do not slice all the way through—leave a hinge so the two sides are still attached. Spread an even, light layer of mayonnaise on both cut sides of the croissants.

In a medium skillet, toast the croissants mayo-side down over medium-low heat until they turn golden, about 3 minutes. Place the croissants on a sheet pan while you cook the eggs and bacon.

In a small bowl, whisk together the eggs and milk.

In a large nonstick skillet, heat the oil over medium-low heat until hot. Add the whisked eggs and cook, using a heatproof spatula to gently push the eggs toward the center of the pan every 30 seconds or so, until the eggs become fluffy and reach your preferred level of doneness. Transfer the eggs to a plate.

In the same pan, cook the bacon over medium heat until it reaches your desired crispiness, about 3 minutes per side. Transfer to the plate with the eggs.

Divide the scrambled eggs and bacon between the two croissants, then top each with two slices of provolone. Bake until the cheese has melted, 5 to 7 minutes.

Remove the pan from the oven and season the tomato slices with salt and black pepper, then add three slices to each sandwich, followed by the onion, avocado (if using), and a generous handful of microgreens. Close the sandwiches and serve immediately!

batata o baid
eggs with curry-spiced potatoes

Serves 2 or 3

Extra-virgin olive oil, for the pan
3 russet potatoes, peeled and cut into 1-inch cubes (see Tip)
1 teaspoon fine sea salt, plus more as needed
1 teaspoon black pepper
1 teaspoon curry powder
6 large eggs
2 tablespoons whole milk
Pita bread, for serving
Pitted olives, for serving

Here's a weekend breakfast classic that made regular appearances at my childhood table when I was growing up. It often doubled as dinner (for a fun breakfast-for-dinner moment)—served with a proper spread of pita, falafel, hummus, and ful.

Heat a large cast-iron or stainless steel skillet over medium-high heat. Add enough oil to fill the skillet by ¼ inch.

If your potatoes are in an ice water bath, drain them and pat them dry with paper towels. Add the potatoes to the skillet, sprinkle with salt, and toss so they're coated in the oil. Reduce the heat to medium, cover the pot, and cook for 10 to 20 minutes, or until fork-tender on the inside and crispy on the outside. Season the potatoes to taste with salt, black pepper, and curry.

Meanwhile, in a medium bowl, whisk together the eggs and milk until smooth.

Push the potatoes to the edge of the skillet and add a drizzle of olive oil to the center if it seems dry. Add the eggs to the skillet and cook, using a heatproof spatula to gently push the eggs toward the center of the pan every 30 seconds or so, until the eggs become fluffy and reach your preferred level of doneness. Remove the pan from the heat.

Season the eggs to taste with salt, then use a spatula to gently fold the potatoes and eggs together to maintain the fluffiness of the eggs.

Serve the dish with pita bread, olives, and any other accompaniments of your choice.

tip If you're prepping ahead, submerge the potatoes in ice water until you're ready to fry.

shakshuka

Serves 4

¼ cup extra-virgin olive oil
1 small yellow onion, finely chopped
1 large red bell pepper, diced
1 small jalapeño, seeded and finely chopped
4 garlic cloves, minced
1½ teaspoons ground cumin
1 teaspoon paprika
1 teaspoon dried oregano
1 teaspoon curry powder
1 teaspoon black pepper
¾ teaspoon fine sea salt
¼ cup tomato paste
4 large tomatoes, chopped
6 large eggs

For Serving

Chopped fresh curly parsley
Red pepper flakes (optional)
Sliced avocado (optional)
Crumbled feta cheese (optional)
Warm pita bread

Shakshuka is a classic dish with origins in North Africa that is a common sight on many Middle Eastern breakfast tables. In my family, we serve it as part of a larger breakfast spread, but it's also wonderful on its own, with some pita bread for dipping.

Make sure to use juicy, bursting-with-flavor tomatoes, as they are the real stars of this dish.

In a 10-inch stainless steel pan, heat the oil over medium heat until hot. Add the onion, bell pepper, and jalapeño and cook, stirring occasionally, until the vegetables become very tender, about 10 minutes. If they are cooking too quickly, reduce the heat.

Add the garlic, cumin, paprika, oregano, curry, black pepper, and salt to the pan. Keep stirring constantly for the next 2 minutes to infuse the flavors.

Add the tomato paste and cook it down for an additional 2 minutes. Stir in the tomatoes and bring the mixture to a gentle boil over medium heat. (If your tomatoes are not super juicy, you may have to add ¼ cup water to achieve the right consistency.) Once boiling, reduce the heat to low and simmer until the mixture is slightly reduced, 3 to 5 minutes.

Using the back of a wooden spoon, create six wells slightly larger than the eggs in the tomato mixture and carefully place an egg in each well. Cover the pan and continue cooking over low heat until the egg whites are set but the yolks remain runny, 5 to 10 minutes, depending on your preferred level of doneness (after 5 minutes, lift the lid to check on the eggs every minute or so).

To serve: Garnish the dish with parsley. If desired, also garnish with pepper flakes, avocado, and feta. Serve immediately with warm pita bread!

smoked salmon and pepper jelly pastry

Makes 6 pastries

- Cooking spray, for the pan
- 1 sheet puff pastry, thawed according to package instructions
- All-purpose flour, for dusting
- Egg wash: 1 egg, beaten with 1 tablespoon milk
- 8 ounces cream cheese, at room temperature
- 2 tablespoons chopped fresh dill
- ¼ cup pepper jelly
- ½ medium cucumber, very thinly sliced
- 4 ounces smoked salmon, thinly sliced into strips
- 2 tablespoons capers, drained
- ¼ red onion, sliced as thinly as possible
- Arugula microgreens, for garnish
- 2 ounces feta cheese, crumbled (about ½ cup, optional)
- Balsamic glaze, for drizzling (optional)

Smoked salmon was my gateway to the wider world of fish. It is so delicious, and I found myself putting it on everything: bagels, sandwiches, avocado toast, eggs.

Salmon might be the star, but pepper jelly is the backup singer who makes the whole dish really shine. I'm relatively new to pepper jelly, which is sweet, savory, and spicy, and is amazing for when you want to add a hint of sweetness without overpowering fruitiness.

I've given some suggestions for how you can decorate these pastries beautifully (see Get Arty! below), but on the simplest level, just arrange the salmon in a wavy pattern or shingle it attractively . . . or have fun with the way you cut and order your toppings!

Get Arty!

For a Beautiful Presentation:

1. Use a spoon to add a thin layer of pepper jelly to the pastry.
2. Transfer the dill cream cheese to a piping bag and pipe on top.
3. For the smoked salmon, make rosettes: Roll one sliver of salmon into a tight curl to make a rosette bud, then roll one or two additional slivers around the rosette bud. Nestle the rosette among the other toppings.

Preheat the oven to 400°F. Line a sheet pan with parchment paper.

Unfold the puff pastry on a lightly floured surface. Roll it out slightly to smooth the creases. Cut the pastry into six equal rectangles and place them on the lined sheet pan.

Using a table knife, gently score a smaller rectangle in the middle of each puff pastry rectangle, about ½ inch in from the edge, without piercing all the way through the dough. This will help create a pocket in the center when baked.

Brush the edges of each pastry rectangle with the egg wash.

Bake until golden brown and puffed, 15 to 20 minutes. Let cool completely on the sheet pan.

In a medium bowl, mix together the cream cheese and dill until smooth and well blended.

Use your fingers or a spoon to gently press down on the center rectangle of puff pastry (using the edges you outlined with a table knife as your guide) to create an indentation for the toppings.

Spoon the dill cream cheese onto each pastry and smooth it out, then use another spoon to add the pepper jelly. Arrange the cucumber slices evenly on top, then layer the smoked salmon slices over the cucumber and top with the capers. Add a few slices of red onion on top.

Garnish each pastry with the microgreens. If desired, sprinkle with crumbled feta and drizzle with balsamic glaze, then serve immediately.

tomato galette *with* za'atar

Makes one 10-inch galette

Galette Dough (recipe follows), chilled

Labneh and Za'atar Filling
½ cup labneh
2 garlic cloves, finely grated (preferably on a Microplane)
1 tablespoon za'atar
1 teaspoon finely grated lemon zest
1 tablespoon extra-virgin olive oil
¼ teaspoon fine sea salt, plus more as needed
¼ teaspoon black pepper, plus more as needed

Assembly
4 ripe heirloom tomatoes, thinly sliced
Fine sea salt, for sprinkling
All-purpose flour, for dusting
¼ cup crumbled feta cheese
1 small red onion, thinly sliced
1 tablespoon extra-virgin olive oil, plus more for serving
Egg wash: 1 egg, whisked with 2 tablespoons water or milk
Flaky sea salt, for sprinkling
Fresh mint and parsley, for garnish
Za'atar, for garnish (optional)

One of our most common snacks as kids was to take a piece of pita and layer it with labneh, za'atar, and tomatoes. We'd roll it up and eat it just like that—sitting at the table if we were feeling polite (or at the very least putting it on a plate) but often just wandering around nibbling at it.

I wanted to take that beloved childhood memory and fancy it up into an "adult" version to add to the dinner table. So I turned the components into a savory galette. This actually uses the same dough as the Apple and Apricot Galette with Maple Crème Fraîche (page 249), so if you'd like, just double the recipe and refrigerate or freeze half the dough to make yourself a sweet treat later.

tip A great way to move a round of rolled-out dough is to gently roll it onto the rolling pin and then transfer it to the sheet pan by rolling it off gently.

Make the dough as directed and refrigerate.

Preheat the oven to 400°F. Line a sheet pan with parchment paper.

Make the labneh and za'atar filling: In a small bowl, mix the labneh, garlic, za'atar, lemon zest, oil, fine salt, and black pepper. Taste and add more salt and pepper, if needed.

Assemble the galette: Sprinkle each side of the tomato slices with the fine salt. Set the tomatoes on paper towels for at least 15 minutes to drain. Use fresh paper towels to pat them as dry as possible.

On a lightly floured surface with a lightly floured rolling pin, roll out the dough into a 12-inch round and transfer (see Tip) to the lined sheet pan.

Spread the labneh mixture evenly over the dough, leaving a 2-inch border. Sprinkle the feta on top of the labneh, then add the onion on top of that.

Arrange the tomatoes in concentric rings over the labneh, feta, and onion (it's okay to overlap, as they will cook down quite a bit—and you might not use all the tomatoes). Drizzle the top of the galette with the oil.

Fold the edges of the dough over the tomatoes, pleating as you go to create a rustic look. Brush the dough edges with the egg wash and sprinkle the entire galette with the flaky salt.

Bake until the crust is golden brown and the tomatoes are tender, 35 to 40 minutes.

Let the galette cool slightly before serving. Garnish with the mint and parsley. Drizzle with a little oil and sprinkle more za'atar on top, if desired.

recipe continues →

tomato galette with za'atar, *continued*

galette dough

Makes enough for one 10-inch galette

1¼ cups / 150g all-purpose flour
1 tablespoon sugar
¼ teaspoon Diamond Crystal kosher salt
½ cup cold unsalted butter, cubed
¼ cup / 60g ice water

In a food processor, combine the flour, sugar, and salt. Pulse a few times until combined, then add the butter and pulse until the mixture resembles coarse crumbs. With the machine running, slowly drizzle in the water, mixing just until the water is incorporated and the dough looks like pebbles. It will still be quite crumbly at this stage but will come together in the next step.

Make a square of plastic wrap (you'll probably need to line up two pieces) and spread it out on your workstation. Flip the contents of the food processor onto the plastic wrap, then pull up the edges of the plastic wrap around the dough and use your hands to shape it into a disk. Fully wrap the disk in plastic, then refrigerate for at least 30 minutes and up to 2 days.

caramelized onion ratatouille tart

Makes one 9-inch tart

I need you all to make this immediately! I placed it in the breakfast and brunch chapter because it's a perfect centerpiece for your weekend table, but it's also delicious as a light dinner or as a hearty side dish if you pair it with breaded chicken.

To answer your next question, yes, this dish is dedicated to one of my favorite Pixar characters, Remy from *Ratatouille*. In traditional ratatouille, all the vegetables are stirred and served together in a stewlike preparation, but in the movie, Remy develops a dish inspired by confit byaldi, where the vegetables are layered in a repeating pattern, creating a beautiful rose shape. I went that route here, because I'll always be nostalgic for the first time I saw that movie and its beautiful namesake dish.

tip To make the tart dough in a food processor, combine all the dry ingredients in a food processor and pulse a few times to combine. Add the butter all at once and pulse until you have coarse crumbs. With the machine running, drizzle in the water until the dough just comes together.

Tart Dough
- 1¼ cups / 150g all-purpose flour, plus more for dusting
- ¼ cup / 25g freshly grated Parmesan cheese
- ⅓ cup / 45g cornmeal
- ½ teaspoon fine sea salt
- ¼ teaspoon mustard powder
- ½ cup / 115g cold unsalted butter, cut into ½-inch cubes
- 3 to 4 tablespoons cold water

Roasted Tomato–Pepper Sauce
- 1 large red bell pepper, quartered
- 2 large heirloom tomatoes, quartered
- 2 shallots, peeled and halved
- 1 garlic bulb, top third trimmed off and any loose skin removed
- Extra-virgin olive oil, for drizzling
- Fine sea salt and black pepper
- 1 teaspoon grated lemon zest
- All-purpose flour, for dusting

Assembly
- ½ cup whole milk ricotta cheese
- ¼ cup freshly grated Parmesan cheese
- 2 tablespoons chopped fresh herbs (such as basil, parsley, or chives)
- Fine sea salt and black pepper
- Caramelized Onions (recipe follows)
- 3 or 4 Roma tomatoes, very thinly sliced
- 1 Chinese eggplant, very thinly sliced into rounds
- 1 zucchini, very thinly sliced into rounds
- 1 yellow squash, very thinly sliced into rounds
- 2 tablespoons extra-virgin olive oil
- 6 to 8 sprigs of fresh thyme, leaves picked, plus more for garnish
- Fresh basil, for garnish

Make the tart dough: In a large bowl, whisk together the flour, Parmesan, cornmeal, salt, and mustard powder. Using your fingers or a pastry cutter, cut in the butter until the mixture resembles coarse crumbs. If you're using your fingers, press the butter and flour between your fingers until the butter pieces are the size of coarse crumbs. Add the water, 1 tablespoon at a time, stirring and massaging with your hands until the dough just comes together. (Alternatively, use a food processor; see Tip.)

Cover the dough in plastic wrap and refrigerate for at least 30 minutes and up to overnight. If you chill it overnight, let it come to room temp for 10 to 15 minutes to soften up.

Make the roasted tomato–pepper sauce: Preheat the oven to 425°F.

On a large sheet pan, arrange the bell peppers, tomatoes, shallots, and garlic bulb. Drizzle with the oil and season generously with salt and black pepper.

recipe continues →

BREAKFAST & BRUNCH

caramelized onion ratatouille tart, *continued*

Roast until the vegetables are soft and lightly charred, 35 to 40 minutes. Leave the oven on but reduce the temperature to 375°F.

Let the vegetables cool slightly, then transfer them to a blender (squeeze the garlic flesh directly into the blender). Add the lemon zest and blend until smooth. Set aside.

On a lightly floured surface, roll out the chilled dough to fit a 9-inch tart pan. Press the dough into the pan and prick the bottom all over with a fork. Line the tart shell with parchment paper and fill it with pie weights.

Bake until the crust is lightly golden, 10 to 12 minutes. Take the pan out of the oven and remove the weights and parchment. Set the crust aside to cool slightly.

Assemble the tart: In a small bowl, mix the ricotta, Parmesan, herbs, and a pinch of salt and black pepper. Spread the ricotta mixture evenly over the partially baked tart crust. Spread the roasted tomato–pepper sauce over the ricotta layer. Spread the caramelized onions over the sauce.

Begin layering the sliced tomatoes, eggplant, zucchini, and yellow squash in overlapping circles on top of the caramelized onions and sauce. Start from the outer edge, working inward to create a spiral pattern. Drizzle with the oil, then sprinkle with salt, black pepper, and thyme. Transfer the tart to the oven.

Bake until the vegetables are tender and lightly browned, 30 to 40 minutes.

Garnish with fresh thyme and basil leaves. Let cool slightly before serving—it's also great at room temp!

caramelized onions

Makes 2 cups

2 tablespoons olive oil or butter
2 large yellow onions, thinly sliced
2 teaspoons sugar
½ teaspoon fine sea salt

In a medium skillet, heat the olive oil over medium-low heat. Add the onions, sugar, and salt and cook, stirring occasionally, until the onions have deeply caramelized and are tender, 20 to 25 minutes. Store in an airtight container in the fridge for up to 3 days.

small plates

fan fave

mama's homemade hummus

Makes about 4 cups

- 1 pound dried chickpeas, rinsed and picked over
- 1 heaping teaspoon baking soda
- 2 teaspoons fine sea salt, plus more as needed
- 1 teaspoon citric acid
- ¼ cup cold water
- 1 cup tahini
- Ice cubes, if needed (see Tip)
- Extra-virgin olive oil and za'atar, for garnish (optional)

This hummus is based on the version my parents made when they ran their restaurant in Cleveland. To make it last a little longer, they used citric acid instead of fresh lemon juice—a small tweak that helped with preserving big batches. It's not a reinvention of hummus by any means, just a small adjustment that stuck with me. You can use lemon juice instead, especially if you're not making a large batch. This is the hummus recipe that my mom has made my entire childhood, that I currently make whenever I want a fresh batch of hummus, and I can't wait to pass it along to all of you.

tips Toward the end of the process, you might have to blend in some ice cubes to achieve the correct consistency. This is one of those times when you have to use your senses to figure out how many ice cubes to add. Every bag of chickpeas is different; if yours are on the older side, they might be very dry and require more ice cubes to reach the creamy texture you want.

You will have several cups of chickpeas left over. Store them in resealable plastic bags and freeze for up to 6 months. Save for your next batch of hummus.

In a large bowl, combine the dried chickpeas and enough water to cover by at least 2 inches. Allow to soak overnight.

Drain the chickpeas and place in a large (at least 5½-quart) pot. Add fresh water to cover by at least 2 inches. Add the baking soda and bring to a boil over high heat. As the water starts to boil, reduce the heat to medium and skim off any white foam that forms on the surface. Continue skimming until the water is about 90 percent clear (the foam may not disappear completely). Boil until the chickpeas are extremely tender, about 1 hour.

Drain and let cool completely. Reserve about ¼ cup of the boiled chickpeas for garnish.

In a small bowl or measuring cup, mix together the salt, citric acid, and cold water. Stir until dissolved and set aside.

Once the chickpeas are completely cool, measure out 4 cups and transfer to a food processor (see Tips). Blend until very smooth. Add the salt/citric acid mixture and the tahini and blend until completely smooth and creamy. If you would like a looser hummus, add ice cubes, two at a time, and blend until smooth. Taste and add more salt, if needed.

To serve, top with the reserved whole chickpeas along with the oil and za'atar, if desired.

Store the hummus in an airtight container in the refrigerator for up to 5 days.

SMALL PLATES

ful medames *with* tatbila

favas with jalapeño sauce

Makes about 15 cups (see Notes)

- 1 pound whole dried fava beans, rinsed and picked over
- 1 pound split dried fava beans, rinsed and picked over

Tatbila
- 4 or 5 jalapeños, seeded and sliced
- 6 to 8 garlic cloves, peeled but whole
- ½ to 1 teaspoon kosher salt, plus more as needed
- 3 tablespoons fresh lemon juice (see Notes), plus more as needed
- ⅓ cup extra-virgin olive oil

For Serving
- Extra-virgin olive oil
- Lemon wedges
- Pita bread (optional)

Ful is a Levantine and North African staple, but for whatever reason, it never got as popular in the non-Arab world as hummus. It's a rich, comforting dish of stewed fava beans that are mashed and served with their liquid to use as a dip for pita. After hours and hours of simmering, the rich, earthy favas break down into a velvety stew consistency. You *could* eat it like a soup—I've definitely seen my dad eat it by the spoonful when he's trying to be healthy (favas are rich in fiber)—but more traditionally, it is served on the breakfast table alongside hummus and falafel, with plenty of pita for dipping.

For me, the earthy flavor of the favas *needs* to be brightened up by tangy, vegetal tatbila. Think of tatbila like Middle Eastern hot sauce; it's great on hummus, falafel, salad, or anything else that needs a bit of acid and heat.

notes:

• I'll admit, this makes a LOT of ful. You can halve the recipe if you'd like, but this recipe is already half of what my mom would make at home, and I didn't want my Palestinian readers raising an eyebrow and asking, "Why is this such a stingy amount of ful?"

• You can also make tatbila the traditional way, using a mortar and pestle: Pound the jalapeños, garlic, and salt into a paste, then add the lemon juice and oil.

• When my parents want to make a batch of tatbila that will last longer in the fridge, they use ⅝ teaspoon citric acid dissolved in 3 tablespoons of water in place of the lemon juice and salt.

In a 5½-quart pot, combine all of the dried favas with enough water to come 2 to 3 inches from the top of the pot. Bring to a boil over medium-high heat and boil for 5 minutes. Skim off any foam or impurities that rise to the surface.

Reduce the heat to its lowest setting. Cover the pot tightly with aluminum foil (you want a tight seal) and use a toothpick to poke many small holes all over the foil to allow it to steam properly. Place the pot's lid on top of the foil. Simmer the favas until the whole beans are tender and the split favas have dissolved into the liquid, 7 to 9 hours. Check every hour or two to make sure the water level is okay: The fava beans should be covered by at least 1 inch of water until the very end, at which point you want the water essentially level with the beans. Add more water, if needed.

Once the beans are very tender, with no firmness, let them cool completely in their cooking liquid. They should absorb most of the remaining liquid during this time, but if there is still a significant amount, you can drain it off to achieve your desired creamy consistency. Store in the fridge for up to 5 days or transfer to resealable plastic bags and freeze for up to 3 months.

Make the tatbila: In a mini food processor, combine the jalapeños, garlic, salt, lemon juice, and oil and blend well. Taste and add more salt and lemon juice, if needed.

Before plating, loosen the ful with water, 1 tablespoon at a time, until you reach your desired creamy consistency. Transfer the warm beans to a serving plate or bowl, add a generous tablespoon of tatbila, and mix it in. Season with salt to taste. Drizzle generously with the oil and tatbila on top, if desired. Squeeze lemon juice over the top. Serve with pita bread or add to your breakfast spread.

I SLEEP IN MY KITCHEN

khiyar bi laban

cucumber yogurt dip

Makes about 2 cups

- 16 ounces plain whole milk yogurt
- 2 garlic cloves, grated
- 3 Persian (mini) cucumbers, finely diced
- 2½ tablespoons minced fresh or dried mint
- 1 tablespoon fresh lemon juice
- 1 teaspoon fine sea salt
- Whole milk (optional)

When I was a girl, I was very picky. I hated vegetables. Really, I hated anything that was good for me. That all changed once I started eating khiyar bi laban, which is a staple Middle Eastern dipping sauce. It is most often served with Kibbeh (page 57), which is meaty, fried, and heavy, but dipping kibbeh in this sauce makes each bite balanced and refreshing. I realized it was the khiyar bi laban that made the dish.

I find this dip to be very versatile; try it paired with any protein or with rice dishes. You could even thin it out with water or milk and use it as a salad dressing.

In a medium bowl, mix together the yogurt, garlic, cucumbers, mint, lemon juice, and salt until well combined. If you want a looser consistency, add 1 teaspoon of milk at a time. Store in an airtight container in the refrigerator for up to 3 days.

SMALL PLATES

baba ghanoush–stuffed eggplant

Serves 6

- 3 medium globe eggplants
- 2 tablespoons extra-virgin olive oil, plus more for drizzling
- 1 teaspoon fine sea salt, plus more for sprinkling
- 3 tablespoons tahini
- 4 garlic cloves, grated
- Juice of 1 lemon
- Paprika, for garnish (optional)
- Chopped fresh parsley, for garnish (optional)
- Pita bread and/or fresh vegetables, for dipping

A few years ago, I went through what is probably best described as my "stuffing things into things" phase. For example, I'd bake a coconut cake inside a coconut. I'd stuff a lemon cake into the hollowed-out skin of a lemon or an orange cake into an orange. I think this comes from my love of anime and especially Studio Ghibli. At night, I spend hours looking at pictures on Pinterest of all the food featured in Studio Ghibli films like *Spirited Away* and think to myself, "How do I make this dish look like the cartoon version of itself?"

That's how I came up with the idea of stuffing baba ghanoush, a simple, classic Middle Eastern eggplant dip, into the shell of a hollowed-out eggplant. It's such a cool way to present something familiar, and I promise if you lay this out on the table at your next dinner party, your friends will be so impressed. I love hosting, and it's the little extra steps like this that make me excited to cook for my loved ones.

tip: Because it is uncooked, the interior of the eggplant shell might oxidize over time. If you're concerned about it browning, you should try to time it so you hollow out the eggplant close to serving time. Or you can rub it with a little lemon juice to slow down oxidation.

Preheat the oven to 425°F. Line a sheet pan with parchment paper.

Cut two of the eggplants in half lengthwise. Score the flesh of the eggplants in a diamond pattern. To do this, make cuts into the eggplant flesh on the diagonal and about 1 inch apart from one end of the eggplant to the other, going to but not through the skin. Repeat on the other diagonal to make the diamond shapes.

Drizzle the cut sides with oil and sprinkle lightly with salt. Place the eggplant halves flesh-side down on the lined sheet pan.

Cut the remaining eggplant in half lengthwise and use a spoon to hollow out each half. Drizzle the flesh with a bit of oil, season it with salt, and wrap it in aluminum foil. Place it on the sheet pan with the eggplant halves. Set the hollowed-out eggplant shells aside (see Tip).

Drizzle the eggplant halves with more oil and sprinkle with more salt. Roast until the flesh is tender and golden brown, about 45 minutes. The foil-wrapped eggplant flesh should also be soft.

When the eggplants are cool enough to handle, scoop the flesh from the roasted halves into a medium bowl. Add the foil-wrapped flesh. Using a fork, mash the roasted eggplant. It should be mostly smooth with some texture.

Mix in the tahini, garlic, lemon juice, the 2 tablespoons oil, and the 1 teaspoon salt.

Spoon the baba ghanoush mixture into the hollowed-out eggplant shells. Drizzle a bit more oil on top for extra richness. For a touch of color and flavor, garnish with paprika and parsley, if desired.

Serve with pita bread and fresh vegetables for dipping.

falafel

Makes about 25 falafel

- 2¼ cups dried chickpeas
- ½ small yellow onion, quartered
- 3 garlic cloves, peeled but whole
- Small handful of fresh parsley leaves
- Small handful of fresh cilantro leaves
- 1 tablespoon falafel spice
- 1 tablespoon sesame seeds
- 2¼ teaspoons ground coriander
- 1½ teaspoons cornstarch
- 1½ teaspoons ground cumin
- 1 teaspoon fine sea salt
- ½ teaspoon ground turmeric
- ½ teaspoon onion powder (optional)
- ½ teaspoon garlic powder (optional)
- ½ teaspoon baking soda
- Vegetable oil, for frying

Falafel has always been a breakfast food for me, which might surprise you if you didn't grow up in an Arab household and are used to eating it for lunch or dinner as part of a mezze platter. While falafel is delicious any time of day, there is something so lovely about enjoying it in the morning as part of a big breakfast spread, along with hummus, butter and jam, potatoes, eggs, and cheese manakeesh. My second-favorite way to enjoy falafel is inside a sandwich . . . which you can and absolutely should do with the recipe below (see Variation). This recipe makes a fair amount of falafel, so you'll have plenty for sandwiches, breakfast, or whenever the falafel craving strikes. Serve with your favorite dips or salads, or in pita bread sandwiches. Khiyar bi Laban (page 49) is a great pairing.

variation

Falafel Sandwich: Start with a nice piece of Pita Bread (page 168), then smother some Creamy Garlic Sauce (page 138) inside. Fill it with Persian pickles, tomatoes, lettuce, pickled or soaked red onion, tahini sauce, hummus (if desired), and plenty of falafel.

tip If you make falafel a lot, you can buy a stainless steel tool with a lever that lets you stuff perfectly shaped falafel. To use it, dip it in water to prevent sticking. Scoop a spoonful of the falafel mixture into the tool and level it off. Add another spoonful and shape it into a dome.

In a large bowl, combine the chickpeas with water to cover by at least 2 inches. Allow to soak overnight.

Drain the chickpeas, transfer to a food processor, and blend until mostly smooth with a bit of texture. Add the onion, garlic, parsley, and cilantro and blend until smooth but still somewhat grainy, scraping down the sides of the processor as needed.

Transfer the chickpea mixture to a large bowl. Add the falafel spice, sesame seeds, coriander, cornstarch, cumin, salt, turmeric, onion powder (if using), and garlic powder (if using) and mix until well combined.

If you don't want to fry all the falafel at once, divide the mixture into two portions and store the portion you don't intend to use immediately in a resealable plastic bag in the freezer for up to 6 months. (Allow to thaw overnight in the refrigerator or for a few hours at room temperature before using.)

To each portion you plan to fry, add ¼ teaspoon of the baking soda and mix well. If you have a falafel tool (see Tip), use it. Otherwise, use a 4-ounce ice cream scoop or a spoon to form 1½-inch balls.

Line a plate with paper towels and have near the stove. Pour 2 to 3 inches oil into a deep heavy-bottomed pot and heat over medium heat until the temperature of the oil reaches 335° to 350°F on an instant-read thermometer. Reduce the heat to medium-low to maintain the oil temperature.

Working in batches so as not to crowd the pot, fry the falafel until golden brown, about 3 minutes. If the exterior is browning before the interior is cooked, reduce the heat. Transfer the falafel to the paper towels to drain.

Serve hot.

SMALL PLATES

sambosas

Makes 24 sambosas

Dough
- 2¼ cups / 280g all-purpose flour, plus more for dusting
- ¼ cup / 60g melted ghee or extra-virgin olive oil
- ¾ teaspoon fine sea salt
- ½ cup / 120g lukewarm water, plus more as needed

Filling
- 3 tablespoons extra-virgin olive oil
- 1 teaspoon cumin seeds
- 1 medium onion, finely diced
- 6 garlic cloves, minced
- 3 tablespoons unsalted butter
- 1 teaspoon ground coriander
- 1 teaspoon ground cumin
- 1 teaspoon garam masala
- ½ teaspoon ground turmeric
- ½ teaspoon seven spice
- ½ teaspoon cayenne pepper
- 1 pound ground beef or lamb
- 1 medium russet potato, peeled and cubed
- ½ cup frozen peas
- Kosher salt and black pepper
- 3 tablespoons finely chopped fresh cilantro

To Finish
- Flour paste (¼ cup all-purpose flour mixed with ¼ cup water), if needed
- Vegetable oil, for frying

This is a very common dish for Muslims to make for Ramadan—we're big on things that can be prepped ahead of time and frozen. (If you do decide to freeze some, you can fry them straight from frozen—just be careful of oil splatters when you lower them into the hot oil.) There is a fair amount of crossover in Indian and Arab flavor profiles, likely thanks to centuries of trade. For example, we use seven spice, which typically contains cardamom, cinnamon, cloves, coriander, cumin, nutmeg, and black pepper. Many Indian cooking traditions use garam masala, which varies from region to region but often includes cinnamon, cumin, mace, black pepper, and coriander. The filling for these sambosas showcases those flavors beautifully, and you can use either lamb or beef as your protein. The trickiest part of the process is the folding, but if you have friends to help you, the work goes by quickly!

Make the dough: In a large bowl, combine the flour, ghee, and fine salt. Rub the ghee into the flour until the mixture resembles bread crumbs. Gradually add the water, kneading as you go, until a smooth and pliable dough forms. Cover with a damp cloth and let the dough rest for 30 minutes.

Make the filling: In a large skillet, heat the olive oil over medium heat. Add the cumin seeds and let them sizzle for a few seconds. Add the onion and cook until soft and translucent, about 3 minutes. Add the garlic and cook for another minute. Add the butter and, once melted, stir in the coriander, cumin, garam masala, turmeric, seven spice, and cayenne, toasting the spices for about 30 seconds until fragrant.

Add the ground meat, breaking it apart with a spoon, and cook until browned, about 7 minutes.

Stir in the potato and cook until slightly tender, about 5 minutes.

Add the peas, cooking until heated through. Season with kosher salt and black pepper to taste. Stir in the cilantro. Let the filling cool completely.

Divide the dough into twelve equal portions (each weighing 35g) and roll each into a small ball. With a lightly floured rolling pin and work surface, flatten each ball into a thin round (about 6 inches in diameter). Cut the round in half to create two semicircles.

recipe continues →

sambosas, CONTINUED

Form each semicircle into a cone by folding it in half, then pinching the edge to seal. Fill the cone with 2 to 3 tablespoons of the meat filling, then seal the top edge by folding and pinching the dough closed. If needed, wet one of your fingers with flour paste and run it along the edge of the dough to strengthen the seal. Repeat with the remaining dough and filling. If you have extra filling, you can enjoy it as a snack! If you don't plan on frying everything, freeze extra sambosas in a resealable plastic bag for up to 3 months.

To finish: Pour 2 inches oil into a deep fryer or deep heavy-bottomed pot and heat over medium heat until the temperature of the oil reaches 350°F on an instant-read thermometer.

Line a tray with paper towels and set near the stove. Working in batches so as not to crowd the pot, gently slide the sambosas into the hot oil, frying until golden brown and crisp, 3 to 4 minutes. Use a slotted spoon or spider to transfer them to the paper towels to drain. Serve hot.

I SLEEP IN MY KITCHEN

kibbeh

beef and bulgur–stuffed shells

Makes 18 kibbeh

Shell Mixture
- 1¾ cups fine cracked wheat (fine bulgur #1)
- ½ cup boiling water
- 1 pound beef chuck, preferably Angus, cut into 1-inch cubes
- ½ yellow onion, chopped
- ½ red bell pepper, chopped
- Finely grated zest of ¼ orange
- Finely grated zest of ¼ lemon
- 1 tablespoon kibbeh spice
- 1 teaspoon fine sea salt
- ½ teaspoon dried marjoram
- ¼ teaspoon ground cinnamon
- ⅛ teaspoon black pepper

Filling
- Extra-virgin olive oil, for drizzling
- 1 pound ground beef (80/20)
- 1 yellow onion, minced
- 2 tablespoons toasted pine nuts
- 1 teaspoon fine sea salt
- ½ teaspoon dried marjoram
- ½ teaspoon black pepper
- ½ teaspoon ground cinnamon
- ½ teaspoon kibbeh spice
- ½ teaspoon ground allspice

To Finish
- Vegetable oil, for frying
- Khiyar bi Laban (page 49), for serving

When I was growing up, my mom, sisters, and I would make this dish together as if in a factory assembly line. My mom would prepare the filling and shell mixtures, then pass the bowls down to us to stuff and shape each kibbeh.

When she was preparing this just for our family, it would be an easy, joyful time. But if we were making it for guests, that's when my mom became a different woman. Suddenly, our misshapen kibbeh weren't acceptable. (In my mom's defense, they're supposed to look like footballs, and ours kind of looked like wonky potatoes.) After we were done, I'd see her step up to the tray of our "finished" kibbeh to reshape them properly.

I don't want this story to intimidate you or stop you from making kibbeh. At the end of the day, they all taste delicious, regardless of whether they're perfect football shapes or not. At home, we always double and sometimes triple this recipe to feed a crowd. They freeze easily so if you make extra, you can save some for later.

Make the shell mixture: In a large bowl, soak the cracked wheat in the boiling water for 15 minutes. Drain and return to a boil.

Add the beef chuck, onion, bell pepper, orange zest, lemon zest, kibbeh spice, salt, marjoram, cinnamon, and black pepper. Use your hands to mix well. Adding one-quarter of the mixture at a time to a food processor, process until very fine and soft, about 4 minutes, then place in a small bowl. (If you find your shell mixture is still not pliable and sticking together easily, return to the food processor and process one or two more times.)

Make the filling: Heat a large skillet over medium heat. Drizzle a bit of olive oil into the pan. Add the ground beef and cook until browned, 7 to 10 minutes. Add the onion and cook until translucent, 4 to 6 minutes.

Remove the pan from the heat and stir in the pine nuts, salt, marjoram, black pepper, cinnamon, kibbeh spice, and allspice. Allow to cool completely for about 20 minutes, then taste and adjust the seasonings.

Now it's time to shape the kibbeh. Keep a cup of ice water nearby. Wet your fingertips and palms. Take about ¼ cup of the shell mixture and roll it into a ball. Use your index finger to create a hole in the center of the ball. This will be the starting point for shaping the shell. Working from the hole in the center, start

recipe continues →

kibbeh, *continued*

gently stretching the edges of the ball outward with your index and middle fingers to form a shallow bowl shape, rotating the bowl in your palm as you work. As you rotate the ball, continue to stretch and thin out the edges evenly to create a thin bowl or shell shape. Add about 3 tablespoons of the filling to the shell, then close the edges around it so they meet, then shape the shell into a tiny football. Wet your hands with the ice water to help smooth out the shape. Repeat until all the shell mixture or the filling mixture has been used.

To finish: Line a plate with paper towels and set near the stove. Pour 2 to 3 inches oil into a deep heavy-bottomed pot and heat over medium heat until the temperature of the oil reaches 350°F on an instant-read thermometer.

Working in batches so as not to crowd the pot, fry the kibbeh until they develop a nice color and crust, about 6 minutes, reducing the heat if they appear to be browning too quickly. Use a slotted spoon or spider to transfer the fried kibbeh to the paper towels to drain.

Serve the kibbeh immediately with the cucumber yogurt dip on the side.

SMALL PLATES

the middle eastern charcuterie board

Serves 12

Extra-virgin olive oil, for drizzling

Cheese and Dairy
Block of Halloumi cheese
Block of feta or Nabulsi cheese
Labneh

Breads and Crackers
Pita bread
Assorted crackers

Dips and Spreads
Mama's Homemade Hummus (page 45)
Extra-virgin olive oil and za'atar
Small jar of fig or apricot jam
Baba ghanoush (optional)

Olives and Pickles
Mix of green and black olives
Pickled veggies (such as cucumbers, turnips, or carrots)

The "Main Event" (aka My Favorite Part)
Cheese Fatayer (page 217) *fan fave*
Falafel (page 53)
Grape leaves (optional)

Fresh Herbs and Vegetables
Cucumber slices
Cherry tomatoes
Radish wedges
Green onions
Sprigs of mint
Sprigs of parsley

If you've spent any time in the Arab world, then you know how much we love our little snacks. Or if you had Arab American friends growing up, you might have visited them at home and noticed that the dad was always wandering around the house nibbling on a green onion or radish. (At least, that's what mine always did.)

Here, I decided to play into the viral trend of grazing or serving charcuterie boards with my own Middle Eastern twist. This recipe was a no-brainer for me, since I grew up with an elaborate spread of hummus, falafel, jam, pickled vegetables, and breads artfully arranged on my family's breakfast table nearly every day.

The last thing I will say—and I know I say this a lot in this book!—is to get creative and artistic when you arrange this! Use my photograph on page 61 and the ingredients list as a jumping-off point for your own beautiful creation. If you don't want to feature every element, that's fine, and if you want to substitute certain components for fresh, in-season produce you find at your market, then do so with my blessing. The most important thing is to try to include a variety of textures, colors, shapes, and heights, almost as if you're making a floral arrangement.

Using a very sharp knife, slice the block of Halloumi into strips that are ¼ to ½ inch thick. Drizzle oil on both sides.

Preheat an outdoor grill or grill pan over high heat. Grill the Halloumi for 2 to 3 minutes per side, until you see grill marks on both sides.

Now is a good time to grill your pita, too. To do it the Arab way, light one of the burners on your stovetop to high heat and toast each side of the pita until warm and lightly toasted, 5 to 10 seconds per side. (Alternatively, you can use your grill.)

Now grab a large wooden cutting board: It's time to assemble your platter! Place the labneh in a bowl and drizzle oil on top. Place the hummus in a separate bowl. Fill another small bowl with oil and sprinkle za'atar on top. Place the baba ghanoush (if using) in a bowl. Arrange all the bowls on the cutting board.

Arrange the falafel and fatayer around the dips for easy grabbing. If you're planning on adding grape leaves, arrange those, too! (Depending on the size of your cutting board, you may also just place the fatayer on a separate plate to the side to make room for the smaller mezze additions.)

Now add the cheese: Arrange the grilled Halloumi on the board. With the feta, you can slice the block neatly or leave it whole and let it naturally crumble when guests cut it for a more casual look. Place the small jar or dish of fig or apricot jam near the cheeses to offer a sweet pairing option.

Arrange the breads and crackers: Cut the fresh or grilled pita into wedges and fan out the pita and crackers next to the dips—you want them close for easy dipping.

Either scatter the olives and pickled veggies throughout the board, or arrange them in small bowls.

Now fill in with the fresh veggies and herbs: Arrange cucumber slices, tomatoes, radish wedges, and green onions around the board to fill in the gaps. Add the mint and parsley sprigs for color and freshness.

Finally, look at your board, and move around anything until you're happy! It should be fun!

salads & sides

crispy potato salad *with* greens

Serves 4 to 6

If you had told my twelve-year-old self that one day she'd be salad-obsessed, she wouldn't have believed you. But here I am, dreaming up creative salads whenever I can and eating them basically for every meal.

This salad balances the richness and comfort of crispy, well-seasoned potatoes with the freshness of arugula and lettuce. One day, I was making my standard crispy potatoes as a side dish, and I thought to myself, "This would taste so good over a fresh salad." The combination is out of this world, if I may say so myself. Unlike the potato salads you might find at a picnic or potluck, this one tastes best when the potatoes are still warm—it's all about the contrast of warm potatoes and cold greens.

Crispy Potatoes

Cooking spray, for the pan
1 pound mini medley potatoes, halved
¼ cup extra-virgin olive oil
1 tablespoon chopped chives
2 tablespoons freshly grated Parmesan cheese
1 teaspoon garlic powder
½ teaspoon onion powder
½ teaspoon red pepper flakes
½ teaspoon fine sea salt
½ teaspoon black pepper

Salad

4 ounces baby lettuce (about 5 cups)
½ cup arugula
¼ red onion, thinly sliced and soaked in ice water for 10 minutes to remove some of the bite (or pickled red onion, if you have it!)
4 radishes, thinly sliced
½ cucumber, halved lengthwise and thinly sliced into half-moons
1 avocado, sliced
Buttermilk Dressing (recipe follows)

Make the crispy potatoes: Preheat the oven to 425°F. Spray a sheet pan with cooking spray.

In a large bowl, toss the potatoes with the oil, chives, Parmesan, garlic powder, onion powder, red pepper flakes, salt, and black pepper until evenly coated.

Spread the potatoes in a single layer on the prepared sheet pan. Roast until golden brown and crispy, about 30 minutes, flipping halfway through. Remove the pan from the oven and let cool slightly.

Assemble the salad: In a large salad bowl, combine the baby lettuce, arugula, onion, radishes, cucumber, and avocado. Toss with as much of the dressing as you like until everything is evenly coated. Gently fold the roasted potatoes into the salad. (Alternatively, divide the salad among serving plates and top each individual salad with crispy potatoes.) Serve immediately!

buttermilk dressing

Makes about 1½ cups

¾ cup buttermilk
¼ cup sour cream
¼ cup plain whole milk Greek yogurt
1 teaspoon extra-virgin olive oil
Finely grated zest of ½ lemon
¼ cup finely grated Parmesan cheese
2 tablespoons chopped fresh chives
½ teaspoon red pepper flakes
3 garlic cloves, finely grated (preferably on a Microplane)
Fine sea salt and black pepper

In a medium bowl, whisk together the buttermilk, sour cream, yogurt, oil, lemon zest, Parmesan, chives, pepper flakes, and garlic until well combined. Season to taste with salt and black pepper. Store in an airtight container in the fridge for up to 3 days.

SALADS & SIDES

fattoush
fried bread salad

Serves 4 to 6

Vegetable oil, for frying
2 pita breads, cut into bite-sized squares
2 cups chopped romaine lettuce
1 cup coarsely chopped fresh parsley
½ cup coarsely chopped fresh mint
1 large cucumber, diced
2 large tomatoes, diced
6 radishes, thinly sliced
1 small red onion, thinly sliced
1 green bell pepper, diced
3 green onions, finely chopped

Dressing
3 garlic cloves, finely grated (preferably on a Microplane)
¼ cup extra-virgin olive oil
3 tablespoons fresh lemon juice
1 tablespoon distilled white vinegar
2 teaspoons sumac, plus more for garnish
1 teaspoon pomegranate molasses
½ teaspoon za'atar
½ teaspoon dried mint
Fine sea salt and black pepper
Pomegranate seeds, for garnish (optional)

Any time you get invited to an Arab's house for dinner, you're going to see either tabbouleh or fattoush on the table—or sometimes both (we do love to be extra). Both salads are so classic, and fattoush in particular pairs beautifully with so many things. Who doesn't love a fresh, citrusy salad with a crunchy bread topping? Fattoush is a perfect side for any of the main dishes in this book or really for any main dish in your existing repertoire. You can even turn it into a main by topping it with chicken or beef shawarma.

There is one thing that separates amazing fattoush from so-so fattoush: You must wait to add the dressing and fried pita until RIGHT before you are about to serve. If you toss it together too far in advance, the pita gets soggy and the veggies don't taste as fresh.

Line a plate with paper towels and set near the stove. Pour 2 to 3 inches vegetable oil into a deep heavy-bottomed pot and heat over medium heat until the temperature reads 350°F on an instant-read thermometer.

Working in batches so as not to crowd the pot, fry the pitas until golden and crispy, 2 to 3 minutes. Use a spider strainer or slotted spoon to transfer to the paper towels to cool.

In a large bowl, combine the romaine, parsley, mint, cucumber, tomatoes, radishes, red onion, bell pepper, and green onion. Toss gently to combine.

Make the dressing: In a small bowl, whisk together the garlic, olive oil, lemon juice, vinegar, sumac, molasses, za'atar, mint, and salt and black pepper to taste. Adjust the seasonings to taste.

Just before serving, pour the dressing over the salad and toss gently to coat all the ingredients. Add the fried pita pieces and give the salad one final, gentle toss to combine.

Transfer the fattoush to a large serving bowl or individual plates. Sprinkle some sumac over the top for color. If desired, garnish with pomegranate seeds.

mediterranean pasta salad *with* sumac vinaigrette

Serves 6 to 8

We had a lot of big family barbecues when I was a kid, and my mom always made sure there was some sort of pasta salad on the table. My favorite was always anything made with tricolor pasta. This recipe is inspired by one she used to make; it's memorable because it was my entryway to enjoying olives. Believe me, being a Palestinian who doesn't like olives is tough, so I'm glad this pasta salad helped me come around.

I encourage you to play around with the amount of ingredients here: If you're an olive or oregano lover, feel free to add more. Just don't skip the banana peppers, because they're always a sleeper hit! This is a recipe that tastes even better the next day, after it marinates in the sumac dressing. Who doesn't love a fresh, cold pasta salad straight from the fridge?

tip For a slightly creamier vinaigrette, in a food processor, combine all the ingredients except the oil. With the motor running, slowly pour in the oil in a steady stream until the vinaigrette is fully emulsified.

Fine sea salt
12 ounces tricolor rotini

Sumac Dressing
⅓ cup extra-virgin olive oil
1 tablespoon distilled white vinegar
1 tablespoon fresh lemon juice
3 garlic cloves, grated
1½ teaspoons sumac
1 teaspoon Dijon mustard
1 teaspoon dried oregano, plus more as needed
¼ teaspoon fine sea salt, plus more as needed
¼ teaspoon black pepper, plus more as needed

Salad
1 cup cherry tomatoes, halved
1 large cucumber, diced
1 small red onion, thinly sliced
½ cup Kalamata olives, pitted and halved
¼ cup crumbled feta cheese
8 ounces fresh mozzarella pearls
¼ cup jarred pickled banana peppers (sliced into rings)
¼ cup chopped fresh parsley
¼ cup chopped fresh dill

Bring a large pot of salted water to a boil over high heat. Add the pasta and cook according to the package instructions. Drain and rinse under cold water to stop the cooking and prevent sticking. Set aside.

Make the sumac dressing: In a small bowl, whisk together the oil, vinegar, lemon juice, garlic, sumac, mustard, oregano, salt, and black pepper. Adjust the seasonings to taste. (See Tip.)

Assemble the salad: In a large salad bowl, combine the pasta, tomatoes, cucumber, onion, olives, feta, mozzarella, banana peppers, parsley, and dill. Pour the dressing over the salad and toss gently to coat all ingredients evenly.

SALADS & SIDES

roasted squash *with* pine nuts and tahini

Serves 6

Seasoning Blend
- ¼ cup extra-virgin olive oil
- 2 garlic cloves, finely grated (preferably on a Microplane)
- 2 tablespoons honey
- 2 teaspoons sumac
- 1 teaspoon ground cumin
- 1 teaspoon ground coriander
- ½ teaspoon fine sea salt, plus more as needed
- ¼ teaspoon black pepper, plus more as needed

Squash
- Olive oil, for the pan
- 3 medium delicata squash or acorn squash (about 2 pounds total), halved lengthwise, seeded, and cut crosswise into half-moons
- 4 shallots, peeled and halved

Tahini Sauce
- ¼ cup tahini
- 2 tablespoons fresh lemon juice
- 2 garlic cloves, grated
- ¼ teaspoon fine sea salt

For Serving
- 2 tablespoons unsalted butter, melted
- ¼ cup toasted pine nuts
- ½ cup chopped fresh parsley
- Pomegranate seeds (optional)

Too many people are sleeping on winter squash! It is such a beautiful and underrated ingredient: It's filling, widely available, and has such a pleasing flavor. Delicata squash in particular is one of my new favorite vegetables. It is so thin-skinned it doesn't need to be peeled, making it easier to prep than some of its autumn squash siblings, like butternut.

This dish is so visually stunning, especially when you consider how easy it is to prepare. Another bonus: You can prepare all the elements the day before you plan to serve. Make the tahini sauce and seasoning blend; chop the parsley; and clean, halve, and store the squash in an airtight container. Then all you have to do is roast and assemble the following day.

Preheat the oven to 400°F.

Make the seasoning blend: In a small bowl, combine the oil, garlic, honey, sumac, cumin, coriander, salt, and black pepper. Taste and add more salt and black pepper, if desired.

Roast the squash: Drizzle a bit of oil onto a large sheet pan. Arrange the squash and shallots on the sheet pan, cut-side up. Brush the seasoning blend generously over the squash and shallots.

Roast until the squash is tender and caramelized and the shallots are soft and golden, 25 to 35 minutes. Flip the squash pieces and shallots halfway through roasting to make sure they cook evenly without burning.

Make the tahini sauce: In a medium bowl, whisk together the tahini, lemon juice, garlic, and salt. Gradually add up to ¼ cup water, whisking until smooth and creamy. The sauce should be thick and pourable but not watery.

To serve: Allow the squash and shallots to cool a tad, then spread a generous layer of tahini sauce on a serving platter. Arrange the squash and shallots over the sauce. Brush as much of the melted butter over the squash as you'd like, then sprinkle with the pine nuts and parsley. If desired, add an extra drizzle of tahini sauce on top and pomegranate seeds for color and brightness.

loaded chickpea salad *with* lemon-garlic shrimp

Serves 6

Lemon-Garlic Shrimp
- 1 pound large shrimp, peeled and deveined
- Fine sea salt and black pepper
- 3 tablespoons extra-virgin olive oil
- 4 garlic cloves, minced
- 1 teaspoon red pepper flakes (optional)
- Grated zest and juice of 1 lemon
- 2 tablespoons unsalted butter
- 2 tablespoons chopped fresh parsley

Bulgur
- 1 yellow onion, diced
- 1 cup bulgur
- 1 teaspoon black pepper
- 1 teaspoon fine sea salt

Chickpea Salad
- ⅓ cup extra-virgin olive oil
- ¼ cup fresh lemon juice
- 1 teaspoon fine sea salt
- 1 cup cooked chickpeas, drained and rinsed
- 1 cup corn (drained if canned)
- 1 red bell pepper, diced
- 1 red onion, diced, soaked in water for 10 minutes, then drained
- 1 cup chopped fresh parsley
- ½ cup chopped fresh dill

For Serving
- Chopped fresh parsley, for garnish
- Lemon wedges, for squeezing

I come from a very large close-knit family—which was why it was especially hard for me to move across the country and away from my mom, dad, and most of my siblings. The distance became even harder to manage once they all started Snapchatting me pictures of food my mom was cooking for them—not fair!

One dish in particular really caught my attention (and spurred my jealousy): a colorful chickpea salad dotted with corn, pepper, red onion, and plenty of fresh herbs. The next time my mom came to visit me in California, she insisted on making it for me—and it was even better than it had looked in pictures!

The best way to make this salad is to cut up all the veggies so the peppers, onions, and corn are all exactly the same size. That way, each bite is perfectly balanced. Adding the lemon-garlic shrimp makes this a complete meal, but you can leave off the shrimp if you'd just like a wholesome salad!

Make the lemon-garlic shrimp: Rinse the shrimp under cold water and pat them dry with paper towels. Season with a pinch of salt and black pepper.

In a medium pot or cast-iron skillet, heat the oil over medium-high heat. Add the garlic and pepper flakes (if using) and sauté until the garlic is fragrant and lightly golden, about 1 minute.

Add the shrimp to the pot in a single layer. Cook the first side until pink, about 2 minutes, then flip the shrimp. Add the lemon zest and lemon juice and stir to coat the shrimp. Add the butter and continue to cook until the shrimp are cooked through and opaque, 2 to 3 minutes.

Transfer the shrimp to a plate and, if you'd like, drizzle the shrimp pan juices over top. Sprinkle with the parsley. Tent with aluminum foil to keep warm.

Cook the bulgur: In the same pot you used for the shrimp, add the yellow onion and sauté over medium-high heat until softened, about 2 minutes. Add the bulgur, black pepper, salt, and 1½ cups water and stir to combine. Bring the mixture to a boil, then turn down the heat to low. Cover and simmer until the bulgur is tender and the water is absorbed, 15 to 20 minutes.

Remove the pot from the heat and let it sit, covered, for 5 minutes. Fluff with a fork before serving.

Meanwhile, make the chickpea salad: In a large bowl, whisk together the oil, lemon juice, and salt. Add the chickpeas, corn, bell pepper, red onion, parsley, and dill. Toss to coat evenly with the dressing.

To serve: You can either add the bulgur to the bowl with the chickpea salad and toss to combine, or you can place it on a plate and add the chickpea salad on top. Top with the warm lemon-garlic shrimp. Garnish with parsley and serve with lemon wedges on the side.

burrata salad *with* steak and labneh chimichurri

Serves 4

This salad is so vibrant and hearty, I like to think of it as "elevated girl dinner." If anyone tells you salads aren't filling, well, just serve them this. I top it with filet mignon because it pairs so beautifully with the tart, herbaceous labneh chimichurri, but you could really use any protein. Or skip the protein entirely for a lighter side. Salads don't have to be boring if you give them the care and attention they deserve!

Labneh Chimichurri
- ½ cup finely chopped fresh curly parsley
- ½ cup finely chopped fresh cilantro
- 1 teaspoon dried oregano
- ¼ cup extra-virgin olive oil
- 2 tablespoons white wine vinegar or red wine vinegar
- 4 garlic cloves, minced
- ½ teaspoon fine sea salt
- ¼ teaspoon red pepper flakes
- 1 cup labneh or plain whole milk Greek yogurt

Filet Mignon
- 2 filet mignons (1½ to 2 inches thick), at room temperature
- Fine sea salt and black pepper
- Olive or avocado oil, for the pan
- 5 tablespoons unsalted butter, at room temperature
- 4 garlic cloves, lightly crushed
- 2 sprigs of thyme
- 2 sprigs of rosemary

Salad
- 3 cups arugula
- 3 heirloom tomatoes, thinly sliced
- 1 blood orange, peeled and thinly sliced
- 1 grapefruit, peeled and thinly sliced
- 1 ball burrata cheese
- 1 red onion, thinly sliced
- Handful of microgreens
- Handful of grape tomatoes, halved

Make the labneh chimichurri: In a medium bowl, mix together the parsley, cilantro, and oregano. Add the oil, vinegar, garlic, salt, and pepper flakes until well combined. Fold in the labneh until smooth. Set aside.

Cook the filet mignon: Pat the filets dry and season both sides generously with salt and black pepper.

In a large cast-iron or stainless steel skillet, heat a drizzle of oil over medium-high heat until just beginning to smoke. Add the steaks—they may splatter, so be careful. You'll know the temperature is correct if you hear a happy sizzle. Without moving the steaks around, sear the steaks for about 4 minutes on each side or until a golden-brown crust forms. Sear the edges of the steaks, about 30 seconds per side.

Add the butter, garlic, thyme, and rosemary to the skillet. Turn off the heat and, using a spoon, baste the steaks with the butter and aromatics for 3 to 5 minutes, flipping the steaks occasionally to ensure even cooking through the residual heat from your skillet.

Transfer the steaks to a cutting board, set the garlic and herbs on top, and let rest for 10 minutes.

Meanwhile, prepare the salad: Add dollops of the labneh chimichurri directly onto one large plate or four individual serving plates. Arrange the arugula on top. Now it's time to get creative and have a little fun with your plating: Arrange the sliced tomatoes in an attractive pattern over the arugula, then alternate slices of orange and grapefruit so they fan out over top. Tear the burrata apart or add it whole to the plate. (If left whole, cut it up with a steak knife when eating the salad.) Top the burrata with as much of the onion as you'd like, then add the microgreens and grape tomatoes. Slice the rested filet mignon into thin strips and arrange them over the salad, then serve.

soups & stews

addas
creamy lentil soup

Serves 4 to 6

⅓ cup extra-virgin olive oil
1 yellow onion, diced
1 teaspoon fine sea salt
1 teaspoon ground white pepper
2 teaspoons ground cumin
2 cups red lentils, rinsed thoroughly
2 chicken bouillon cubes

Optional Accompaniments
Lemon slices or wedges
Chopped green onions
Halved radishes
Pitted olives

This comforting soup, which is made throughout the Levant, is typically served during the colder months and is a staple during Ramadan, probably because it's so nutritious and filling. Every family has their own take on it—my version is simply the one I grew up watching my mom make for me and my siblings.

In a medium pot, heat the oil over medium heat. Add the onion and cook until translucent and aromatic, about 4 minutes. Add the salt, white pepper, and cumin and toast for about a minute, so the spices become fragrant. Add the lentils and stir to combine.

Add 6½ cups water and the bouillon cubes and bring the mixture to a boil. Cover the pot and simmer over medium-low heat, stirring every 5 minutes, until the lentils are very tender and almost melt in your mouth, 25 to 30 minutes.

You can use an immersion blender to puree the soup, or you can leave it as is if you prefer a bit of texture. Taste and adjust the seasonings as needed.

Serve with lemon, green onions, radishes, and olives on the side, if desired.

spiced butternut squash soup

Serves 4 to 6

- 1 medium butternut squash, peeled, seeded, and cubed
- 1 large carrot, peeled and coarsely chopped
- 2 tablespoons extra-virgin olive oil, plus more for drizzling
- Fine sea salt and black pepper
- ¼ cup unsalted butter
- 1 medium onion, diced
- 6 garlic cloves, minced
- 2 teaspoons grated fresh ginger (from a 1-inch piece)
- 6 fresh sage leaves
- 2 teaspoons garlic powder
- 1½ teaspoons onion powder
- 1 teaspoon ground cumin
- ½ teaspoon ground turmeric
- ½ teaspoon ground white pepper
- 4 cups vegetable broth
- 1 (13.5-ounce) can unsweetened full-fat coconut milk
- Cornstarch slurry: 1 tablespoon cornstarch, mixed with ¼ cup water (optional)
- Toasted pumpkin seeds, for garnish (optional)

If you ask me, everyone needs a go-to autumn soup in their lives. Mine is this creamy, lightly spiced butternut squash soup, which is warm and filling and perfect for the moment the weather gets chilly. Fresh ginger and coconut milk give this a pop of sweetness that complements the natural sweetness of the squash. I love sage and use it here to add an almost minty, wintry note to the soup. If you'd like, you can fry up some of the sage for a tasty edible garnish (see Tip), or you can top the soup with coconut milk and/or toasted pumpkin seeds for a little crunch. Try this paired with the Garlic-Bread Grilled Cheese (page 91) for a perfect cold-weather lunch.

tip **Crispy sage-leaf garnish:** If you decide not to blend the sage leaves into the soup, you can still add a lovely sage garnish. Just melt a little butter in a small saucepan or skillet, then fry a few fresh sage leaves until the edges start to brown and crisp up, no more than 30 seconds. Remove the sage from the pan and season with a bit of salt.

Preheat the oven to 400°F.

In a large bowl, combine the squash and carrot. Drizzle in some oil, season with salt and black pepper, and toss to coat. Spread out on a sheet pan and transfer to the oven.

Roast until golden and tender, 25 to 30 minutes.

In a large pot, heat the oil and butter over medium heat. Add the onion and cook until softened, 3 to 5 minutes.

Add the garlic, ginger, sage leaves, garlic powder, onion powder, cumin, turmeric, and white pepper and cook, stirring, until fragrant, 1 to 2 minutes.

Add the roasted squash and carrot and the broth to the pot. Bring to a boil, then turn down the heat and simmer for 10 minutes. If you don't want too much of a sage-y flavor, remove the leaves now. (If you want, you can turn them into a garnish; see Tip.) If you love sage, continue on with the next step!

Use an immersion blender (or transfer the mixture to a regular blender) to puree the soup until smooth. Set aside about ¼ cup of the coconut milk for the garnish, then stir the remaining coconut milk into the soup. If you prefer an even thicker consistency (I do!), whisk the cornstarch slurry to loosen it up and add it to the pot.

Taste and adjust the seasoning with more salt and black pepper, if desired, then ladle into bowls. Garnish each bowl with a drizzle of coconut milk, then use a toothpick, if you'd like, to swirl it into an attractive pattern. Top with the pumpkin seeds or crispy sage leaves, if desired.

french onion soup

Serves 6 to 8

I absolutely love onions, so any recipe that has a mountain of onions involved—I'm in. Many French onion soup recipes call for alcohol, but I wanted to develop a version without it. You know me . . . I love to cook for a crowd, so the yield is rather large here. You can cut the recipe in half if you're serving fewer people. And if you go that route, you can divide the soup among four Sourdough Bread Bowls (page 186), which adds an extra-special touch.

Garlic-Butter Toast
- Cooking spray, for the pan
- ½ cup unsalted butter, melted
- 4 garlic cloves, minced
- 1 teaspoon dried thyme
- 1 teaspoon red pepper flakes
- 1 teaspoon chopped fresh parsley
- Fine sea salt
- 1 baguette, cut into 6 to 8 (1-inch) slices

Soup
- ½ cup unsalted butter
- 3 tablespoons extra-virgin olive oil
- 6 large yellow onions, thinly sliced
- Fine sea salt
- 2 tablespoons distilled white vinegar
- 2 tablespoons all-purpose flour
- 1 cup white grape juice
- 8 cups beef broth, plus more as needed
- 1 teaspoon black pepper
- 1 teaspoon garlic powder
- A few sprigs of thyme

For Serving
- Sourdough Bread Bowls (page 186; optional)
- 6 ounces Gruyère cheese, freshly shredded

Preheat the oven to 350°F. Spray a sheet pan with cooking spray.

Make the garlic-butter toast: In a medium bowl, stir together the butter, garlic, thyme, pepper flakes, parsley, and salt to taste. Brush the garlic butter on one side of the baguette slices. Arrange the slices, buttered-side up, on the sheet pan.

Bake until toasted, about 20 minutes. Set aside.

Make the soup: In a Dutch oven, melt together the butter and oil over medium heat. Add the onion, generously seasoning with a big pinch of salt. Cook, stirring every couple of minutes, until the onion caramelizes—it will be very soft and tender, golden brown, and its wonderful aroma will fill your house—about 45 minutes.

Once the onion has caramelized, add the vinegar to deglaze the bottom of the pan, loosening any flavorful bits with a wooden spoon. Sprinkle in the flour and cook, stirring constantly, for about 2 minutes to create a roux. Add the grape juice, letting it simmer for about 3 minutes to cook down a bit. Add the broth and stir to incorporate. Add more broth as desired to achieve your desired soup consistency. Season with 1 teaspoon salt, the black pepper, garlic powder, and thyme sprigs. Taste and adjust the seasoning to your liking.

Bring the mixture to a boil, then reduce the heat to a simmer, cover, and let the soup simmer for 30 minutes to meld the flavors. Discard the thyme stems.

To serve: When you are about 30 minutes away from serving, preheat the oven to 350°F.

Arrange six to eight ovenproof soup bowls or the bread bowls (if using) on a sheet pan. Ladle the soup into the bowls, topping each with a slice of garlic-butter toast and a generous amount (about ¼ cup) of Gruyère.

Bake until the cheese is melted and golden, about 8 minutes. Then turn the oven to broil and broil until the cheese is browned and crispy in spots, about 2 minutes longer.

Serve immediately.

clam chowder

Serves 6

- ¼ cup extra-virgin olive oil
- 1 small yellow onion, diced
- 6 medium celery stalks, chopped
- 8 garlic cloves, minced
- 2 tablespoons unsalted butter
- ½ cup all-purpose flour
- 1 cup bottled clam juice
- 3 cups no-salt-added chicken broth
- 2½ cups half-and-half
- 2 sprigs of fresh thyme
- 1 bay leaf
- 3½ teaspoons fine sea salt
- 1½ teaspoons black pepper
- 1½ teaspoons garlic powder
- 1½ teaspoons onion powder
- 1 pound russet potatoes (about 3 medium), peeled and diced
- 3 (10-ounce) cans whole baby clams, drained and rinsed

For Serving
- Freshly grated Parmesan cheese
- Chopped fresh parsley
- Chopped green onions
- Red pepper flakes
- Crackers (optional)

Clam chowder was the one canned thing my mom always kept in the pantry—for my brother. He loved it, and she made sure it was there. It wasn't until years later that I tried a homemade version, and it completely changed my relationship with chowder. Now, it's one of my comfort foods. This version is rich and thick, with a creamy base, tender potatoes, and plenty of herbs for garnish. It's exactly how I like it.

In a large pot, heat the oil over medium heat. Add the onion and celery and sauté until softened, about 5 minutes. Add the garlic and sauté for 1 minute until fragrant.

Add the butter and cook until melted. Add the flour in two additions, stirring constantly to prevent lumps. Cook, stirring frequently, for 4 minutes to remove the raw flour taste. Pour in the clam juice, stirring to combine well with the roux. Stir in the chicken broth, then stir in the half-and-half. Bring the mixture to a simmer over medium heat. Add the thyme, bay leaf, salt, black pepper, garlic powder, and onion powder and continue to simmer for 15 minutes, stirring every few minutes to prevent sticking or burning, until the flavors have melded. Discard the thyme stem and bay leaf.

Add the potatoes and continue to simmer for an additional 25 to 30 minutes, or until the potatoes are perfectly tender. Gently stir in the clams and simmer for 5 minutes, but be careful not to overcook, as clams can become rubbery if cooked too long.

To serve: Ladle the chowder into bowls and top with the Parmesan, parsley, green onions, and a dash of pepper flakes. Serve with crackers on the side, if desired.

chicken noodle soup

Serves 6

- 1 teaspoon garlic powder
- 1 teaspoon onion powder
- 1 teaspoon paprika
- 2 teaspoons black pepper, plus more as needed
- ½ teaspoon fine sea salt
- 3 tablespoons extra-virgin olive oil, plus more as needed
- 3 pounds bone-in, skin-on chicken parts (I like using half thighs, half breasts)
- 5 tablespoons unsalted butter
- 1 large yellow onion, diced
- 3 large carrots, peeled and cut into ½-inch rounds
- 3 celery stalks, cut into ½-inch pieces
- 4 to 6 garlic cloves (depending on how much you love garlic!), minced
- 8 cups chicken broth
- 2 bay leaves
- 2 sprigs of thyme
- 2 chicken bouillon cubes
- 1½ teaspoons fine sea salt, plus more as needed
- ½ teaspoon ground white pepper
- 8 ounces egg noodles or your preferred pasta
- ¼ cup chopped fresh parsley
- Fresh lemon juice, for serving (optional)

This is what you need to make your loved ones whenever they're feeling down and need a little comfort. It's so easy but so flavorful—and it tastes like health in a bowl. I love to augment the flavor of fresh aromatics with their powdered counterparts; that is why you will find both fresh and powdered garlic and onion here. A small hit of the powdered version makes the fresh vegetables really sing.

In a small bowl, mix together the garlic powder, onion powder, paprika, black pepper, and fine salt.

Drizzle 1 tablespoon of the oil onto the chicken pieces, then rub the seasoning mix evenly over all the pieces.

In a large Dutch oven or deep heavy-bottomed pot, heat the remaining 2 tablespoons oil over medium-high heat until hot. Working in batches, sear the chicken until it develops a golden crust, 4 to 5 minutes per side, then transfer to a plate. Add more oil as needed for subsequent batches.

Reduce the heat to medium and melt the butter. Add the onion, carrots, and celery and sauté, stirring occasionally, until the vegetables soften and the onion turns translucent, 4 to 6 minutes. Add the garlic and cook for 1 to 2 minutes until fragrant.

Pour in the chicken broth and bring to a gentle simmer. Add the bay leaves, thyme, bouillon cubes, salt, black pepper, and white pepper. Return the chicken pieces to the pot, ensuring they are submerged in the broth. Reduce the heat to medium-low, cover, and simmer gently until the chicken is tender and cooked through, 25 to 30 minutes.

Pull out the chicken and when cool enough to handle, shred into bite-sized pieces, discarding the skin and bones. Set the chicken aside.

Discard the bay leaves and thyme stems. If you prefer a clear broth, strain the broth through a fine-mesh sieve, discarding the vegetables, then return the strained broth to the pot. For a soup with more texture, skip the straining step and leave the vegetables in the soup.

Return the broth to a gentle boil. Stir in the egg noodles and cook until al dente according to the package instructions.

Reduce the heat to a simmer. Return the shredded chicken to the pot, along with the parsley. Simmer for another 5 to 10 minutes to meld the flavors—the chicken should be fully heated and the noodles tender. Taste and adjust the seasoning with more salt or pepper, if needed, and serve with a squeeze of lemon juice, if desired.

creamy chicken gnocchi soup

Serves 4 to 6

- 2 chicken breasts (see Notes), patted dry
- Kosher salt and black pepper
- Garlic powder
- ⅓ cup olive oil, plus more for drizzling
- 3 tablespoons unsalted butter
- 4 celery stalks, chopped
- 1 medium onion, chopped
- 1 large carrot, shredded on the large holes of a box grater
- 6 garlic cloves, minced
- 4 cups chicken broth
- 1 teaspoon onion powder
- 1 teaspoon fresh thyme leaves
- 1 (16-ounce) package gnocchi (see Notes)
- 2 cups half-and-half
- Cornstarch slurry: 1 tablespoon cornstarch, mixed with ¼ cup water
- 4 cups baby spinach (about 2 large handfuls)
- Freshly grated Parmesan cheese, for garnish (optional)
- Red pepper flakes, for garnish (optional)

While this soup is a beloved menu item at Olive Garden, funny enough, I created this version without ever trying the original—or even stepping foot in an Olive Garden. I was younger, standing in my parents' kitchen, when my sister and I came across a video that mentioned the idea of putting soft, pillowy gnocchi in a creamy, veggie-packed broth. It just sounded so wonderful and comforting . . . so we made it once and never stopped. It became a go-to in our house, and honestly, it's a recipe I know I'll be making for the rest of my life.

note:
- You can substitute 2 cups cubed rotisserie chicken if you don't want to cook the chicken breasts from scratch.
- If you've never cooked with gnocchi before, look for packages in the refrigerated section of the grocery store, near the fresh pastas and raviolis, or shelf-stable versions in the pasta aisle.

Season both sides of the chicken breasts with a dusting of salt, black pepper, and garlic powder.

Drizzle a little oil into a medium skillet and heat over medium-high heat. Add the chicken breasts (you should hear a sizzle) and cook until the first side is slightly golden, 3 to 4 minutes. Flip and brown the second side for 3 minutes.

Add ¼ cup water to the pan, reduce the heat to medium, cover, and cook until an instant-read thermometer inserted into the thickest part of a breast reads 165°F, about 6 minutes. Remove the chicken from the pan and let it rest for 10 minutes before cutting into cubes.

In a large pot or Dutch oven, heat the oil and the butter over medium heat. Add the celery, onion, and carrot and sauté until the vegetables are softened and the onion is translucent, about 4 minutes. Add the garlic and sauté until fragrant, about 1 minute.

Stir in the cubed chicken, chicken broth, 1 teaspoon salt, 1 teaspoon black pepper, 1 teaspoon garlic powder, onion powder, and thyme. Bring the mixture to a boil, add the gnocchi, and cook for 3 minutes. Reduce the heat to achieve a gentle simmer, cover, and simmer for 10 minutes to meld the flavors.

Pour in the half-and-half, then whisk the cornstarch slurry to loosen it up and add it to the pot. Increase the heat to bring the mixture back to a gentle boil, stirring frequently, until you achieve a creamy and slightly thickened consistency.

Remove the pot from the heat and stir in the spinach until wilted. Taste and adjust the seasoning if necessary.

Ladle the soup into serving bowls. If desired, garnish with the Parmesan and/or pepper flakes.

tomato soup *with* garlic-bread grilled cheese

Serves 6

Tomato Soup

- 6 tomatoes (such as Romas), chopped
- 1 red bell pepper, chopped
- ¼ cup unsalted butter
- ¼ cup extra-virgin olive oil
- 1 onion, minced
- 6 garlic cloves, minced
- 1 (6-ounce) can tomato paste
- 2 tablespoons chopped fresh basil, plus whole or chopped leaves for garnish
- 2 to 2½ cups chicken broth
- 2 tablespoons brown sugar
- 1 tablespoon dried oregano
- 1½ teaspoons fine sea salt
- 1½ teaspoons black pepper
- 1 teaspoon onion powder (optional)
- 1 teaspoon garlic powder (optional)
- 1 teaspoon dried basil
- ½ teaspoon ground white pepper
- Cayenne pepper
- 2 cups heavy cream, plus more for garnish

Garlic-Bread Grilled Cheese

- ½ cup unsalted butter, at room temperature
- 6 garlic cloves, minced
- 2 tablespoons chopped fresh basil
- 1 teaspoon red pepper flakes, plus more as needed
- Pinch of fine sea salt
- 12 (½-inch) slices of your preferred bread (such as white or sourdough)
- 12 slices nice-quality mild Cheddar cheese
- 8 ounces freshly grated extra-sharp Cheddar cheese (about 2 cups)
- Mayonnaise, for spreading on bread slices
- Butter or cooking spray, for the pan

I didn't grow up eating tomato soup with grilled cheese, but once I tried it, it became an instant classic in my repertoire. But of course, I wanted to put my own spin on things. First, I decided to roast the tomatoes to give the soup a depth of flavor you can never get from raw or boiled tomatoes. I'm obsessed with garlic—as you get further along in this cookbook, you'll see it pop up everywhere—so I decided that the best way to sneak more garlic in here was to use garlic bread as the base for my grilled cheese. But the garlic is hidden *inside* the sandwich, rather than on the outside, so when you take a bite you get this garlicky surprise.

I still remember the first time I made this for my family. (I always find it exciting to make food that is a bit new to us, to see their reaction.) Of course, they loved it, and now it has become an annual fall tradition for me to make a huge batch of tomato soup with garlic-bread grilled cheese sandwiches.

Make the tomato soup: Preheat the oven to 425°F.

Arrange the tomatoes and bell pepper in an even layer on a sheet pan. Roast until tender, about 20 minutes. Turn the oven to broil and broil until the tomatoes develop a nice char, about 3 minutes.

Meanwhile, in a large pot, heat the butter and oil over medium heat until the butter melts. Add the onion and sauté until translucent, about 2 minutes. Add the garlic and sauté until fragrant, 2 to 3 minutes. Add the tomato paste and fresh basil and sauté for 2 to 3 minutes.

Transfer the roasted tomatoes and bell pepper to the pot. Add the broth and stir to combine. Add the brown sugar, oregano, salt, black pepper, onion powder (if using), garlic powder (if using), dried basil, white pepper, and cayenne to taste. Adjust the seasonings as needed. Cooking doesn't have to be strict, so tailor it to your preference.

recipe continues →

tomato soup with garlic-bread grilled cheese, *continued*

Cook until the flavors have melded, about 15 minutes. Use an immersion blender to puree the soup until smooth. (Or allow the soup to cool slightly, then blend in batches in a standard blender. Once blended, return the soup to the pot.) Add the cream and simmer for 5 minutes until incorporated. At this point, you can either keep the soup warm on the stove (cover it to retain the heat) or refrigerate it and reheat it before serving.

Make the garlic-bread grilled cheese: Preheat the oven to 350°F.

In a small bowl, stir together the butter, garlic, fresh basil, pepper flakes, and salt.

Generously spread the garlic-butter mixture on one side of each slice of bread. Arrange the slices of bread on a sheet pan, garlic butter–side up, and bake until golden and fragrant, about 10 minutes. Remove the pan from the oven.

Top the garlic-butter side of each of six slices of bread with two slices mild Cheddar and a generous portion of extra-sharp Cheddar. Close the sandwich with the other slices of bread, buttered-side down. Spread a thin layer of mayo on both unbuttered sides of the sandwiches.

Heat a medium skillet over low heat. Lightly grease the pan with a small amount of butter or cooking spray. Working in batches, add the sandwiches to the pan. Cover the pan with a lid and toast until the first side is golden brown, about 3 minutes. Flip the sandwiches, cover the pan, and toast the other side until golden and the cheese is thoroughly melted, about 3 minutes more. Keep a close eye on things—the sandwich can burn, even on low heat!

Cut the sandwiches as desired, ladle the tomato soup into bowls, drizzle with some heavy cream, and garnish with fresh basil leaves. Serve with the grilled cheese on the side—dipping in the soup is encouraged!

shishbarak
beef dumplings in yogurt sauce

Serves 4 to 6

Dough
- 3 cups / 375g all-purpose flour, plus more for dusting
- ¼ cup / 60g extra-virgin olive oil
- 2 teaspoons fine sea salt

Filling
- ¼ cup extra-virgin olive oil
- 1 onion, minced
- 1 pound ground beef (80/20)
- 2 tablespoons ground allspice
- 1 tablespoon ground cumin
- 2 teaspoons seven spice
- 1½ teaspoons ground cardamom
- 1½ teaspoons black pepper
- 1½ teaspoons fine sea salt
- ½ teaspoon ground turmeric
- ½ teaspoon ground white pepper
- ¼ teaspoon ground cinnamon
- ½ cup toasted pine nuts

Yogurt Sauce
- 32 ounces (1 quart) plain whole milk Greek yogurt
- 2 cups boiling water or chicken broth, plus more as needed
- 1 egg white
- Cornstarch slurry: 1½ teaspoons cornstarch, dissolved in 2 tablespoons warm water
- 1 tablespoon sugar
- 1 teaspoon fine sea salt, plus more to taste

To Finish
- 2 tablespoons extra-virgin olive oil
- 4 garlic cloves, minced
- ¼ cup chopped fresh cilantro or curly parsley, plus more for garnish (optional)
- Toasted pine nuts (optional)

Shishbarak is widely loved throughout the Arab world. You start by making small wheat-based dough wrappers, then stuffing them with a spiced meat filling we call mashi. The result is a shape somewhat reminiscent of Italian tortellini that we then bake until golden and somewhat crisp. Then comes the best part, in my opinion: We simmer the dumplings in a beautifully tart, yogurt-based soup to cut through the richness of the warm spiced beef. Traditionally, this soup base would be made with jameed, a hard ball of dehydrated yogurt. This product is widely available at well-stocked Arab groceries, but I wanted to make sure everyone could make this dish at home, so in the recipe below, I start with plain yogurt instead.

The process of stuffing and simmering the dumplings isn't difficult, but it does take time. If you grew up in an Arab household, shishbarak is probably very sentimental for you: It's a labor of love, so when someone takes the time to cook it for you, you know they really care.

Make the dough: In a large bowl, combine the flour, oil, salt, and 1 cup / 240g water. Mix with your hands until combined, adding up to ¼ cup / 60g additional water if necessary for the dough to come together. Your dough should have the consistency of Play-Doh.

Lightly flour or oil your hands, then knead the dough in the bowl or on a clean, lightly floured surface until it comes together into a cohesive, elastic mass, about 5 minutes. Cover with plastic wrap and let the dough rest while you prepare the filling.

Make the filling: In a large skillet, heat the oil over medium heat. Add the onion and sauté until softened, 2 to 3 minutes. Add the beef and cook, breaking it up into small crumbles, until browned, 7 to 10 minutes.

Stir in the allspice, cumin, seven spice, cardamom, black pepper, salt, turmeric, white pepper, and cinnamon. Mix well and cook for 2 to 3 minutes to meld the flavors. Fold in the pine nuts and set the filling aside to cool.

recipe continues →

shishbarak, *continued*

On a lightly floured surface, roll out the dough into a sheet about ⅛ inch thick. Use a 2- to 3-inch round cookie cutter or glass and cut the dough into rounds. Gather and reroll the scraps once, if needed. You should end up with 50 to 60 rounds.

Place a heaping teaspoon of filling in the center of each dough round. Fold the round in half, pressing the edges to seal. Bring the two ends together, pinching to form a dumpling shape. Make sure to pinch tightly to prevent the filling from spilling out later on. As you finish shaping the dumplings, arrange them on two sheet pans lightly dusted with flour and cover them with a cloth.

Preheat the oven to 375°F.

Uncover the dumplings and bake until lightly golden and crisp, 15 to 20 minutes.

Make the yogurt sauce: In a large pot, combine the yogurt, water or chicken broth, egg white, cornstarch slurry, sugar, and salt. Use an immersion blender or whisk vigorously until completely combined. While blending or whisking continuously, turn on the heat to medium-high. Cook, blending or whisking, until it begins to bubble. The sauce should have the consistency of tomato soup.

Gently add the baked dumplings to the simmering yogurt sauce and cook until the dumplings are slightly softened and immersed in the flavor of the sauce, about 5 minutes.

To finish: In a small skillet, heat the oil over medium heat. Add the garlic and sauté until fragrant, 2 to 3 minutes. Stir in the cilantro and cook for another 30 seconds to 1 minute, just to infuse the flavor.

Traditionally, you'd pour the garlic and cilantro into the yogurt sauce and stir until combined. Alternatively, you can plate the shishbarak and drizzle the garlic, cilantro, and oil over top, as pictured. Serve warm, garnished with additional pine nuts if desired.

tip If your sauce *does* split, an immersion blender is your best friend. Just blend the sauce until it emulsifies.

I SLEEP IN MY KITCHEN

molokhia

mallow stew with chicken

Serves 4 to 6

- 1 whole chicken, cut into 8 pieces, or 4 chicken leg quarters
- 1 large onion, quartered
- 2 tablespoons chicken bouillon powder
- 1 teaspoon black pepper
- Extra-virgin olive oil, for drizzling
- 1 tablespoon smoked paprika
- 1 tablespoon adobo or chicken bouillon powder

Molokhia
- Extra-virgin olive oil, for drizzling
- 1 medium yellow onion, finely minced
- 1 small tomato, quartered
- 12 garlic cloves, minced
- 2 (14-ounce) bags frozen chopped molokhia, thawed
- 1 tablespoon ground coriander

For Serving
- Lemon wedges
- Vermicelli Rice (page 110) or pita bread

Molokhia is found throughout the Levant and North Africa and likely has origins in Egypt. This dish is named for its main ingredient, *molokhia*, which is a leafy vegetable that in English is called "jute," "jute leaves," or "jute mallow." Like okra, molokhia can be a bit controversial; it is quite bitter and has a specific almost-sticky texture that some people find off-putting. I love it, and when you top the stew with rich roasted chicken, the flavors and textures are quite harmonious.

This is a good dish to make in advance. Boil the chicken and prepare the stew, then transfer the boiled chicken to a baking pan, cover with foil, and refrigerate. Then, all you have to do is rewarm the stew and roast the chicken when you're ready to eat.

In a 5½-quart pot, combine the chicken pieces, onion, bouillon powder, black pepper, and enough water to come 1 to 2 inches from the top of the pot. Bring to a boil over medium-high heat. Once boiling, skim off any foam or impurities that rise to the surface. Reduce the heat to low and simmer gently until the chicken is fully cooked and tender, about 45 minutes.

Meanwhile, preheat the oven to 425°F.

Reserving the cooking liquid, transfer the chicken to a baking pan and drizzle all over with oil.

tip To make sure you get all of that goodness out of the skillet you sautéed the garlic in, dip it into the molokhia pot, swirl it around, then dump the contents back into the pot.

In a small bowl, mix together the smoked paprika and adobo and dust it evenly over the chicken. I like to use my hands to rub the seasoning into the oil for a beautiful even color, but this is optional. Add 1 to 2 cups of the chicken cooking liquid to the bottom of the pan to keep the chicken nice and juicy when baking. Transfer the pan to the oven.

Roast until the skin is golden and crisp, about 15 minutes. Set aside.

Cook the molokhia: In a large pot, heat a drizzle of oil over medium heat. Add the onion and cook until softened, about 4 minutes. Stir in the tomato and cook until softened, about 4 minutes. Add half the garlic and sauté just until fragrant.

Gradually add the molokhia to the pot, stirring well to incorporate with the onion-tomato mixture. When simmering, slowly ladle 1 to 2 cups of the reserved chicken cooking liquid, a little at a time, stirring as you go. Use just enough so the molokhia becomes slightly thick, but not too watery. Skim off any foam that forms.

In a small skillet, heat a touch more oil over medium heat. Add the remaining garlic and the coriander and sauté until aromatic, about 1 minute. Stir this mixture into the molokhia pot and simmer for another 5 minutes (see Tip). Before serving, fish out the quartered tomato—that was just there to help with the stew's texture.

To serve: Serve the molokhia hot, with the roasted chicken arranged on top or on the side, with lemon wedges for squeezing into the stew. Pair with the vermicelli rice or pita bread.

bamia

okra stewed in tomato sauce with lamb

Serves 4 to 6

- 3 pounds boneless leg of lamb, cut into large chunks
- 1 large onion, chopped
- 1 (6-ounce) can tomato paste
- Neutral oil, for frying
- 2 (14-ounce) bags frozen okra, thawed
- 1 small green bell pepper, minced
- 1 tablespoon chicken bouillon powder
- ½ teaspoon black pepper
- ½ teaspoon curry powder
- ¼ teaspoon ground cinnamon
- 2 tablespoons ghee or clarified butter
- 4 garlic cloves, minced
- Vermicelli Rice (page 110) or warm pita bread, for serving

Just like the Molokhia (page 97), people have conflicting opinions on bamia, a traditional Middle Eastern stew of okra, tomatoes, and lamb . . . either you love it, or you hate it. I happen to love it; otherwise, I wouldn't have included it in the book!

In my opinion, all the controversy comes from okra, which can be mucilaginous (a nice word for slimy) when stewed. But in my version, I fry the okra, which not only adds flavor but also improves the texture. If you ask me, frying is the answer to everything!

In a 5½-quart pot, combine the lamb with enough water to come 1 to 2 inches from the top of the pot. Bring to a boil over medium-high heat, skimming off any foam or impurities that rise to the surface.

Add the onion and tomato paste and stir until the tomato paste dissolves. Reduce the heat to medium, cover, and simmer until the lamb is just about tender but not fully cooked through, about 45 minutes. Remove the pot from the heat but keep the lamb and broth in the pot.

Meanwhile, line a plate with paper towels, set a colander on top, and set near the stove. Pour 2 inches oil into a deep heavy-bottomed pot and heat over medium heat to 350°F.

Pat the okra as dry as you can with paper towels. Working in batches so as not to crowd the pot, fry the okra until it develops a light golden color but doesn't brown, about 5 minutes. Use a slotted spoon to transfer the okra to the prepared colander.

Once the lamb is about 15 minutes away from being done, add the bell pepper, bouillon powder, black pepper, curry powder, and cinnamon to the pot. Carefully add the fried okra, stirring gently to keep the pieces intact. Simmer until the okra is fully cooked but not mushy, about 15 minutes.

In a small skillet, melt the ghee over medium heat. Add the garlic and sauté until fragrant, about 1 minute. Stir this garlic-ghee mixture into the pot with the lamb, mixing carefully to keep the okra intact.

Serve hot with the vermicelli rice or pita bread.

pasta & rice

three-cheese creamy baked mac and cheese

fan fave

Serves 8 to 10

- Butter, for the pan
- Fine sea salt
- 1 pound macaroni
- 1 to 2 tablespoons plus ½ cup unsalted butter
- 3 cups heavy cream
- 1 cup canned evaporated milk
- 4 ounces cream cheese
- 2 teaspoons ground white pepper
- 2 teaspoons paprika
- 2 teaspoons garlic powder
- 2 teaspoons onion powder
- 1 shallot, minced
- 6 garlic cloves, minced
- 3 tablespoons all-purpose flour
- 8 ounces freshly grated sharp or mild yellow Cheddar cheese (about 2 cups)
- 8 ounces freshly grated Gouda cheese (about 2 cups)
- 8 ounces freshly grated sharp or mild white Cheddar cheese (about 2 cups)
- 8 ounces freshly grated cheese of your choice (any of the above; about 2 cups), for topping
- Sliced green onions, for garnish (optional)

Mac and cheese is one of those dishes where I think you need to have a go-to recipe. So when I set out to develop mine, I thought about all the things that I love about mac and cheese. Personally, I think all mac and cheeses should be layered. You have to go all the way here—none of this "Well, that maybe seems like too much cheese." There is no such thing! On that note, I think you need to use a mix of cheeses. If you use just one cheese, the flavor is one-note. Three complementary cheeses take it to the next level. I also like to bake my mac and cheese so there's a little bit of crisp, textural contrast on the top but not a ton of browning.

Preheat the oven to 350°F. Butter a 9 × 13-inch rectangular or a similar 4-quart baking dish.

Bring a large pot of salted water to a boil over high heat. Add the macaroni and cook to al dente according to the package instructions. Reserving ½ cup of the cooking water, drain the pasta. Rinse it with cold water, transfer to a bowl, and add 1 to 2 tablespoons of the butter to stop the pasta from sticking to itself. Set aside.

In a medium saucepan, combine the cream, evaporated milk, cream cheese, 2 teaspoons salt, the white pepper, paprika, garlic powder, and onion powder. Simmer over low heat (but don't let it boil), stirring occasionally, until warmed through, about 5 minutes. Set aside.

In the same pot you used to boil the pasta, melt the remaining ½ cup butter over medium heat. Add the shallot and sauté until slightly translucent and fragrant, about 3 minutes (reduce the heat if it starts to brown). Reduce the heat to medium-low, add the garlic, and sauté until fragrant, about 3 minutes.

Gradually add the flour to the butter mixture, stirring constantly until it develops a light golden color, about 4 minutes. As soon as the roux is golden, slowly pour in the warmed cream mixture, stirring constantly to prevent lumps. Add the reserved pasta water and mix well. Gradually add the yellow Cheddar, Gouda, and white Cheddar to the sauce, stirring until melted and creamy. Taste the sauce and adjust the seasonings, if needed.

Add the cooked macaroni to the cheese sauce, stirring until well coated. Transfer half of the mac and cheese mixture to the prepared baking dish. Sprinkle with half the topping cheese. Repeat with the remaining macaroni mixture and topping cheese. Transfer to the oven.

Bake until the top layer of cheese is golden and bubbling, 10 to 20 minutes. If you like, pop it under the broiler for the last 3 to 5 minutes to ensure the cheese gets a bit browned. Garnish with green onions, if desired, and serve.

roasted yellow pepper pasta

Serves 4

- 4 large yellow bell peppers, halved
- 2 large shallots, peeled and halved
- 1 garlic bulb, top cut off to expose the cloves
- ¼ cup extra-virgin olive oil
- Fine sea salt and black pepper
- 1 teaspoon garlic powder
- 1 teaspoon onion powder
- 1 pound fusilli or pasta of your choice
- ¼ cup chopped fresh basil, plus more for garnish
- 6 tablespoons unsalted butter
- Grated zest of 1 lemon
- Flaky sea salt, for garnish

Sometimes, my best kitchen moments happen when I'm not trying so hard. One day, after a string of recipe-development fails, I was feeling defeated and just wanted to cook something simple and comforting—not for the cookbook, not for content—just for me. I had a few peppers, garlic, and shallots lying around, so I roasted them and blended them into a silky, all-veggie sauce. Stirred into hot pasta with a generous amount of butter, it became one of those meals that made me stop and say, "Wait, this is actually incredible."

The recipe couldn't be simpler: Roast and blend your veg, toss with pasta, and swirl in six tablespoons of butter. Yes, six. It sounds like a lot, but it's what gives the sauce that rich, glossy finish. Serve it with the Slow-Roasted Jalapeño Salmon (page 132), a piece of roast chicken, or just eat it on its own if you're leaning into an all-carb girl dinner!

Preheat the oven to 425°F.

Place the bell peppers and shallots, cut-side down, on a sheet pan. Place the garlic bulb on the same sheet. Drizzle everything with the oil and season with fine salt and black pepper. Wrap the seasoned garlic bulb in aluminum foil.

Roast until the peppers are charred and the garlic cloves are soft and caramelized, 25 to 30 minutes, turning the vegetables halfway through.

Squeeze the garlic cloves out of their skins into a blender. Add the roasted peppers and shallots and the garlic and onion powders to the blender and set aside.

Bring a large pot of salted water to a boil. Add the pasta and cook to al dente according to the package instructions. Reserving 1 cup of the pasta water, drain the pasta and set aside.

Add ½ cup of the pasta water to the blender with the roasted veg and blend until smooth.

Pour the sauce into a large saucepan and gently reheat over low heat. Stir in the basil. If your sauce seems too thick, gradually add more pasta water until it's nice and loose, keeping in mind the sauce will thicken as it sits.

Toss the pasta directly into the sauce, stirring to coat every strand and adding more pasta water, if needed; you want the sauce to stay loose and silky.

Stir in the butter and lemon zest and season with fine salt and black pepper to taste. Garnish with basil and a pinch of flaky salt and serve immediately.

fan fave

macarona béchamel

egyptian-style pasta bake

Serves 8

Fine sea salt
1 pound penne pasta
2 tablespoons extra-virgin olive oil, plus more as needed
1 pound ground beef (80/20)
1 medium onion, diced
1 tomato, preferably heirloom, diced
1 heaping tablespoon tomato paste
1 chicken bouillon cube
1 teaspoon dried oregano
1 teaspoon black pepper
¼ teaspoon ground nutmeg

Béchamel
5 tablespoons unsalted butter
4½ tablespoons all-purpose flour
4 cups whole milk, warmed
1 teaspoon fine sea salt
1 teaspoon ground white pepper
1 chicken bouillon cube
¼ teaspoon ground nutmeg

Assembly
1¾ cups freshly grated mozzarella cheese
Chopped fresh parsley, for garnish

This Egyptian dish might just be my favorite pasta recipe of all time. The first thing you will notice is the warm, comforting notes of béchamel, a classic French sauce made with a decadent amount of butter and finished with delicate, fragrant nutmeg. Then you bite into the happy amount of cheese and beef and think, "*What's not to love?*"

Preheat the oven to 400°F.

Bring a large pot of salted water to a boil over high heat. Add the penne and cook to al dente according to the package instructions. Drain the pasta, transfer to a large bowl, and toss with a bit of oil to prevent sticking. Set aside.

In a large cast-iron skillet or saucepan, heat the 2 tablespoons oil over medium heat. Add the beef and cook until lightly browned and no longer pink, 7 to 10 minutes.

Add the onion, tomato, tomato paste, bouillon cube, and 1 cup water. Cover and simmer for 5 minutes, stirring every minute or so to prevent sticking. Remove the pan from the heat and stir in the oregano, 1 teaspoon salt, the black pepper, and nutmeg. Taste and adjust the seasoning.

Make the béchamel: In a small pot, melt the butter over medium heat. Add the flour, stirring quickly and constantly to avoid lumps. Cook the flour, stirring constantly, until it develops a light golden color, 2 to 3 minutes.

While whisking constantly, pour in the warmed milk. Stir in the salt, white pepper, bouillon cube, and nutmeg, reduce the heat to medium-low, and simmer until the mixture thickens to a creamy and smooth consistency, 5 to 10 minutes.

To assemble: Add half the pasta to a 9 × 13-inch or 4-quart baking dish. Pour on half of the béchamel (about 2 cups), top with all the meat mixture, then add half of the mozzarella. Layer on the rest of the pasta and pour the remaining béchamel on top. Cover the baking dish with aluminum foil or a lid and transfer to the oven.

Bake for 20 minutes. Uncover and add the remaining mozzarella. Turn the oven to broil and broil until the cheese is melted and slightly golden, 5 to 10 minutes, depending on your broiler. Make sure to keep your eye on it!

Garnish with parsley and serve.

pasta *with* mussels and shrimp

Serves 4 to 6

- Fine sea salt
- 1 pound spaghetti
- ¼ cup unsalted butter
- 3 tablespoons extra-virgin olive oil
- 1 shallot, finely chopped
- 6 garlic cloves, minced
- 1½ to 3 teaspoons red pepper flakes
- ½ teaspoon black pepper
- ¼ cup tomato paste
- 16 ounces cherry tomatoes (2 pints), halved
- ½ cup seafood stock
- Juice of 1 lemon
- 2 pounds extra-jumbo shrimp, peeled and deveined
- 2 pounds mussels, cleaned and debearded
- Grated zest of ½ lemon
- ½ cup freshly grated Parmesan cheese (optional)
- ½ cup chopped fresh parsley, plus more for garnish
- Lemon wedges, for serving

When we were kids, if my mom made us a pasta dish like spaghetti and meatballs, my siblings and I would eat as many meatballs as we could and leave most of the pasta behind.

So I figured that if everyone's favorite part of a pasta dish is the add-ons, I might as well emphasize that. This recipe is heavy on the seafood, in part because I'm a big seafood lover, but also because I reasoned if someone tried to sneakily pick off shrimp and mussels before dinner was served, there would still be plenty left when the dish hit the table.

Bring a large pot of salted water to a boil over high heat. Add the spaghetti and cook to al dente according to the package instructions. Reserving ½ cup of the pasta cooking water, drain the pasta and set aside.

In a large Dutch oven, heat the butter and oil over medium heat. Add the shallot and sauté for 1 minute. Add the garlic and sauté until fragrant, about 2 minutes.

Stir in the pepper flakes (the amount will depend on your desired level of heat) and black pepper and sauté for 1 minute. Add the tomato paste and cook, stirring frequently, until it deepens in color, 2 to 3 minutes.

Add the cherry tomatoes and sauté until the tomatoes begin to soften, about 3 minutes.

Pour in the stock and lemon juice. Bring the mixture to a simmer and cook for 8 minutes to meld the flavors.

Add the shrimp and mussels, give them a toss to coat, then cover and cook until the mussels open and the shrimp are 95 percent cooked, 6 to 7 minutes, giving the pot a gentle shake every 2 minutes to encourage the mussels to open.

Using a slotted spoon or tongs, transfer the shrimp and mussels to a separate bowl. If you come across any mussels that have not opened fully, throw them out—we don't want them!

Add the spaghetti and reserved pasta water to the pot. Set over medium-high heat and cook, stirring occasionally with tongs or a spoon, until the sauce thickens and clings to the pasta, about 5 minutes. Season with salt if needed; start with 1 teaspoon, taste, and add more if desired.

Return the shrimp and mussels to the pot along with the lemon zest, Parmesan (if using), and parsley. Toss everything together and cook for an additional minute, so your shrimp fully cook from the residual heat from the pasta and sauce. Transfer to serving bowls, then garnish with parsley and serve with lemon wedges on the side.

vermicelli rice

Serves 6 to 8

3 cups basmati rice
2½ tablespoons ghee or olive oil
¾ cup broken-up vermicelli noodles
2½ teaspoons fine sea salt
¼ teaspoon ground turmeric

This is a classic side dish in our family, perfect with so many dishes in this book. Try it with Molokhia (page 97), Bamia (page 99), Saniyeh Kofta (page 161) . . . the sky's the limit!

Rinse the rice under cold water until it runs clear. This helps remove excess starch, so you get separate, fluffy grains instead of a gummy texture.

In a large pot, melt the ghee over medium heat. Add the vermicelli and cook, stirring frequently, until they turn a deep golden brown, about 5 minutes. Watch them closely, since they can quickly go from perfectly toasted to burnt.

Pour in the salt, turmeric, and 4¼ cups water, stirring to combine. Bring everything to a boil.

Add the rice, give it a quick stir, then cover the pot with a tight-fitting lid. Reduce the heat to low and let cook, undisturbed, for 15 to 20 minutes, until the rice is tender and has absorbed all the liquid.

Remove the pot from the heat and let sit, with the lid on, for 10 minutes to allow the rice to steam and fluff up.

Use a fork to gently separate the grains before serving.

oozi

spiced rice with beef, peas, and carrots

Serves 4 to 6

3 tablespoons extra-virgin olive oil
1 large onion, finely diced
1¼ pounds ground beef (80/20)
1 (16-ounce) bag frozen peas and carrots, thawed
2 teaspoons fine sea salt
2 teaspoons curry powder
2 teaspoons ground allspice
2 teaspoons black pepper
2 teaspoons seven spice
½ teaspoon ground cinnamon
½ teaspoon ground turmeric

Spiced Rice

2 cups basmati rice
3 tablespoons ghee or olive oil
1 tablespoon ground allspice
1 tablespoon curry powder
1 tablespoon seven spice
2 teaspoons fine sea salt
2 teaspoons Vegeta seasoning or chicken bouillon powder
2 teaspoons black pepper
½ teaspoon ground turmeric
¼ teaspoon ground cinnamon

For Serving

Chopped fresh parsley
Toasted pine nuts

Oozi is my lazy-girl meal for those "I don't know what to make for dinner and it's already 6:00 p.m." nights—we all have them! The foundation is rice, frozen peas and carrots, and ground beef, ingredients I almost always have on hand. And it uses only a couple of dishes, so there isn't even a bunch of cleanup at the end. When you remove the lid of the pot, a plume of spice-fragrant steam will waft into your kitchen, and you'll be greeted with plump colorful rice, dotted with pretty veggies. No one will believe you when you tell them it came together in only 30 minutes! Traditionally, we serve oozi with chicken leg quarters (if you'd like to go that route, follow the chicken instructions for Msakhan, page 139), but it's also delicious on its own for a simple dinner.

In a large saucepan, heat the oil over medium heat. Add the onion and sauté until softened and translucent, 3 to 4 minutes. Stir in the beef, breaking it apart with a spoon as it cooks, and cook until evenly browned, 5 to 7 minutes.

Add the peas and carrots, salt, curry powder, allspice, black pepper, seven spice, cinnamon, and turmeric. Stir to coat the beef and vegetables in the fragrant spices. Let the mixture cook for 5 to 7 minutes to meld the flavors. Remove the pan from the heat and set aside.

Make the spiced rice: Rinse the rice under cold water until it runs clear. This helps remove excess starch, so you get separate, fluffy grains instead of a gummy texture.

In a large pot, melt the ghee over medium heat. Stir in the rice, coating each grain with ghee, and toast for 3 minutes, stirring constantly so it doesn't burn.

Add the allspice, curry powder, seven spice, salt, Vegeta, black pepper, turmeric, and cinnamon. Stir well to evenly distribute the spices. Add 4 cups water and bring to a rolling boil. Reduce the heat to low, cover, and let simmer, undisturbed, until the rice is fully cooked and tender, 15 to 20 minutes. Remove the pot from the heat and let stand, covered, for 10 minutes to allow the rice to absorb any remaining moisture and to become fluffy.

To serve: Fluff the rice gently with a fork and transfer to a serving platter. Layer the spiced beef mixture over the rice. Garnish with the parsley and pine nuts.

maklouba

upside-down rice with chicken legs

Serves 6 to 8

3½ cups long-grain white rice
Neutral oil, for frying
¾ cup broken-up vermicelli noodles
2 medium globe eggplants, cut into ¼-inch-thick slices
Fine sea salt
3 large russet potatoes, peeled and cut into ¼-inch-thick slices
1 large head cauliflower, cut into medium florets
6 to 8 chicken leg quarters (as many as will fit in the bottom of your pot)
1 small onion, chopped
6 garlic cloves, sliced or crushed
2 bay leaves
¼ cup Vegeta seasoning or chicken bouillon powder
2½ tablespoons black pepper
1 tablespoon seven spice
1 tablespoon curry powder
1 teaspoon ground turmeric
1 teaspoon maklouba spice (optional)

For Serving
Toasted pine nuts or almonds
Chopped fresh parsley
Plain whole milk Greek yogurt or laban

Maklouba is a very traditional Palestinian-style upside-down rice, made for large gatherings, celebrations, or as a comforting weekend dinner. It is cooked in a large pot—I love to use my *siti*, or "grandma pot," which is a tapered aluminum pot, but you can use any 8-quart pot with a wide, flat bottom (nonstick if you have it!). Every family makes theirs differently—which I find so beautiful—but the one thing they have in common is that at the end of cooking, a serving plate is arranged on top of the pot and the whole thing is dramatically flipped so that the cooked meat, vegetables, and rice land, beautifully molded, on the serving plate.

In our family, it was a big deal to be chosen to do the flip. After all, everyone was watching you. You needed to be quick and confident. If you got anxious and stopped halfway, boom, you'd just spilled dinner all over the table! But I have some guidance for how to avoid this disaster on page 116.

This recipe is the way my Palestinian mother taught me to make maklouba, with striking layers of fried eggplant, fried cauliflower, fried potatoes, chicken, and rice, and a wonderful amount of flavor. She loved to use boxed parcooked rice, which is harder to mess up, but any long-grained rice will work. Her other secret tip? She'd always fry up a few extra potatoes to hold us over until dinnertime, so we wouldn't snack on the potatoes meant for the dish while she was cooking.

In a large bowl, soak the rice in enough cold water to cover it.

In a deep heavy-bottomed pot, add enough oil to just coat the surface (about 2 tablespoons). Heat over medium heat and add the vermicelli. Cook, stirring frequently, until they turn a deep golden brown, about 5 minutes. Watch them closely, since they can quickly go from perfectly toasted to burnt. Drain the rice, add it to the pot, and toast for 1 to 2 minutes more. Transfer to a bowl and set aside.

Line one or two sheet pans with paper towels and set near the stove. Wipe clean the pot you used to toast the vermicelli and pour in 2 inches oil. Heat over medium heat to 350°F.

Meanwhile, line a third sheet pan with paper towels and arrange the eggplant slices on it. Sprinkle salt on top.

When the oil is hot, working in batches so as not to crowd the pot, fry the potato slices until golden brown, 5 to 6 minutes. Transfer to the paper towels to drain. No need to salt them—they will be salted later on!

Allow the oil to return to temperature. Working in batches, fry the cauliflower until golden, 7 to 10 minutes. Transfer to the paper towels to drain.

Allow the oil to return to temperature. Pat the eggplant dry, then, working in batches, fry until golden, about 5 minutes. Transfer to the paper towels to drain. Set all the vegetables aside for later.

recipe continues →

maklouba, *continued*

Place the chicken leg quarters in an 8-quart pot and add enough water to come 2 to 3 inches from the top of the pot. Bring to a simmer over medium-high heat. Keep an eye on the pot and constantly skim and discard any impurities that rise to the surface. Cook until no more foam rises and the water is clear, 10 to 15 minutes. (Keep in mind, once you add the seasonings in the next step, you don't want to skim anymore, because you'll end up taking flavor away from the dish!)

Add the onion, garlic, bay leaves, Vegeta, black pepper, seven spice, curry powder, turmeric, maklouba spice (if using), and 2 teaspoons salt. Bring to a boil. Reduce the heat to medium, cover, and simmer for 30 minutes. Add boiling water, if needed, to keep about 3 inches of liquid above the chicken.

Remove the chicken and arrange it in a clean large (about 8-quart) pot or Dutch oven. You might have to play a bit of Tetris to get the leg quarters to fit; it's okay if they overlap slightly, but if your pot isn't wide enough to accommodate all eight leg quarters, just add as many as you can fit and save the others for another use. Strain, reserving the chicken broth. Taste and adjust seasoning as needed.

Make layers on top of the chicken in the following order: eggplant, potato, and cauliflower. Pour the rice mixture in an even layer over the cauliflower. Now add enough of your reserved chicken broth to come ¼ inch above the other ingredients. This is usually 9 cups for me, but it depends on the size of your pot.

Set the pot over medium heat and bring to a simmer. Reduce the heat to low and cover with a lid. You want to see a couple of happy bubbles on the surface, but we're not looking for an aggressive simmer. Cook without stirring until the rice is perfectly tender, 40 to 60 minutes. Check often, starting around the 30-minute mark. If at the one-hour mark you feel like there is still a substantial amount of liquid, uncover your maklouba, reduce the heat to medium-low, and simmer for an additional 10 to 15 minutes so the liquid can evaporate. Make sure to re-cover the pot once the liquid is reduced.

Remove the pot from the heat and carefully wrap the whole thing in a heavy blanket to keep warm. Let the maklouba sit for at least 30 minutes and up to 2 hours. This is essential! It allows the steam to distribute properly, so the texture of your rice will be perfect from top to bottom. It also helps the maklouba set and will make it easier for the next step—flipping it out onto a serving tray!

Call all of your guests into the kitchen so they can see all your hard work beautifully pay off! Remove the lid, cover the pot with a large, round serving tray, and then, using oven mitts, flip the pot so it's upside down on top of the tray. Everyone will be holding their breath at this point . . . so, with confidence, lift up the pot to reveal a gorgeous layered mountain of chicken, vegetables, and rice!

To serve: Place the maklouba in the center of the table along with a big serving spoon and encourage your guests to scoop out their portion. Garnish each serving with the pine nuts and fresh parsley. Pass some yogurt on the side and enjoy!

mansaf
rice with lamb and fermented yogurt sauce

Serves 4 to 6

Lamb Shanks
- 6 lamb shanks
- 1 large onion, coarsely chopped
- 8 green cardamom pods
- 2 bay leaves

Yogurt Sauce
- 2 quarts drinkable yogurt (aka laban; see Tips, page 119)
- 1 large egg, whisked
- 1 box (2 packets) jameed soup starter (see Tips, page 119)
- Fine sea salt, as needed
- ¼ cup ghee or clarified butter
- 3 garlic cloves, minced

Turmeric-Spiced Rice
- 3 tablespoons ghee or clarified butter
- 3 cups basmati rice
- 2½ teaspoons fine sea salt, or to taste
- ½ teaspoon ground turmeric

For Serving
- Shrak (Jordanian flatbread) or pita bread (not traditional for this, but more widely available)
- ¼ cup toasted pine nuts or slivered almonds
- Chopped fresh parsley (optional)

Mansaf is a beautiful layered dish of flatbread, topped with fragrant turmeric-spiced rice, stewed lamb shanks, and a distinctive yogurt sauce. It is the national dish of Jordan, and if you enjoy other yogurt-based dishes, I can promise you're going to love this. One of the essential ingredients in mansaf is jameed (see page 13), which is made from dehydrated salted sheep or goat's milk yogurt. The flavor of jameed is really unique and hard to replicate with other ingredients. It is salty, tangy, and essential to the dish, so I encourage you to seek out jameed soup starter (see Tips on page 119) in an Arab market or online. Of course, if you can find the more traditional jameed balls, you can definitely use those here, but the dehydrated soup starter is more readily available.

Mansaf takes some time to make because the lamb shanks need a few hours to cook, but most of that time is inactive. You can prep most of it in advance if you'd like, then gently reheat it and assemble the layers on a platter when it's time to serve.

Prepare the lamb shanks: In a large pot, combine the lamb shanks with enough water to cover by several inches. Add the onion, cardamom pods, and bay leaves. Bring to a boil over medium-high heat, skimming off any foam or impurities that rise to the surface. Reduce the heat to medium-low, cover, and simmer until the lamb is about halfway to tender, 1 to 1½ hours. Add more water as needed to keep the shanks covered.

Remove the lamb shanks and reserve the broth, discarding the solids. Keep the broth warm to use later.

Meanwhile, make the yogurt sauce: In a separate large pot, combine the yogurt drink and the egg. Whisk until the egg is fully incorporated; this will help stabilize the yogurt sauce and prevent curdling during cooking.

You may hate me for this step, but believe me when I say you have to whisk constantly! Whisking constantly in one direction, heat the sauce over medium-low heat. Once it reaches a gentle bubble, add the jameed soup starter and continue whisking in one direction. Gradually add 4 to 6 cups of the reserved lamb broth, stirring after each addition, until the sauce is thick enough to coat the back of a spoon but not overly dense; it should look like a loose gravy. Taste the sauce and add salt, if needed. You may feel that it's not needed at all—and that's normal! Jameed and laban are both naturally salty.

Once the yogurt sauce is smooth and warmed through, add the partially cooked lamb shanks to the pot. Simmer gently until the lamb is tender and the flavors have melded together, 30 to 45 minutes.

recipe continues →

mansaf, *continued*

In a small skillet, melt the ghee over medium heat. Add the garlic and sauté until fragrant, about 1 minute. Stir this mixture into the pot with the lamb and laban.

Make the turmeric-spiced rice: Rinse the rice under cold water until it runs clear. This helps remove excess starch, so you get separate, fluffy grains instead of a gummy texture.

In a large pot, combine the ghee and rice and stir to coat each grain in the ghee. Sprinkle in the salt and turmeric.

Bring the remaining lamb cooking broth to a simmer. You'll need 4¼ cups liquid to cook the rice; if you don't have enough broth, add boiling water to reach 4¼ cups. Pour over the rice and stir briefly to combine.

Set the pot of rice over medium-high heat and bring to a gentle boil. Reduce the heat to low, tightly cover, and simmer until the rice is fully cooked and the broth is absorbed, 15 to 20 minutes. Remove the pot from the heat and let it sit, covered, for 5 to 10 minutes to allow the rice to steam and fluff up.

Fluff the rice with a fork, being careful not to mash the grains.

To serve: While your rice is cooking, shred up enough shrak by hand to cover the entire surface of your serving platter.

Spread the rice on top of the shrak, then arrange the lamb shanks on top. Pour the warm yogurt sauce over the rice and lamb and serve any extra on the side for guests to ladle as desired.

Serve, garnished with the pine nuts and parsley (if using).

tips Drinkable yogurt, called *laban* in Arabic, is a salted yogurt drink popular throughout the Middle East. Look for it in Arab grocery stores or online. Karoun is a popular brand.

Jameed soup starter is found at Arab grocery stores and online. Most often, each box contains two pouches—use both for this recipe.

PASTA & RICE

warak dawali *(stuffed grape leaves with beef ribs)* recipe on page 122

warak dawali

(stuffed grape leaves with beef ribs)

Serves 6

Stuffed Grape Leaves
- 4 cups medium-grain white rice
- 1 (16-ounce) jar grape leaves
- 1 pound ground beef (80/20)
- 1 small yellow onion, grated on the large holes of a box grater
- 12 garlic cloves (about 1 bulb), minced
- 1 cup chopped fresh curly parsley
- ⅓ cup ghee, melted
- 2½ tablespoons pomegranate molasses
- 2 tablespoons extra-virgin olive oil
- 2 tablespoons seven spice
- 1½ tablespoons fine sea salt
- 1 tablespoon curry powder
- 2 teaspoons black pepper
- 1½ teaspoons ground turmeric
- ½ teaspoon ground cinnamon

Beef Ribs
- 2 tablespoons vegetable oil
- 1 medium yellow onion, thinly sliced
- 2 large tomatoes, thinly sliced
- 1 rack beef short ribs (3 to 4 pounds)
- 1 (6-ounce) can tomato paste
- ½ cup fresh lemon juice
- 2 tablespoons pomegranate molasses
- 2 tablespoons extra-virgin olive oil
- 2 teaspoons fine sea salt

If I had to guess, you've probably encountered stuffed grape leaves at some point in your life, maybe in a Greek restaurant (where they might be called dolmas) or anywhere specializing in Mediterranean and Arab cuisine. For me, and for many people who grew up in Arab households, *warak dawali* ("stuffed grape leaves") are a celebration food, something you make as a group with your friends and loved ones. I'll admit, this is one of those dishes that takes a bit of time to put together; that is why you're going to want to set up an assembly line to help you fill and wrap the grape leaves.

My advice to first-timers is, avoid the temptation to overfill the leaves. If you do that, the delicate leaves might tear. Each jar of grape leaves is slightly different, but there are usually sixty to seventy grape leaves per jar—which means you might run out of grape leaves and have a bit of filling left over. My mom usually steamed the leftover filling in a pot, cooking it like you would plain rice. We'd snack on the filling during the three-plus hours it took for the grape leaves to cook on the stovetop.

Like the Maklouba (page 114), this dish involves theatrically flipping the finished dish onto a serving platter. Don't worry if some of the grape leaves tumble down the sides of the beef when you flip it; you can serve it as is, or you can neatly restack them on top. I feel like this recipe could be a full meal on its own, but you can also add sliced radishes, whole green onions, and olives on the side if you'd like!

Make the stuffed grape leaves: Place the rice in a sieve and rinse until the water runs clear. Transfer the rice to a large bowl filled with warm water and soak for 30 minutes. Drain the rice, then return the rice to the bowl.

Meanwhile, drain the grape leaves and rinse them under cold water to remove excess brine. Bring a large pot of water to a boil over high heat.

Working in batches of ten to fifteen leaves at a time, use a spider strainer to carefully transfer the grape leaves to the boiling water. Blanch for 1 to 2 minutes, or until they are tenderized but not mushy. Use the spider to transfer the leaves to a sieve set over the sink or to a sheet pan lined with paper towels to drain.

To the bowl with the rice, add the beef, onion, garlic, parsley, ghee, molasses, olive oil, seven spice, salt, curry powder, black pepper, turmeric, and cinnamon. Use your hands to mix until thoroughly incorporated. Set aside.

Place a grape leaf on a clean cutting board with the shiny-side down and the stem facing toward you. If there is a stem, cut it away. If any of the leaves are significantly larger than the others, you can cut them in half through the stem, then fill and roll each half.

Transfer about 1 teaspoon of the rice mixture to the center of the leaf, near the bottom (stem) end. Fold the bottom of the leaf over the filling, then fold in the sides. Tightly roll the leaf (taking care not to tear the leaf) the rest of the way over the filling. Repeat this process with the remaining grape leaves and rice mixture. Set the stuffed grape leaves aside.

Prepare the beef ribs: In a 5½-quart Dutch oven or deep heavy-bottomed pot, heat the vegetable oil over medium-low heat. Add the onion and sauté until softened, 3 to 5 minutes. Remove the pot from the heat.

Layer the tomatoes evenly on the bottom of the pot over the sautéed onions. Arrange the beef back ribs in as even a layer as possible (if you have to stack a few on top of each other, that's okay), with the bone of the ribs facing up, on top of the tomatoes. Neatly arrange a layer of the stuffed grape leaves over the ribs, making sure they all face in the same direction. Arrange a second layer of grape leaves on top of the first, all facing in the direction perpendicular to the first layer. If you have more grape leaves, make a third layer of grape leaves that faces the same direction as the first.

In a large measuring cup or bowl, combine 3½ cups water, the tomato paste, lemon juice, molasses, olive oil, and salt. Mix well to combine. Pour the prepared broth mixture over the stuffed grape leaves, ensuring they are submerged. If they are not, add water just until the grape leaves are covered.

Place a large plate upside down on top of the grape leaves to weight them down and prevent them from unfolding.

Set the pot over high heat and bring to a boil. Once boiling, cover the pot tightly with aluminum foil and then with a lid to create a tight seal. Turn down the heat to medium-low and simmer until the grape leaves are tender and the rice is cooked through, 3½ to 4½ hours (see Note). To check, take a grape leaf from the middle of the pot and check the doneness of the rice; it should be beautifully tender.

Remove the foil wrapping. If there is any broth left in the pot, with an oven mitt, VERY carefully hold down the plate (taking care not to burn yourself) and tip the pot to drain the broth into a large bowl (in case you want to save the broth for something else). With the oven mitt, remove the plate from the top of the grape leaves. Place a large round platter (it must be wider than the pot) on top of the pot and carefully flip the pot onto the platter. Lift up the pot, revealing the grape leaves and beautifully cooked beef ribs, then serve!

note: If your onions and tomatoes are a bit burned, don't worry; they're mostly there to prevent your beef ribs from charring too much during the cooking period.

PASTA & RICE

seafood, poultry & meat

bang bang shrimp tacos *with* cabbage slaw

Serves 4 to 6

Bang Bang Sauce
½ cup mayonnaise (preferably Kewpie)
3 tablespoons Thai sweet chili sauce
1 tablespoon sriracha
1 teaspoon honey

Fried Shrimp
½ cup cornstarch
½ cup all-purpose flour
½ cup panko bread crumbs (optional, for extra texture)
1 teaspoon garlic powder
1 teaspoon onion powder
1 teaspoon ground white pepper
1 teaspoon fine sea salt
½ teaspoon black pepper
½ cup buttermilk
1 pound large shrimp, peeled and deveined
Neutral oil, for frying

For Serving
12 to 18 fresh corn tortillas, warmed
Shredded green cabbage
Chopped fresh cilantro
Sliced green onions
Lime wedges

Fried shrimp with a sweet and spicy bang bang sauce are the perfect accompaniment for soft corn tortillas. If you've never had bang bang sauce before, what have you been doing with your life? It's so good . . . it's a sweet, spicy mayonnaise sauce that is good on pretty much every sandwich or taco I can imagine. Just make sure to serve the tacos soon after frying the shrimp, so they're extra crispy when you take your first bite!

tip When dredging food, I am a big fan of the dry hand, wet hand technique: Use one hand to dredge the food in the flour and the other hand for dredging in a wet mixture like buttermilk.

Make the bang bang sauce: In a bowl, whisk together the mayonnaise, chili sauce, sriracha, and honey until smooth. Set aside.

Make the fried shrimp: In a medium bowl, whisk together the cornstarch, flour, panko (if using), garlic powder, onion powder, white pepper, salt, and black pepper.

In a separate medium bowl, combine the buttermilk and ¼ cup of the cornstarch-flour mixture. Set up a dredging station with the flour mixture and the buttermilk mixture.

Line a plate with paper towels and set near the stove. Pour 1 to 2 inches oil into a deep heavy-bottomed pot and heat over medium heat to 350°F.

Line a sheet pan with parchment paper.

Working with one or two shrimp at a time so you get a nice coating, toss them in the flour mixture, pressing lightly to make the coating stick. Dip them into the buttermilk mixture, allowing excess to drip off. Then return them to the flour mixture for a final dredge. Arrange the shrimp on the lined sheet pan.

Working in batches so as not to crowd the pot, fry the shrimp until golden and crispy, 2 to 3 minutes per side. Transfer to the paper towels to drain.

To serve: Toss the fried shrimp in bang bang sauce until coated. Place a few pieces on each warm tortilla and top with shredded cabbage, cilantro, green onions, and a squeeze of lime. Serve immediately, while hot and crispy!

spiced jumbo crab cakes *with* lemon aioli

Serves 6

- 1 cup mayonnaise
- 3 garlic cloves, finely grated (preferably on a Microplane)
- 3 tablespoons fresh lemon juice
- 2 tablespoons Dijon mustard
- 2 tablespoons Frank's RedHot sauce or your favorite cayenne hot sauce
- 1 tablespoon grated onion
- 1 tablespoon Worcestershire sauce
- 2½ teaspoons garlic powder
- 2 teaspoons Old Bay seasoning
- ½ teaspoon cayenne pepper (optional, for extra kick)
- 1½ teaspoons black pepper
- ½ teaspoon ground ginger
- 2 large eggs
- 2 pounds jumbo lump crabmeat
- 1 generous handful of chopped fresh parsley
- ½ cup panko bread crumbs, plus more for topping
- 6 teaspoons unsalted butter, cold
- Lemon Aioli (recipe follows), for serving

This recipe is jumbo in every sense: big on flavor, big on crabmeat, and, well, just BIG! Jumbo crab cakes are the only way to make them in my eyes—I just want a beautiful mound of crab on my plate. But if you prefer them smaller, you can divide the mixture into twelve smaller cakes.

Make sure to use jumbo lump crabmeat here—you will find it frozen or refrigerated in a plastic tub in the seafood section—so that each bite will be bursting with crabmeat.

Cut six 6-inch squares of parchment paper and arrange them on a sheet pan.

In a large bowl, whisk together the mayonnaise, garlic, lemon juice, mustard, hot sauce, onion, Worcestershire sauce, garlic powder, Old Bay, cayenne (if using), black pepper, and ginger. Whisk in the eggs until the mixture becomes smooth and well blended.

Gently fold in the crab, being careful not to break up the pieces. Fold in the parsley and panko.

Form the mixture into six large mounds, each about 2 inches thick and 4 inches in diameter. Place each on a parchment square on the prepared sheet pan, then cover the sheet pan with plastic wrap and refrigerate for at least 30 minutes and up to 1 hour. This will help them hold their shape during baking.

Preheat the oven to 400°F.

Remove the crab cakes and add 1 teaspoon butter and a sprinkling of panko on top of each. Transfer the pan to the oven.

Bake until golden brown and slightly crisp on the outside, 20 to 25 minutes.

To serve, spoon a dollop of aioli on each of six serving plates and use the back of a spoon to spread it in a pretty pattern. Place a crab cake on top and serve immediately with any extra aioli on the side!

lemon aioli

Makes about 1 cup

- 1 large egg yolk, at room temperature
- 3 garlic cloves, finely grated (preferably on a Microplane)
- 1½ teaspoons Dijon mustard
- ½ teaspoon fine sea salt
- 1 cup olive oil
- 1½ tablespoons fresh lemon juice
- ½ teaspoon black pepper

Choose one of the following methods for blending the ingredients:

- **Food processor:** In a food processor, combine the egg yolk, garlic, mustard, and salt. Pulse until well mixed. With the machine running, slowly drizzle in the oil, starting with just a few drops. Once it begins to emulsify, add the oil in a slow, steady stream until the mixture is smooth and creamy—if you add the oil too fast, you risk your aioli separating. Add the lemon juice and black pepper and pulse a few more times to combine.
- **By hand:** In a medium bowl, whisk together the egg yolk, garlic, mustard, and salt until smooth. Whisking constantly, slowly drizzle in the oil, starting with just a few drops. As it thickens, gradually add the rest of the oil in a slow, steady stream, whisking until the aioli is smooth and creamy—if you add the oil too fast, you risk your aioli separating. Whisk in the lemon juice and black pepper until fully combined.
- **Immersion blender:** Follow the steps for the hand method, but instead of whisking, use your immersion blender!

For all methods, taste and adjust the seasoning as needed. If it's too thick, stir in a little cold water to loosen it up. Store in an airtight container in the fridge for 2 or 3 days.

teriyaki salmon *with* mango salsa and quinoa

Serves 4 to 6

Teriyaki Salmon
- ½ cup soy sauce
- 4 garlic cloves, grated
- 1-inch knob fresh ginger, grated
- 2 tablespoons honey
- 2 tablespoons brown sugar
- 2 tablespoons toasted sesame oil
- 1 tablespoon distilled white vinegar
- 1 teaspoon cornstarch
- ¼ teaspoon red pepper flakes
- 4 to 6 Atlantic salmon fillets (about 6 ounces each)

Mango Salsa
- 2 mangoes, diced
- 1 avocado, diced
- 1 red bell pepper, diced
- 1 small onion, diced
- 1 handful of chopped fresh cilantro
- 1 habanero, seeded and diced
- 1 tomato, diced
- ¼ cup extra-virgin olive oil
- Juice of 1 lime
- ½ teaspoon garlic powder
- Fine or flaky sea salt and black pepper

Quinoa
- 1 cup quinoa, rinsed
- 1¾ cups vegetable broth
- Pinch of fine sea salt

For Serving
- Thinly sliced green onions
- Sesame seeds
- Balsamic glaze (optional)

This is one of my go-to weeknight dinners. I love salmon because it's healthy, delicious, and, I promise, one of the easiest fish to cook. Here, I marinate it in a sweet and umami-packed teriyaki sauce. Mango and salmon are a match made in heaven, so I love to make a fresh and fruity salsa with mango, bell pepper, avocado, and red onion. I dice the veg so they're exactly the same size—that way, every bite is perfectly balanced and none of the ingredients overwhelms the others.

Prepare the teriyaki salmon: In a large bowl, whisk together the soy sauce, garlic, ginger, honey, brown sugar, sesame oil, vinegar, cornstarch, pepper flakes, and ¼ cup water. Add the salmon and toss gently with your hands to coat evenly. Cover with plastic wrap and refrigerate for at least 30 minutes and up to 2 hours.

Make the mango salsa: In a large bowl, combine the mango, avocado, bell pepper, onion, cilantro, habanero, and tomato.

In a small bowl, whisk together the olive oil, lime juice, and garlic powder. Pour the dressing over the mango mixture and toss gently to combine. Season to taste with salt and black pepper. Set aside.

Preheat the oven to 400°F. Line a sheet pan with parchment paper.

Cook the quinoa: In a medium saucepan, combine the quinoa, broth, and salt. Bring to a boil over medium-high heat, then reduce the heat to low, cover, and simmer until the water is absorbed, about 15 minutes. Remove the pan from the heat and let it sit, covered, while you cook the salmon.

Cook the salmon: Reserving the marinade, place the salmon skin-side down on the lined sheet pan.

Bake until it registers 145°F on an instant-read thermometer, 12 to 15 minutes.

Meanwhile, pour the reserved teriyaki marinade into a small saucepan and simmer over medium-low heat until it thickens slightly, 3 to 5 minutes.

Brush the baked salmon with the thickened teriyaki sauce.

To serve: Fluff the quinoa with a fork and divide among serving plates. Set a salmon fillet on top. Spoon the salsa over the salmon and garnish with the green onions and sesame seeds. If desired, drizzle with more of the thickened teriyaki sauce or balsamic glaze.

SEAFOOD, POULTRY & MEAT

slow-roasted jalapeño salmon *with* citrus chimichurri

Serves 4 to 6

- 1 (2- to 3-pound) skin-on salmon fillet
- ½ cup unsalted butter, at room temperature
- 3 garlic cloves, finely grated (preferably on a Microplane)
- 2 tablespoons chopped fresh chives
- 1 teaspoon smoked paprika
- 1 teaspoon fine sea salt
- 1 teaspoon garlic powder
- 1 teaspoon black pepper
- ½ teaspoon onion powder
- 1 medium red onion, thinly sliced
- 2 jalapeños (seeded if you wish less heat), thinly sliced
- 1 lemon, thinly sliced

Citrus Chimichurri
- ½ cup finely chopped parsley leaves
- ¼ cup finely chopped cilantro leaves
- Grated zest and juice of 1 orange
- Grated zest and juice of 1 lemon
- Grated zest and juice of 1 lime
- 4 garlic cloves, finely grated (preferably on a Microplane)
- 1 teaspoon dried oregano
- ¼ teaspoon red pepper flakes
- ½ cup extra-virgin olive oil
- 2 tablespoons distilled white vinegar
- Fine sea salt and black pepper

This is my go-to salmon when I want dinner to feel a little special without spending the whole day in the kitchen. I know cooking fish can feel intimidating—people always say it's easy to overcook or hard to tell when it's done—but this slow-roasting method fixes all that. Cooking it low and slow at 275°F makes the salmon super tender and flaky every time. The fat gently melts and basically bastes the fish as it cooks. Add spicy jalapeños, sliced red onion, and a good hit of citrus to balance out all that richness, and you've got a really solid, flavor-packed dinner that's actually super easy to make. It's a beautiful dish, one you'll definitely put on your weeknight dinner rotation.

Preheat the oven to 275°F. Line a large baking dish with parchment paper. The parchment paper will help you transfer the salmon without its falling apart—a spatula alone will not be enough for this recipe!

Place the salmon skin-side down in the prepared baking dish. Pat the flesh side dry with paper towels so the seasonings stick.

In a small bowl, mix together the butter, garlic, chives, smoked paprika, salt, garlic powder, black pepper, and onion powder. Rub this seasoned butter all over the exposed salmon flesh until evenly coated. Arrange the sliced onion (you might not need a whole onion, depending on the size of your fillet) and the jalapeños on top of the salmon and arrange the lemon slices on top. Transfer the pan to the oven.

Slow-roast until the salmon flakes easily with a fork or reads 125°F on an instant-read thermometer, 45 to 50 minutes.

Meanwhile, make the citrus chimichurri: In a medium bowl, mix together the parsley, cilantro, all the citrus zest and juices, the garlic, oregano, and pepper flakes. Stir in the oil and vinegar until well combined. Season with salt and black pepper to taste.

Once the salmon is done, carefully transfer it (including the parchment paper you cooked it on—this will help keep the lemon slices, red onions, and jalapeños on top) to a serving platter using a spatula. Carefully pull out and discard the parchment, then drizzle the fish with the chimichurri and serve.

pan-seared lemon-caper sea bass

Serves 4

Tomatillo Salsa Verde
- 1 pound tomatillos, husked and rinsed
- 1 jalapeño, halved and seeded
- 2 garlic cloves, peeled but whole
- ¼ cup extra-virgin olive oil, plus more for drizzling
- ½ cup fresh cilantro leaves
- ¼ cup fresh parsley leaves
- Juice of 1 lime
- 1½ tablespoons distilled white vinegar
- 1 teaspoon honey
- Fine sea salt and black pepper

Fennel-Radish Salad
- 1 fennel bulb, thinly sliced
- 6 radishes (such as Cherry Belle or watermelon, or a mix), thinly sliced
- ¼ cup chopped fresh dill
- 2 tablespoons fresh lemon juice
- 2 tablespoons extra-virgin olive oil
- Fine sea salt and black pepper

Sea Bass
- 4 skin-on sea bass fillets (about 6 ounces each), left at room temperature for 15 to 30 minutes
- Fine sea salt and black pepper
- 2½ tablespoons extra-virgin olive oil
- 6 tablespoons unsalted butter
- 4 garlic cloves, smashed
- Juice of 1 lemon
- 4 sprigs of fresh thyme
- 2 tablespoons capers, drained
- Chopped fresh parsley, for garnish

I recently spent time with my eight-year-old nephew and was so impressed by his adventurous palate. If it comes from the sea, he *loves* it, even sushi and other raw fish preparations. When I was eight, I wouldn't touch seafood, which is so sad . . . I didn't know what I was missing. Now of course, I am far more open-minded and love cooking fish. I developed this dish for people who are maybe a little on the fence about fish. I find sea bass to be extremely mild and not too fishy. It pairs beautifully with the herbaceous salsa verde and the freshness of the fennel-radish salad. When you see this plate with all its colors and textures, you might even forget that fish is the main event . . . until you take a bite of the buttery, tender flesh. At that point, I promise you'll be a fish convert!

Make the tomatillo salsa verde: Preheat the oven to 425°F.

Place the tomatillos, jalapeño, and garlic on a sheet pan. Drizzle with a little oil and toss to coat.

Roast until the tomatillos are blistered and softened and the jalapeño and garlic are slightly charred, 15 to 20 minutes. Remove the pan from the oven and let cool slightly.

Transfer the roasted vegetables to a blender. Add the cilantro, parsley, lime juice, and ¼ cup water. Blend until smooth. With the motor running, slowly add the ¼ cup oil, the vinegar, and honey until emulsified. Season with salt and black pepper to taste. Set aside.

Make the fennel-radish salad: In a large bowl, combine the fennel, radishes, and dill.

In a small bowl, whisk together the lemon juice and oil. Pour the dressing over the salad and toss to combine. Season with salt and black pepper to taste. Set aside.

Cook the sea bass: Pat the fillets dry with paper towels. Season both sides with salt and black pepper.

In a large skillet, heat the oil over medium-high heat. Add the fillets, skin-side down, and cook until the skin is crispy and golden brown, 4 to 5 minutes. Flip the fillets and cook until the fish is opaque and flakes easily with a fork, 2 to 3 minutes.

Reduce the heat to medium and add the butter, garlic, lemon juice, thyme, and capers to the skillet. Spoon the melted butter mixture over the sea bass fillets for 1 to 2 minutes to baste them with the sauce. Remove the fillets from the skillet and let them rest for a minute.

Divide the fennel-radish salad among serving plates and arrange a sea bass fillet on top. Drizzle the tomatillo salsa verde over the top of each fillet and around the plate. Garnish with the parsley and serve!

chicken shawarma wraps

Serves 6

Chicken Shawarma
- 5 pounds boneless, skinless chicken pieces (half thighs and half breasts)
- 1 cup distilled white vinegar
- ¼ cup vegetable oil, plus more for the pan
- 2 tablespoons hot sauce (your choice)
- 1½ heaping teaspoons paprika
- 1½ teaspoons fine sea salt
- 1 heaping teaspoon black pepper
- 1 heaping teaspoon ground turmeric
- ½ heaping teaspoon ground cinnamon

Wraps
- 6 pita breads, warmed
- 1 cup Creamy Garlic Sauce (page 138) or store-bought toum
- 3 Persian pickles (see Note), halved or quartered lengthwise
- 3 large tomatoes, sliced
- 1 red onion, sliced

One of the things I struggled with in writing this book was coming up with reasonable recipe yields for most home cooks. You see, growing up in a household of twelve with a mother who loved to cook, our yields were always *enormous*. Take this chicken shawarma, for example: When my mom originally developed the recipe, it called for *10 pounds* of chicken! She would keep the cooked shawarma in the fridge, and whenever one of us would tug at her clothes and say we were hungry, she could say, "There's shawarma in the fridge; go make yourself a sandwich."

I scaled this recipe back to use 5 pounds of chicken, which may still seem like a lot . . . but the Arab in me cannot tell you to make less. The warmly spiced, vinegary chicken is great in a sandwich, on a salad, or on its own—perfect for meal prep.

Make the chicken shawarma: Slice the chicken into very thin strips of uniform thickness.

In a large bowl, combine the chicken, vinegar, oil, hot sauce, paprika, salt, black pepper, turmeric, and cinnamon. Toss the chicken well so each strip is evenly coated in the marinade. Cover the bowl tightly with plastic wrap and refrigerate for at least 4 hours and preferably overnight.

Heat a large skillet over medium-high heat and add a bit of oil. Working in batches so as not to crowd the pan, add the chicken and cook, stirring occasionally, until all the liquid has evaporated and the chicken takes on a rich, golden-brown color, 7 to 10 minutes.

Build the wraps: Generously slather a warm piece of pita with garlic sauce. Add the chicken, pickles, tomatoes, and onion. Wrap the pita tightly around the filling, tucking in the sides to secure everything. Continue building the remaining wraps.

Serve immediately as is or toast them in the skillet that you cooked the chicken in or in a panini press.

note: Persian pickles are what I call the small cornichon pickles you'd buy at a Middle Eastern grocery store. They're a bit tangier and more sour than an American-style dill pickle, and I think they're perfect for wraps and sandwiches.

recipe continues →

chicken shawarma wraps, *continued*

creamy garlic sauce

Makes about 4 cups

3 tablespoons (packed) minced garlic
1 teaspoon fine sea salt
5 large egg yolks
1½ tablespoons fresh lemon juice
3 cups vegetable oil

In a food processor, pulse the garlic and salt for 1 minute, pausing at the 30-second mark to scrape down the sides with a spatula. You want a smooth, well-blended garlic paste.

Add the egg yolks and process until the mixture is thick and creamy, about 30 seconds.

With the machine running, pour in the lemon juice and process until fully combined. With the processor still running, add the vegetable oil in a slow, steady stream. Aim for a very thin ribbon of oil to avoid breaking the emulsion. Patience is important here! If the oil is added too quickly, the mixture might separate.

Once all the oil has been incorporated, turn off the food processor immediately. Your sauce should have a thick, glossy finish. Transfer it to a clean jar or airtight container and store it in the fridge for up to 1 week.

tip If your sauce breaks (it looks curdled or separated), transfer the broken mixture to a separate bowl. Clean out the food processor, add a fresh egg yolk, and turn on the food processor. Slowly add back in the broken sauce and process until it comes back to life.

fan fave

msakhan

flatbread with chicken, sumac, and caramelized onions

Serves 6

6 chicken leg quarters
1 small yellow onion, diced
2 bay leaves
1½ teaspoons fine sea salt
1½ tablespoons adobo
1½ tablespoons paprika
1½ tablespoons sumac

Caramelized Onions
6 large red onions, chopped
2 cups extra-virgin olive oil
5 tablespoons sumac
1 tablespoon fine sea salt
1½ to 3 teaspoons black pepper

Assembly
4 large flatbreads, such as Khubiz Taboon (page 172)
Extra-virgin olive oil
Sumac, for dusting (optional)
Chopped fresh curly parsley, for garnish
Toasted pine nuts (see Tip, page 141), for garnish

Msakhan is the national dish of Palestine and a staple in every Palestinian household. I grew up with my mom making it all the time, especially for Ramadan, when it was often the centerpiece of the first night's meal.

Traditionally made to celebrate the olive harvest, msakhan is built on the ingredients that have shaped Palestinian kitchens for generations—fresh-pressed olive oil being the closest to my heart. Msakhan is the kind of meal that feels generous by nature—it's meant to be placed at the center of a table, torn apart with your hands, and shared with the people you love most.

The foundation is khubiz taboon, our traditional flatbread, which is then topped with heaps of caramelized onions, succulent stewed chicken, fresh parsley, and toasted pine nuts. Growing up, I didn't realize how much power there was in something as simple as bread soaked with olive oil. But that's what msakhan is: simple ingredients carrying generations of history and love. It's a dish that says, "We're still here. Our trees are still standing. Our stories are still alive." Simply by enjoying time in the kitchen, we are participating in an act of cultural preservation, and for that reason, msakhan will always feel like the heart of Palestine to me.

In a large pot or Dutch oven, combine the chicken with enough water to cover (don't come any higher than 3 to 4 inches from the top so the water doesn't boil over) and bring to a boil. Skim and discard the foam that rises to the top until the water is clear.

Once boiling, add the onion, bay leaves, and salt. Reduce the heat to a steady boil, cover, and cook for 30 minutes.

Reserving the cooking liquid, remove the chicken from the pot and pat dry.

Preheat the oven to 550°F or as high as it will go.

Arrange the leg quarters in a large sheet pan or roasting pan and season the skin side with the adobo, paprika, and sumac. Pour enough liquid into the pan to come up the sides ½ inch (this keeps the chicken juicy), then transfer the pan to the oven.

Bake until the juices run clear and the internal temperature in the thickest part of the thigh reads 165°F on an instant-read thermometer, 10 to 15 minutes. Remove the pan from the oven.

Make the caramelized onions: In a large saucepan, combine the red onions and olive oil and cook until they are soft, about 10 minutes. Lower the temperature, if needed, to make sure the onions don't burn.

Add the sumac, salt, and black pepper and cook until the onion becomes soft with a bit of structure and is nearly translucent, 30 to 45 minutes. Remove the pan from the heat, cover, and set aside.

Preheat the broiler.

recipe continues →

SEAFOOD, POULTRY & MEAT

msakhan, *continued*

Assemble the msakhan: Brush one of the flatbreads generously on both sides with some of the reserved chicken cooking liquid, then use your hands or a pastry brush to rub a generous amount of oil on both sides. (If you'd like, you can use some of the oil that you used to caramelize the onions.)

Lay a flatbread on a sheet pan. Use a slotted spoon to transfer one-quarter of the caramelized onions to the bread. If desired, add a light dusting of sumac on top of the onions. Coat another flatbread with chicken cooking liquid and olive oil, stack it on top of the onions, and top it with one-quarter of the onions. Repeat with the remaining flatbreads until you have a stack of four.

Use tongs to transfer as many of the chicken leg quarters as you'd like on the top layer of onions. (For aesthetics, I like to arrange two on top; my mom typically piles all the chicken on top when she's serving our family.) Serve the remaining chicken leg quarters on the side in a separate serving dish or plate.

Pop the pan under the broiler and cook just until the edges of the bread are crisp (to your liking), about 5 minutes. Everyone's broiler is different, so keep a close eye on it. Remove the pan from the oven and sprinkle parsley and pine nuts on top.

To serve, divide the chicken among your serving plates, then cut the flatbreads into six slices, as you would a pizza. Eating this meal with your fingers is encouraged!

tip To toast the pine nuts, in a small skillet, add a bit of your favorite oil—olive oil and avocado oil are good choices. Warm over low heat, then add the pine nuts and cook, giving the pan a shimmy-shake every so often. As soon as they start browning, remove the pan from the heat (they go from perfect to burned really quickly) and drain on paper towels.

garlic-parmesan fried chicken sandwiches

Makes 4 to 6

I feel like everybody needs to have their back-pocket fried chicken sandwich recipe, and this is mine. It's rich and decadent, with plenty of umami flavors from the garlic sauce and Parmesan cheese. If you'd like, you can dress the sandwich simply, with lettuce, tomatoes, and pickles. But I think it's best with a simple homemade coleslaw, which helps cut through the richness and gives you a nice crunchy contrast.

Marinated Chicken
- 2 cups buttermilk
- ½ cup hot sauce, such as Frank's RedHot
- 2 teaspoons fine sea salt
- 1 teaspoon garlic powder
- 1 teaspoon onion powder
- ½ teaspoon chili powder
- ½ teaspoon black pepper
- ½ teaspoon mustard powder (optional)
- 4 to 6 boneless, skinless chicken thighs, trimmed of excess fat and patted dry

Coating
- 2 cups all-purpose flour
- ½ cup cornstarch
- 1 tablespoon fine sea salt
- 2 teaspoons smoked paprika
- 1½ teaspoons onion powder
- 1½ teaspoons garlic powder
- 1 teaspoon chili powder
- 1 teaspoon black pepper
- 1 large egg

Neutral oil, for frying

Garlic Sauce
- ¼ cup unsalted butter
- 4 garlic cloves, minced
- ½ cup mayonnaise
- 2 tablespoons heavy cream
- 1 teaspoon garlic powder
- ½ teaspoon smoked paprika
- ¼ teaspoon red pepper flakes
- Fine sea salt and black pepper

Sandwiches
- ½ cup freshly grated Parmesan cheese
- 4 to 6 Brioche Buns (page 191) or store-bought, split and toasted
- Lettuce
- Sliced tomatoes
- Bread and butter pickles
- Coleslaw (recipe follows; optional)

coleslaw

Makes about 3 cups

- 2 cups finely shredded romaine or iceberg lettuce
- 1 cup shredded green cabbage
- ½ cup shredded carrots
- ⅓ cup mayonnaise
- ¼ cup chopped fresh parsley
- ¼ cup freshly grated Parmesan cheese
- 2 tablespoons fresh lemon juice
- 1 teaspoon garlic powder
- Fine sea salt and black pepper

In a large bowl, stir all the ingredients together until well combined. Taste and add more salt and black pepper, if needed. Store in an airtight container in the fridge for up to 5 days.

Marinate the chicken: In a large bowl or 1-gallon resealable plastic bag, combine the buttermilk, hot sauce, salt, garlic powder, onion powder, chili powder, black pepper, and mustard powder (if using). Add the chicken thighs, making sure they are fully coated. Cover the bowl with plastic wrap or seal the bag and refrigerate for at least 4 hours or preferably overnight.

Make the coating: In a large shallow dish, mix the flour, cornstarch, salt, smoked paprika, onion powder, garlic powder, chili powder, and black pepper. Remove the chicken from the marinade, allowing any excess to drip off, and pour the marinade into a bowl. Dip each thigh into the flour mixture, coating evenly, and set aside on a wire rack.

Whisk the egg into the remaining marinade. Dip each thigh back into the marinade, then into the flour mixture again for a double coating. Shake off excess flour and place the coated chicken on the wire rack. Let the coated chicken rest for 10 minutes.

Pour 2 to 3 inches oil into a deep heavy-bottomed pot and heat over medium heat to 325°F.

I SLEEP IN MY KITCHEN

stove. Working in batches so as not to crowd the pot, carefully lower the thighs into the oil. Fry, turning occasionally, until the chicken is golden brown and the internal temperature reaches 165°F, 8 to 10 minutes. Transfer to the rack to drain.

Make the garlic sauce: In a large saucepan, melt the butter over medium heat. Reduce the heat to medium-low, add the garlic, and sauté until fragrant but without any color, about 1 minute. Stir in the mayonnaise, cream, garlic powder, smoked paprika, pepper flakes, and salt and black pepper to taste. Cook until smooth and warmed through, 1 to 2 minutes.

choices: You can either use the garlic sauce like you would a traditional mayonnaise, and slather it on the buns. Or you can transfer the fried chicken to a large bowl, thin the garlic sauce with a bit of water, then pour in the bowl with the chicken and toss gently until each piece is coated. Add the Parmesan and toss again to evenly distribute the cheesy coating.

Serve the chicken on the buns with lettuce, tomato, and pickles, or with coleslaw, if desired—whatever seems most delicious to you!

buttermilk-brined chicken and waffle sliders

Serves 4 to 6

Marinated Chicken
- 1 cup buttermilk
- 1 teaspoon garlic powder
- 1 teaspoon paprika
- 1 teaspoon fine sea salt
- 1 teaspoon black pepper
- 4 to 6 boneless, skinless chicken thighs, patted dry

Honey Butter
- ½ cup salted butter, at room temperature
- 2 tablespoons honey
- ½ teaspoon ground cinnamon

Waffles
- 2 cups / 250g all-purpose flour
- 1 tablespoon baking powder
- ¾ teaspoon fine sea salt
- ½ teaspoon baking soda
- ¼ cup chopped fresh chives
- 2 cups / 450g buttermilk
- ¼ cup unsalted butter, melted
- 2 large eggs, whisked
- ¼ cup / 50g sugar
- 1½ teaspoons vanilla extract

Fried Chicken
- ¾ cup all-purpose flour
- 2 tablespoons cornstarch
- 2 teaspoons onion powder
- 2 teaspoons garlic powder
- 2 teaspoons cayenne pepper
- 1½ teaspoons fine sea salt
- 1 teaspoon paprika
- 1 teaspoon baking soda
- 1 teaspoon black pepper
- Vegetable oil, for frying
- Maple syrup, for serving (optional)

I've always had a soft spot for chicken and waffles, a beautiful comfort food classic. A few years back, I started turning them into sliders, and I haven't made them any other way since. I like adding fresh chives to the waffle batter—it keeps things savory enough to hold up to the honey butter without tipping too sweet.

Marinate the chicken: In a medium bowl, whisk together the buttermilk, garlic powder, paprika, fine salt, and black pepper. Add the chicken thighs and toss to fully coat. Cover with plastic wrap and refrigerate for at least 1 hour and preferably 24 hours.

Make the honey butter: In a stand mixer fitted with the whisk attachment (or using a hand mixer), whip the softened butter, honey, and cinnamon on medium speed until fluffy, about 5 minutes. Set aside.

Make the waffle batter: In a large bowl, sift together the flour, baking powder, kosher salt, and baking soda. Stir in the chives.

In a separate bowl, whisk together the buttermilk, melted butter, eggs, sugar, and vanilla until smooth. Pour the wet ingredients into the dry and stir until just combined (be careful not to overmix). Set aside.

Coat and fry the chicken: In a medium bowl, whisk together the flour, cornstarch, onion powder, garlic powder, cayenne, sea salt, paprika, baking soda, and black pepper.

Line a plate with paper towels. Pour 2 to 3 inches oil into a deep heavy-bottomed pot and heat over medium heat until the temperature reaches 350°F.

Remove the chicken thighs from the marinade, allowing any excess to drip off. Coat the chicken in the flour mixture, pressing to ensure even coverage.

Working in batches so as not to crowd the pan, fry the chicken until golden brown and the internal temperature reaches 165°F, 5 to 7 minutes. Drain on the paper towels.

Preheat a waffle iron according to the manufacturer's instructions.

Spoon a heaping ¼ cup (or as much as you need to fill your waffle iron) of batter onto the waffle iron and cook until the waffles are golden brown and crisp, 3 to 5 minutes, depending on your waffle iron. Repeat with any remaining batter.

Cut the waffles into slider-size squares, about 3 inches. Spread honey butter on one side of each waffle. Place a fried chicken thigh between two waffle pieces to form a slider. Serve, drizzled with a bit of maple syrup, if desired, with extra honey butter on the side.

mini chicken alfredo pizzas

recipe on page 148

fan fave

mini chicken alfredo pizzas

Makes eight 5-inch pizzas

2 boneless, skinless chicken breasts, patted dry

Fine sea salt and black pepper

Extra-virgin olive oil, for drizzling

Alfredo Sauce

½ cup unsalted butter

10 garlic cloves (or to taste), minced

1 cup heavy cream

1 cup freshly grated Parmesan cheese

Fine sea salt and black pepper

Garlic powder

Pizza Dough

2½ cups / 315g all-purpose flour, plus more for dusting

1 cup / 240g lukewarm water

2 tablespoons sugar

1 tablespoon active dry yeast

¼ cup / 55g olive oil

2 teaspoons fine sea salt

Assembly

20 ounces (about 5 cups) freshly grated mozzarella cheese

Egg wash: 1 egg, whisked with 2 tablespoons water

Chopped fresh parsley

Red pepper flakes (optional)

This recipe is a combination of the three things that hold my heart: pizza, Alfredo, and anything mini. If you're skeptical of Alfredo sauce on a pizza, just trust me, it's a magical combination. This to me is a fun dish to make for brunch with friends—you can even have them help you shape the pizzas—or for a casual dinner party.

Dust both sides of the chicken with salt and black pepper. In a medium skillet, heat a drizzle of olive oil over medium-high heat until hot. Add the chicken and cook until the first side is slightly golden, 3 to 4 minutes. Flip and brown the second side for 3 minutes. Add ¼ cup water, reduce the heat to medium, cover, and cook until an instant-read thermometer inserted into the thickest part of the breast reads 165°F, 5 to 6 minutes.

Remove the chicken from the pan and let rest on a plate for 10 minutes before cutting into ½-inch cubes.

Make the Alfredo sauce: In a medium skillet, melt the butter over medium heat. Add the garlic and sauté until fragrant, 2 to 3 minutes, being careful not to burn the garlic. Stir in the cream and then the Parmesan and cook, stirring, until the cheese is melted. Season with salt, black pepper, and garlic powder, starting with ¼ teaspoon of each and then adding more, if needed. Set aside.

Make the pizza dough: In the bowl of a stand mixer (or in a large bowl), combine 1 cup / 125g of the flour with the water, sugar, and yeast. Mix with a fork until integrated, then cover with a damp paper towel and let rest until it bubbles and foams, about 10 minutes.

I SLEEP IN MY KITCHEN

Add the remaining 1½ cups / 190g flour, the oil, and salt. Snap on the dough hook and mix on medium-low speed for 10 minutes. (If working by hand, lightly flour your hands and a work surface and knead the dough for 8 to 10 minutes until smooth. See Hands-On Bread Basics, page 169). If needed, you can add up to ½ cup / 63g of additional flour to this recipe—but you might not need it. The dough is done if it bounces back when it passes the Poke Test (see page 169). Cover it with a kitchen towel and let it rest for 15 minutes

Use a knife or bench scraper to cut the dough into eight equal portions (about 70g each). Roll into balls, cover with a damp towel, and let rise until the balls are one and one-half times their original size, 10 to 15 minutes.

Assemble the pizzas: Lightly flour a work surface and roll out each dough ball into a round about ¼ inch thick. Sprinkle a small handful of the mozzarella just around the edge of each dough round. Fold the edges of the dough over the mozzarella, pressing down to seal them.

Preheat the oven to 425°F. Line two sheet pans with parchment paper (you may need to bake in batches, depending on the size of your oven).

Use your hands to transfer the shaped crusts to the lined sheet pans. Brush the edges of the crusts with the egg wash. Spoon about 2 tablespoons Alfredo sauce in the centers. Sprinkle about 2 tablespoons chicken on top of each pizza, then top each with about ⅛ cup mozzarella. Sprinkle with some parsley and pepper flakes, if you like a bit of heat.

Bake the pizzas until the bottoms and crusts are beautifully golden, 15 to 20 minutes.

Let the pizzas cool for a couple minutes before serving. Store any leftovers in an airtight container or wrapped tightly in the refrigerator.

sumac and lemon roast chicken *with* tahini salad

Serves 4

Seasoned Butter
- ½ cup unsalted butter, at room temperature
- 2 tablespoons extra-virgin olive oil
- 4 garlic cloves, finely grated
- ½ teaspoon finely grated lemon zest
- 2 tablespoons fresh lemon juice
- ½ teaspoon fresh thyme leaves
- ½ teaspoon fresh rosemary leaves
- ½ teaspoon sumac
- ¼ teaspoon paprika
- ¼ teaspoon lemon pepper
- ¼ teaspoon garlic powder
- ¼ teaspoon onion powder

Chicken
- 1 whole chicken (3 to 4 pounds), spatchcocked (see Tip), at room-temperature
- 1½ teaspoons paprika
- 1½ teaspoons sumac

Tahini Salad
- ½ cup tahini
- 3 tablespoons fresh lemon juice
- ½ teaspoon fine sea salt
- 2 Persian (mini) cucumbers, diced
- 2 large tomatoes, diced
- 1 small habanero, seeded and minced
- ½ red onion, diced and soaked in ice water for 10 minutes, then drained
- ¼ cup chopped fresh parsley

Every cookbook worth its salt needs a roast chicken recipe, IMO. And I've got to say, I'm pretty proud of this one. The sumac adds a complex flavor and aroma that is at the same time sour, sweet, and savory and pairs so beautifully with the acidity of fresh lemon and the earthiness of tahini. All we need to fully round out the meal is fresh, crisp veg, so I serve it with a quick salad of cucumber, tomato, chile, onion, and parsley. Spatchcocking, also called butterflying, is when you remove the backbone of your chicken and press it flat to allow it to cook more quickly and evenly. You can ask your butcher to do this for you, or you can do it yourself (see Tip).

Make the seasoned butter: In a small bowl, mix together the butter, oil, garlic, lemon zest, lemon juice, thyme, rosemary, sumac, paprika, lemon pepper, garlic powder, and onion powder until well combined.

Season the chicken: Use paper towels to pat the chicken dry. Tuck the wing tips under the chicken, or trim them off. Gently loosen the skin of the chicken, taking care not to tear it. Spread the butter mixture evenly under the skin as well as on the surface of the skin. Cover the chicken with plastic wrap and refrigerate it for at least 1 hour and preferably 24 hours.

Preheat the oven to 400°F.

Place the spatchcocked chicken in a roasting pan or on a sheet pan, breast-side up. Ensure the chicken is as flat as possible for even cooking. Sprinkle the paprika and sumac evenly over the chicken, then use your hands to rub it all over.

Roast the chicken until an instant-read thermometer inserted into the thickest part of the thigh registers 160°F, 45 to 55 minutes. If desired, broil for the last 3 to 5 minutes for extra-crispy skin. For an extra-tasty dipping sauce, pour any of the buttery gravy in the bottom of the roasting pan into a small bowl.

Let the chicken rest for 10 minutes before carving.

Meanwhile, make the tahini salad: In a small bowl, whisk together the tahini, lemon juice, salt, and ¼ cup water. Whisking vigorously, drizzle in ¼ to ½ cup water until the mixture is smooth and your desired consistency; I like it pourable but not runny.

In a separate bowl, mix together the cucumbers, tomatoes, habanero, red onion, and parsley. Pour the tahini dressing over the salad and toss to combine.

Carve the rested chicken and serve with the tahini salad and the buttery pan sauce.

tip To spatchcock a chicken, using a knife or kitchen shears, cut down either side of the backbone. You might have to use a little force to cut through the ribs and to disconnect the backbone where it connects with the thigh bones. Save the backbone for stock. Flip the chicken over so it's breast-side up and push down on it to crack the rib bones a bit and to flatten the bird as much as possible.

cast-iron chicken *with* tarragon, olives, and charred lemon

Serves 4

- 1 whole chicken (3 to 4 pounds), cut into 6 pieces (see Tip)
- Kosher salt and black pepper
- 4 tablespoons extra-virgin olive oil
- 1 large lemon, cut into ½-inch slices
- 4 tablespoons unsalted butter
- 6 garlic cloves, minced
- 1 shallot, finely chopped
- 1½ cups no-salt-added chicken broth
- 2 tablespoons chopped fresh tarragon
- 1 cup heavy cream
- ½ cup crushed and pitted green olives

Who doesn't love a chicken recipe that comes together in well under an hour but feels elevated and classy? My inspiration for this dish was the Marry Me Chicken recipe that took the Internet by storm a few years ago, but my twist is to add salty olives, shallot, and my secret weapon, fragrant tarragon, which unlocks a new level of flavor. Pair this with roasted vegetables, a crusty Sourdough Loaf (page 184), or mashed potatoes.

Let the chicken come to room temperature before cooking, about 1 hour.

Preheat the oven to 375°F.

Pat the chicken pieces dry with paper towels and season generously with salt and black pepper.

In a large cast-iron skillet, heat 1 tablespoon of the oil over medium-high heat. Add the lemon slices and cook until they are charred and caramelized, 2 to 3 minutes per side. Remove the lemon slices and set aside.

Add the remaining 3 tablespoons oil and 2 tablespoons of the butter to the skillet. Once the butter is sizzling, add the chicken, skin-side down, and sear until the skin is golden and crisp, 8 to 10 minutes. If the chicken is browning too quickly, reduce the heat to medium.

Flip the chicken and sear the other sides for 6 minutes. Transfer the chicken to a plate and set aside.

Add the remaining 2 tablespoons butter to the skillet. Add the garlic and shallot and sauté until fragrant and softened, 2 to 3 minutes. Pour in the broth, scraping up any browned bits from the bottom of the skillet. Return the seared chicken pieces to the skillet, nestling them into the broth. Sprinkle the tarragon over the top.

Transfer the skillet to the oven and bake until the chicken is cooked through and the internal temperature of the thighs reaches 165°F and of the breasts reaches 150°F (there will be carryover cooking), 20 to 30 minutes. Remove the skillet from the oven and transfer the chicken to a plate.

Set the skillet over medium heat and stir in the cream, letting the sauce simmer and thicken for about 5 minutes.

Return the chicken to the skillet, spooning the sauce over the top. You can serve the chicken in the skillet, or you can transfer it to a serving platter. Arrange the charred lemon slices and crushed olives as a garnish.

Let the chicken rest for a few minutes before serving.

tip Ask your butcher to cut your chicken into six pieces: two bone-in breasts, two wings, and two leg quarters.

SEAFOOD, POULTRY & MEAT

lamb shoulder *with* labneh and fennel-orange glaze

Serves 6 to 8

Marinated Lamb
- ½ cup labneh
- 8 garlic cloves, finely grated (preferably on a Microplane)
- 2 tablespoons fresh orange juice
- 1 tablespoon ground turmeric
- 2 teaspoons black pepper
- 1½ teaspoons fine sea salt
- 1½ teaspoons ground cumin
- 1½ teaspoons ground coriander
- 1 teaspoon smoked paprika
- 1 bone-in lamb shoulder (5½ to 6½ pounds)

Fennel-Orange Glaze
- Grated zest of 1 orange
- ½ cup fresh orange juice
- ¼ cup honey
- 2 tablespoons balsamic vinegar
- 1½ tablespoons fennel seeds
- 2 tablespoons extra-virgin olive oil
- Fine sea salt and black pepper

Charred Orange and Fennel
- Extra-virgin olive oil, for the pan and for the orange and fennel
- 2 large oranges, cut into ½-inch slices, seeds removed
- 2 large fennel bulbs, cut into quarters
- Kosher salt and black pepper

For Serving
- Fresh herbs (such as parsley or fennel fronds)
- Toasted pine nuts (optional)

Lamb is a staple protein in Palestinian culture but for some people, certain cuts of lamb have an assertive, gamey flavor that they can't move past. I wanted to develop a recipe that even lamb skeptics could get behind; that is why I paired lamb shoulder with orange and fennel. The orange in the marinade and glaze contributes acid; both the orange and the fennel contribute sweetness; and the fennel adds a subtle anise-y note. I coat this shoulder with turmeric because once the shoulder is roasted, it creates a lovely crust.

I highly recommend marinating overnight for the best result; this will also make the following day much easier for you, since you'll only have to pop the dish in the oven. (If time is short, four hours of marinating will do.) Because it is a make-ahead dish, I think this is perfect for big gatherings, dinner parties, or for when you want a high-key meal that's stress free.

tip Try this marinade with other cuts of lamb, too.

Marinate the lamb: In a medium bowl, combine the labneh, garlic, orange juice, turmeric, black pepper, fine salt, cumin, coriander, and smoked paprika. Mix until well combined.

Pat the lamb shoulder dry with paper towels. Rub the marinade all over the lamb, making sure it is evenly coated on all sides. Place the lamb in a roasting pan, cover with aluminum foil, and refrigerate for at least 4 hours and preferably overnight.

Make the fennel-orange glaze: In a small bowl, combine the orange zest, orange juice, honey, vinegar, and ¼ cup water. Stir to mix and set aside.

In a small stainless steel skillet, toast the fennel seeds over medium heat until they are fragrant, 2 to 3 minutes. Be careful not to burn them.

In a medium saucepan, heat the oil over medium heat. Add the toasted fennel seeds and sauté for 1 to 2 minutes to infuse the oil with their flavor; again, keep your eye on them so they don't burn. Stir in the orange juice–honey mixture and bring the mixture to a simmer. Reduce the heat to low and let the glaze simmer gently, stirring occasionally, until it thickens slightly, about 15 minutes. It should have a slightly thicker consistency, not jamlike. Season with fine salt and black pepper.

recipe continues →

SEAFOOD, POULTRY & MEAT

lamb shoulder with labneh and fennel-orange glaze, *continued*

Strain the glaze through a fine-mesh sieve, discarding the solids. You can prepare this a day ahead—let it cool to room temperature, then store it in a sealed jar in the refrigerator.

When ready to cook, remove the lamb from the refrigerator and allow it to come to room temperature for about 1 hour.

Preheat the oven to 325°F.

Make sure the roasting pan with the lamb is tightly covered with foil, then roast the lamb until the meat is tender and easily pulls away from the bone, about 4 hours.

Make the charred orange and fennel: Preheat a lightly oiled cast-iron skillet over medium-high heat. Brush both sides of the orange slices and the fennel quarters with oil and season with kosher salt and black pepper.

Cook the fennel until nicely charred on each cut side and until caramelized but still slightly crisp, 3 to 4 minutes per side. Remove the fennel from the skillet and set aside. Add the orange slices to the skillet and cook until nicely charred and caramelized, 2 to 3 minutes per side. Remove the orange slices from the skillet and set aside.

Once the lamb has cooked for 4 hours, increase the oven temperature to 400°F. Remove the foil from the pan and generously brush the lamb with the fennel-orange glaze. If you have a needle injector, you can inject some of the glaze into the lamb for extra flavor (but if you don't have one, don't worry; this is optional).

Roast the lamb for an additional 25 minutes, basting with the glaze every 10 minutes, until the lamb is golden brown and caramelized.

Allow to rest for 15 minutes before carving and transferring to a serving dish.

To serve: Serve the lamb with a drizzle of the remaining glaze, along with the charred orange slices and charred fennel quarters. Garnish with the herbs and pine nuts, if desired.

surf and turf *with* filet mignon and crab-stuffed lobster

Serves 4

4 lobster tails (about 4 ounces each)

Butter Mixture
- 6 tablespoons unsalted butter, melted
- 3 garlic cloves, finely grated
- 1 tablespoon chopped fresh parsley
- 1 teaspoon finely grated lemon zest
- 1 teaspoon Cajun seasoning
- ¾ teaspoon Old Bay seasoning
- ½ teaspoon paprika
- ½ teaspoon lemon pepper
- ¼ teaspoon onion powder

Crab Mixture
- ½ cup mayonnaise
- 1 large egg, whisked
- 2 tablespoons Dijon mustard
- 2 tablespoons panko bread crumbs
- 1½ tablespoons Worcestershire sauce
- 1 tablespoon fresh lemon juice
- 2¼ teaspoons Old Bay seasoning
- ½ teaspoon Cajun seasoning
- ½ teaspoon red pepper flakes
- 16 ounces fresh crabmeat (lump or claw or a mixture of both)

Steak
- 4 filet mignons (1½ to 2 inches thick), at room temperature
- Fine sea salt and black pepper
- Olive or avocado oil, for the pan
- 10 tablespoons unsalted butter, at room temperature
- 8 garlic cloves, slightly crushed
- 4 sprigs of fresh thyme
- 4 sprigs of fresh rosemary
- Chopped fresh parsley, for garnish

I used to get so nervous about cooking steak—especially the pricier cuts. I'd overthink every step and psych myself out before I even turned the heat on. But one day I decided to just go for it. I picked up some lobster tails and crab, to make it feel like the kind of dinner I'd want to book a reservation for, and suddenly the whole thing didn't feel so intimidating anymore. It ended up being fun—and way less dramatic than I made it out to be in my head.

tip **Getting steak right:** The key to really getting the steak right is to use a heavy-bottomed cast-iron skillet. When you add the steak to the skillet, don't move it around. You want a crust to form, and if it's constantly being fiddled with, your sear won't be even. And I'm sure you've read this before, but it really is important that you let your steak rest before cutting it!

Preheat the oven to 400°F. Line a sheet pan with parchment paper.

Using kitchen shears, carefully butterfly the lobster tails by cutting through the center of the top shell and stopping right before the tail fin (make sure you cut just the shell and not the meat; be gentle so you don't crack the shell while you're cutting it). Using your fingers, gently spread the shells apart. Push the lobster meat above the shell halves. You may have to use your fingers to detach the meat from the shell a bit. Then very carefully close the shell and lay the attached meat on top of the shell. Squeeze the shell halves closed. Use a knife to cut away the vein that runs down the center of the meat.

Place the lobster tails on the lined sheet pan and set aside.

Make the butter mixture: In a small bowl, combine the butter, garlic, parsley, lemon zest, Cajun seasoning,

recipe continues →

SEAFOOD, POULTRY & MEAT

surf and turf with filet mignon and crab-stuffed lobster, *continued*

Old Bay, paprika, lemon pepper, and onion powder. Mix well and set aside.

Prepare the crab mixture: In a large bowl, mix together the mayonnaise, egg, mustard, panko, Worcestershire sauce, lemon juice, Old Bay, Cajun seasoning, and pepper flakes until well combined. Gently fold in the crabmeat until evenly distributed, taking care not to break apart the crab lumps too much. Set aside.

Using a pastry brush, generously brush the butter mixture over the exposed lobster meat. If you have extra butter mixture, save it for serving. Divide the crab mixture into four equal portions and spoon a portion onto each lobster tail, pressing gently to adhere.

Bake the lobster tails until the lobster meat is just opaque and the crab mixture is heated through, 7 to 10 minutes.

Meanwhile, prepare the steak: Pat the filets with a paper towel and generously season both sides with salt and black pepper.

In a large cast-iron or stainless steel skillet, heat a drizzle of oil over medium-high heat. Once the oil is just beginning to smoke, add two of the steaks—the oil may splatter, so be careful. You'll know the temperature is correct if you hear a happy sizzle. Without moving them around, sear each side of the steaks until a golden-brown crust forms, about 4 minutes per side. Sear the edges of the steaks about 30 seconds per side.

Add 5 tablespoons of the butter, 4 of the garlic cloves, 2 sprigs of the thyme, and 2 sprigs of the rosemary to the skillet. Turn off the heat and, using a spoon, baste the steaks with the melted butter and aromatics for an additional 3 to 5 minutes, flipping the steaks occasionally to ensure even cooking through the residual heat from the cast iron.

Transfer the steaks to a cutting board and allow to rest, topped with the garlic cloves and the remaining herbs and tented with aluminum foil, while you sear the remaining steaks.

Wipe your pan clean, add more oil, and repeat the searing and basting process with the remaining two steaks and the remaining 5 tablespoons butter, 4 garlic cloves, 2 sprigs of thyme, and 2 sprigs of rosemary. Let the steaks rest for at least 5 minutes.

Start plating your dishes while the last two steaks are resting. Remove the herbs but leave the garlic, then slice the steaks against the grain into slices of your preferred thickness. Plate the sliced steak alongside the stuffed lobster tails. If desired, brush the lobster tails with more of the butter mixture and garnish with parsley before serving.

saniyeh kofta

beef patties in tomato sauce

Serves 6

Meat Patties
- 1 yellow onion
- 2 pounds ground beef (80/20)
- ½ cup finely chopped fresh parsley
- 4 garlic cloves, grated
- 1 tablespoon fine sea salt
- 1 tablespoon black pepper
- 1 teaspoon ground cumin (not traditional, but tasty; optional)

Fried Potatoes
- Neutral oil, for frying
- 3 russet potatoes, peeled and sliced into ¼-inch-thick rounds

Sauce
- 1 (6-ounce) can tomato paste
- 1 tablespoon pomegranate molasses, or to taste
- 2½ teaspoons fine sea salt
- 2 teaspoons black pepper
- 1 teaspoon curry powder

Assembly and Serving
- 3 large tomatoes, cut into ¼-inch-thick slices
- 3 large green bell peppers, cut into ¼-inch half-rings
- ¼ cup toasted pine nuts, for garnish
- Chopped fresh parsley, for garnish (optional)
- Vermicelli Rice (page 110) or pita bread, for serving

This dish is perfect for those nights when I want something comforting but without much effort.

Traditionally, saniyeh kofta can be simmered in a tangy tahini sauce or a tomatoey red sauce. My mom used to make both, but the tomato sauce was always my favorite, so that's the version I offer here.

Make the meat patties: Grate the onion on the large holes of a box grater. Wrap the onion in a clean kitchen towel and squeeze out as much moisture as possible. Place in a large bowl, then add the ground beef, parsley, garlic, salt, black pepper, and cumin (if using). Knead the mixture until thoroughly combined.

Shape the mixture into small patties about 1 inch thick and 2 to 3 inches in diameter. Arrange them on a plate or sheet pan and set aside.

Fry the potatoes: Line a second plate or sheet pan with paper towels and set near the stove. Pour 2 inches oil into a deep heavy-bottomed pot and heat over medium heat until the temperature reaches 350°F on an instant-read thermometer.

Working in batches so as not to crowd the pot, fry the potato slices until golden and slightly crispy, about 4 minutes. Transfer the slices to the paper towels to drain.

Make the sauce: In a medium bowl, whisk together the tomato paste, pomegranate molasses, salt, black pepper, curry powder, and 2 cups water until smooth. Taste and adjust the seasonings as needed.

Preheat the oven to 350°F.

Assemble the dish: In a 10½-inch round ovenproof baking dish or skillet, arrange the ingredients in a spiral pattern, starting at the outer edge of the dish and alternating them in this order: Start with one meat patty arranged vertically (like the wheel of a car), followed by a slice of tomato, then a slice of fried potato, and a strip of bell pepper. Repeat, working from the outside in, until you reach the center of the pan. Pour the sauce evenly over the assembled ingredients.

Cover the dish with aluminum foil and bake for 45 minutes. Remove the foil and bake until slightly caramelized on top, 10 to 15 minutes longer.

Sprinkle the pine nuts and parsley, if desired, over the dish just before serving. Serve with the rice or pitas.

fan fave

triple-stack smash burgers

Serves 2

Sauce
- ½ cup mayonnaise
- 2 tablespoons ketchup
- 1 tablespoon Dijon mustard
- 1½ teaspoons Worcestershire sauce
- 1 teaspoon garlic powder
- Fine sea salt and black pepper
- Honey (optional)
- Hot sauce (optional)

Burgers
- Olive oil, for the pan
- 1½ pounds ground beef (80/20)
- Unsalted butter, for the buns
- 2 hamburger buns (such as sesame seed, potato, or brioche; page 191)
- Fine sea salt and black pepper
- 6 slices Cheddar or American cheese

Topping Ideas
- Romaine lettuce leaves
- Sliced tomato
- Sunny-side-up fried eggs
- Sliced white onions
- Pickles
- Caramelized Onions (page 40)

Smash burger or regular juicy burger? Let's break it down: With a traditional seared burger, you get a nice, juicy patty with a little bit of caramelized flavor from where the burger hits the cook surface. With a smash burger, you still get that rich, juicy mouthfeel—but even more caramelization because so much more meat is in direct contact with the pan. And here's the best part of all—you get *crispy texture* from all those seared edges. It's practically impossible to get this with a classic burger—the texture is more homogenous, dominated by that juicy interior.

"So," I thought to myself, "how do I solve that initial problem of a smash burger seeming so itty-bitty and looking as if I'd need three of them to feel full?" Easy: Stack three of them on top of each other! The result is filling and beautiful, with triple the amazing texture and crunch of a single smash burger.

Make the sauce: In a small bowl, combine the mayonnaise, ketchup, mustard, Worcestershire sauce, garlic powder, and salt and black pepper to taste. If using, stir in the honey and hot sauce to taste. Taste and adjust the seasonings as needed. Set aside for later. (Store in an airtight container in the refrigerator for up to 5 days.)

Cook the burgers: Lightly oil a griddle or large cast-iron skillet and preheat over high heat for at least 5 minutes.

Divide the ground beef into six equal portions (4 ounces each) and shape them into balls.

Generously butter the cut sides of the buns. Place the buns on the griddle, buttered-side down, and toast until they are a nice golden color, about 1 minute. Remove the buns from the griddle and set aside.

Working in batches, if needed, place each burger ball on the hot griddle or skillet and immediately smash it down with a metal spatula to form a thin patty. Press down firmly to ensure that the patty is thin—a little more than ¼ inch—and has good contact with the cooking surface. Season each patty with salt and black pepper.

Cook the patties until the bottoms are browned and crispy, 1 to 2 minutes. Flip and cook for an additional 1 to 2 minutes. Place a slice of cheese on top of each patty during the last 30 seconds of cooking to allow it to melt.

Spread the sauce on the cut side of the top and bottom buns of each smash burger.

Assemble the burgers with three patties per bun, add your desired toppings, and serve immediately.

marinated brisket *with* olive and fig tapenade

Serves 8 to 10

Brisket
- 2 tablespoons chopped fresh rosemary
- 2 tablespoons chopped fresh thyme
- 2 tablespoons chopped fresh oregano
- ¼ cup extra-virgin olive oil, plus more as needed
- 8 to 10 garlic cloves, finely grated (preferably on a Microplane)
- 1 tablespoon kosher salt
- 1½ teaspoons black pepper
- 1 beef brisket (about 5 pounds)
- 3 cups beef broth

Fig Tapenade
- 1¼ cups dried figs, stemmed
- 1 cup pitted kalamata olives
- ¼ cup capers, drained
- 3 garlic cloves, finely grated (preferably on a Microplane)
- 2 tablespoons fresh lemon juice
- ¼ cup extra-virgin olive oil
- ¼ teaspoon black pepper

For Serving
- 4 to 6 fresh figs, halved
- Fresh herbs (such as parsley leaves, rosemary sprigs, or thyme sprigs)

My favorite recipe in this chapter, inspired by the ninety-fifth chapter of the Qur'an, "Surah At-Tin" ("The Fig"), came to life on a quiet afternoon when I opened the fridge and realized I had more ripe figs than I could possibly eat in time. They were sitting next to a large jar of olives.

Figs are an unusual fruit. They're rich and almost meaty in texture, which made me wonder if they could work in something savory. I paired them with olives and blended them into a tapenade, then layered that over a slow-cooked brisket. I served the dish at my next dinner party. To my surprise, everyone loved it more than I could have hoped for.

Try serving this over mashed potatoes or with fresh sourdough slices on the side. You can also use the beef and tapenade to make a rich and unique sandwich; try it on Cast-Iron Sourdough Focaccia (page 176)!

Prepare the brisket: In a small food processor, combine the rosemary, thyme, and oregano and process until finely chopped. Add the oil, garlic, salt, and black pepper and process until combined. (Alternatively, you can do this by hand.)

Place the brisket in a baking pan and pat it dry with a paper towel. Pour the garlic and herb marinade over the brisket, coating it well on all sides. Cover the pan with aluminum foil and refrigerate for at least 8 hours and preferably overnight.

Remove the brisket from the refrigerator and let it come to room temperature for 30 to 60 minutes.

Preheat the oven to 325°F.

Heat a Dutch oven over medium-high heat. Add a bit of oil and sear the brisket on all sides until browned and caramelized, 3 to 4 minutes per side. Transfer the brisket to a plate.

Add any leftover marinade from the baking pan to the Dutch oven, along with the beef broth. Bring to a simmer, scraping up any browned bits from the bottom. Return the brisket to the Dutch oven, cover, and transfer to the oven.

Oven-braise until the meat is tender and easily shreds with a fork, about 4 hours.

Meanwhile, make the fig tapenade: In a food processor, combine the dried figs, olives, capers, garlic, lemon juice, oil, and black pepper. Pulse until the mixture is finely chopped. Taste and add more black pepper, if desired. (You can make this a day ahead and store refrigerated.)

To serve: Let the brisket rest on a plate or cutting board for 15 minutes before slicing. Slice against the grain and arrange on a serving platter. Spoon the tapenade over the brisket, then arrange the fresh figs between the slices of meat. Garnish with the herbs and serve.

breads & savory baked goods

fan fave

pita bread

Makes fourteen 6-inch pitas

1⅓ cups / 315g lukewarm water
1 tablespoon active dry yeast
3 tablespoons sugar
4 cups / 500g all-purpose flour, plus more for dusting
1 teaspoon baking powder
2 teaspoons distilled white vinegar
1½ teaspoons Diamond Crystal kosher salt

The first time I made pita bread, I was fifteen years old and standing at my mom's side—as I always was when she was baking in the kitchen. I used to say that I "made" the pita bread, but really, I was just acting as her assistant, taking everything in and doing whatever she asked of me. She would have her huge, oversized stainless steel mixing bowl out on the counter and would be making enough bread to feed a village. Growing up with nine other siblings, that was not an unusual sight in our house. I will always have the image of one particular day and the image of her making the pita bread in my head. Considering how often I've seen my mother cook, it's hard to say why this one image is embedded in my brain (don't get me wrong; I'm not mad about it!), but it probably has to do with how delicious and fragrant this pita is—so much better than anything you'll find at the store.

In the bowl of a stand mixer (or in a large bowl by hand), combine 1 cup / 240g of the water, the yeast, and 1 tablespoon of the sugar. Mix with a fork until integrated, then cover the top of the bowl with a damp paper towel and let it rest until it bubbles and foams, about 10 minutes.

Once the yeast is activated, sift in the flour, the remaining 2 tablespoons sugar, the baking powder, vinegar, and salt. Snap on the dough hook attachment and, with the mixer on low speed, gradually pour in the remaining ⅓ cup / 75g water, 1 tablespoon at a time—keeping in mind that you may not need the entire ⅓ cup to achieve the perfect dough texture. (If working by hand, stir with a spoon.) Scrape down the bowl periodically to ensure the ingredients are evenly combined. Mix until the dough is firm and elastic and pulls beautifully from the sides of your bowl, about 10 minutes. (If mixing by hand, lightly flour or oil your hands, then knead the dough for 10 to 15 minutes until smooth. See Hands-On Bread Basics, page 169.)

Add a bit of flour to the sides of the mixer bowl so that the dough doesn't stick while it rises. (If working by hand, place the dough in a lightly floured or oiled bowl.) Cover the bowl with plastic wrap and let it rest in a warm place until doubled in size, 1 to 2 hours.

Divide the dough into fourteen equal portions (about 60g each) and roll into balls. Cover them with a towel and let rest for 20 minutes to allow the gluten to relax.

Roll out each dough ball to about 6 inches in diameter and ⅛ inch thick (no thinner). Cover and let them rest for another 20 minutes.

Meanwhile, preheat the oven to 550°F or as high as it will go. Set a sheet pan on the oven rack to preheat.

Carefully transfer as many pitas as will fit on the sheet pan (likely two or three) and bake until the bottoms develop a beautiful golden color, 3 to 4 minutes. Use your hands (being careful not to burn yourself!) or a spatula to flip the pitas and bake until the other sides develop color, 1 to 2 minutes. Keep a close eye to avoid burning.

Use a spatula to carefully transfer the baked pitas to a bread basket and cover with a towel to keep warm. Repeat to bake the remaining pitas.

Store the pitas in an airtight container at room temperature for up to 2 days or in the refrigerator for up to 5 days. For longer storage, seal in a resealable plastic bag and store in the freezer for up to 3 months.

hands-on bread basics

To knead by hand: Drizzle a bit of olive oil on the dough. Use the palm of your hand to push the dough away from you, then bring it back to the center of the dough mass and repeat. Give the dough mass a quarter-turn every four stretches or so. You'll know the dough is done when it passes the Poke Test (see below).

The Poke Test: If you poke the dough with your pointer finger and the dough bounces back, it's ready. If the indentation made by your finger *does not* bounce back, then the dough is not elastic enough, and you need to keep kneading.

To form smooth dough balls: After pinching off the dough into the portions specified in the recipe, gently roll them in the palms of your hands until they're smooth, uniform balls. Don't be too rough here; you're really just trying to roll the surface of the ball without deflating all the air pockets in the interior.

To form dough rings: For recipes like Ka'ak al-Quds (page 171) and Everything Bagels (page 205), here is the way to make dough rings:

Holding a dough ball in one hand, take your index finger and press a hole through the center of the ball. Lightly flour your hands and thread your pointer finger and thumb through the hole of the dough circle, bringing those two fingers together to make an O-shape. Use your other hand to rotate the dough 360 degrees—as you turn it, your O-shaped fingers should help the dough maintain its shape. Your goal is to slightly stretch the dough without ruining the overall shape.

To stretch and fold the dough: Wet your hands lightly with water, then grab a portion of the dough (while it's still in the bowl), stretch it upward, and fold it over itself. Rotate the bowl a quarter-turn and repeat this action four times, or until the dough feels more elastic and cohesive. Re-cover the dough and let rest for 30 minutes.

Repeat the stretch-and-fold process, followed by a 30-minute rest, for the number of times specified in the recipe.

pita bread
recipe on page 168

fan fave

khubiz taboon

traditional Palestinian flatbread

Makes eight 9-inch flatbreads

- 3 cups / 720g lukewarm water
- 1 tablespoon active dry yeast
- 1 tablespoon sugar
- 7 cups / 875g all-purpose flour, plus more for dusting
- ¼ cup / 30g powdered milk
- 4 tablespoons olive oil, plus more for oiling hands
- 1 tablespoon fine sea salt

Khubiz taboon is a traditional Palestinian flatbread that holds a special place in our cuisine. It is a staple that we use in so many ways: dipped in fresh olive oil and za'atar or eaten for breakfast alongside falafel, hummus, and olives. My dad likes to add labneh, za'atar, and flattened falafel and fold it into a sandwich. Topped with olive oil, caramelized onions, sumac, chicken, parsley, and pine nuts, it becomes Msakhan (page 139), the national dish of Palestine. For me and other Palestinians, khubiz taboon is more than just bread; it's a part of our daily life that connects us to tradition and makes every meal feel a little more like home.

Traditionally, this bread is cooked over hot stones within a *taboon*, or "clay oven," which is how it gets its name. The intense heat of the stones gives the bread its signature crisp exterior while maintaining a soft and airy inside. Since most people do not have clay ovens in their backyards, ingenious home cooks like my mama adapted the recipe to cook over stones in a standard oven. (For more on this method, see How to Bake on Stones on page 175.)

This dough is quite sticky, which might feel unusual to bakers who are used to working with stiffer, more floury doughs. But my advice is to embrace this tacky, loose dough. Coat your hands with olive oil and make sure to flour your work surface so the dough is easier to work with. As you are kneading and folding it, add more olive oil to help the dough mass become smooth and cohesive. The result of your efforts will be a beautiful, airy bread with a crisp crust and pillowy interior—all worth the effort.

In a measuring cup or small bowl, combine 1 cup / 240g of the water with the yeast and sugar. Mix with a fork until integrated, then cover with a damp paper towel and let it rest until it bubbles and foams, about 10 minutes.

In a large bowl, combine the flour, powdered milk, 2 tablespoons of the oil, and the salt. Add the yeast mixture along with the remaining 2 cups / 480g water. You may find you don't need the full 480g, depending on the hydration level you're aiming for. Slowly incorporate the water until you reach the desired dough consistency.

Oil or dampen your hands with water and use your fingers to stir the ingredients into a rough mixture. Once everything is integrated, squeeze the dough to bring it together. Don't worry if it seems a bit loose and sticky; this dough is meant to be airy. Your goal at this stage is to have a rough, sticky dough ball but without any visible patches of flour.

Drizzle about 1 tablespoon of the oil over the dough. Using both hands (dampen them with water, if needed to avoid sticking), stretch some of the dough away from you, then fold it down into the center of the dough mass. Then use one hand to stretch a corner of the dough and fold and punch it down into the center. Alternate this stretching, folding, and punching process until the dough becomes smoother, about 3 minutes. Once it's somewhat smoother, add a bit more olive oil (around 1 tablespoon) and keep folding until the dough is completely smooth. To see if the dough is ready, try the Poke Test (see page 169).

Cover the dough with a damp cloth and let it rest until it doubles in size, 1½ to 2 hours.

recipe continues →

I SLEEP IN MY KITCHEN

za'atar manakeesh
(za'atar flatbread)
recipe on page 211

khubiz taboon, *continued*

Either remove the oven racks or position them in the highest position so you have room to work. Place baking stones in a 15-inch round ovenproof baking pan (see How to Bake with Stones on page 175) and place the pan directly on the floor of your oven. Preheat the oven to 550°F or as high as it will go to superheat the stones.

Gently punch any air bubbles out of the dough. Using oiled hands, pinch off the dough into eight equal portions and then gently roll them into balls (see page 169). Place the dough balls on a lightly floured work surface, cover them with a dry cloth, and let them rest until they're about one and one-half times their original size, 15 to 30 minutes.

Lightly flour a work surface and your hands. Flatten a dough ball with your hands to about ¼ inch—thin but not so thin that it's see-through. (I prefer a flatbread with a slightly poofy rim, so I don't make it uniform. You don't have to leave a rim if you don't want to.) Use your fingers to spread out the dough on the work surface or lift the dough and stretch it between your hands, allowing gravity to help you shape it—I usually do a combination of both. The finished disks will be about 9 inches in diameter.

Working with one piece at a time, use your hands to transfer the dough onto the preheated baking stones. You might have to stretch the dough a bit to help it maintain its shape, but you're not looking to stretch it any thinner.

Bake until the pockets of the bread that are in contact with the stones turn a lovely golden brown, about 5 minutes. Keep an eye on the bread, as every oven performs differently and your cooking time will vary. Using your hands, *very* carefully remove the baked flatbread, transfer it to a bread basket or serving plate, and loosely cover it with a towel to keep it soft and warm. Repeat the process with the remaining dough pieces.

The flatbreads are best served fresh, but they'll hold at room temperature for 1 to 2 days if stored in an airtight container. For even longer storage, you can do what my mama does and store them in a resealable plastic bag in the freezer for up to 3 months. Thaw at room temperature, then warm in the oven before serving.

I SLEEP IN MY KITCHEN

how to bake on stones

Our staple Palestinian bread, Khubiz Taboon (page 172), is baked in a clay oven (called a taboon) over rocks. The rocks ensure that the bread is attractively dimpled and, unlike pita bread, does not have a pocket. Since few of us have clay ovens in our backyards, home cooks have adapted the process to work in a standard oven. To do this, you'll need the following:

• **About 15 pounds of river rocks.** When I was growing up, my mom would literally go into our backyard and collect rocks the day before she planned to bake. You want rocks that are about the size of two quarters—larger than that could also work, but you'll get fewer dimples, and I personally like the look of lots of cute little dimples. If you are unable to forage for rocks, you can buy river rocks at a landscaping or garden store like Home Depot; that is what I do. Make sure they are natural stone and do not have any coating.

• **A 15-inch round ovenproof pan to place the rocks in during baking.** I use a stainless steel pan. A paella pan with handles also works. Any ovenproof material that can be heated to a high temperature, such as stainless steel or cast iron, will work.

To prepare the stones, wash and scrub them so there is no dirt or debris. Fill your sink or a large bowl or bucket with soapy water with a splash of vinegar, then let them soak for at least 10 and up to 30 minutes. Rinse the rocks thoroughly, then set them aside to dry completely overnight. It is essential that the rocks be completely dry before you use them. If there is any moisture in the stones, they might explode when they are heated in the oven, and we don't want that!

When you're ready to bake, arrange the stones in an even layer in the baking pan.

You don't need to go through this cleaning process every time you bake—you can reuse the stones until they start looking crusty; this might not happen until after ten bakes or so. If you do feel like your stones are looking crusty and decide to clean them again, just make sure to allow them to completely dry before you reuse them.

cast-iron sourdough focaccia

Makes one 10- to 12-inch focaccia

- 1¾ cups / 425g lukewarm water
- 80g active Sourdough Starter (page 188)
- 3¾ cups / 500g unbleached bread flour
- 2 teaspoons fine sea salt
- ¼ cup / 50g extra-virgin olive oil, plus more for greasing
- Flaky sea salt

Focaccia is wonderful because it's so much more forgiving than a sourdough loaf. Whereas you really have to practice to get a feel for how long to proof a sourdough loaf, focaccia is ready once you see a few bubbles on the top and it has risen a bit. For this reason, a lot of people decide to turn their overproofed sourdough into focaccia instead!

I've kept this recipe simple, but you should feel free to add whatever decorative and edible garnishes you'd like, such as fresh rosemary leaves (make sure to coat them well in olive oil so they don't burn), coarse salt, halved cherry tomatoes, pitted olives, or pickled red onions.

In a large bowl, combine the water and sourdough starter. Stir gently to dissolve the starter, then add the flour and fine salt. Using a dough whisk (or a wooden spoon), mix until the dough comes together and there are no dry bits of flour remaining. This is a high-hydration recipe, which means the dough will be loose—that's exactly what you want. Cover the bowl with plastic wrap and let the dough rest at room temperature for 1 hour to allow the gluten to relax.

Stretch and fold the dough: Perform a total of three stretches and folds (see Hands-On Bread Basics, page 169).

Re-cover the dough with plastic and allow to rest in a warm draft-free area for its bulk fermentation, about 5 hours. (Alternatively, if you prefer to hold the dough longer, you can place the covered dough in the refrigerator for 8 to 24 hours for a cold fermentation.)

Generously oil a 10- to 12-inch cast-iron skillet with oil. Transfer the dough from the bowl into the skillet. With lightly oiled hands, fold the dough like a letter: First, fold the bottom third toward the center, then fold the top third over it. Next, flip the dough so the seam is facing down. Cover the skillet with plastic wrap and let the dough rest until it rises and nearly fills the skillet, about 2 hours.

Lightly oil your hands again and dimple the dough evenly across the surface, spreading it a bit to fit the skillet if it didn't fully spread out while resting.

Cover with plastic or a clean cloth and let rest for 1 more hour.

Preheat the oven to 450°F.

Just before baking, drizzle the ¼ cup oil over the top of the dough, then sprinkle with the flaky salt.

Bake until the focaccia is golden brown and crisp on the edges, 25 to 30 minutes.

Remove the pan from the oven and transfer the focaccia to a wire rack to cool for at least 10 minutes before serving.

fan fave

ka'ak al-quds
jerusalem bread

Makes 6 breads

Dough

1 cup / 240g lukewarm water, plus more as needed
1½ teaspoons active dry yeast
1½ teaspoons sugar
2¾ cups / 345g all-purpose flour, plus more for dusting
2 tablespoons extra-virgin olive oil, plus more for greasing
1½ tablespoons powdered milk
1½ teaspoons fine sea salt
1½ teaspoons baking powder
Cooking spray, for the pan

Pomegranate Wash

1 cup whole milk or water
1 tablespoon pomegranate molasses
1 tablespoon honey
8 ounces sesame seeds, toasted or untoasted

Ka'ak al-quds is a fluffy ring-shaped bread with a sesame seed crust that has a long history in Jerusalem and has become an iconic street food. It's a staple among Palestinians and perfect for any time of the day. Slice it in half and enjoy it as a sandwich with olives and fresh cheese or tear off pieces to dip into olive oil and za'atar. Or simply enjoy it on its own with a cup of tea! With its beautiful, crunchy exterior and soft, pillowy interior, it's hard to go wrong.

The method here calls for mixing the dough by hand, which I quite enjoy. Alternatively, you can use your stand mixer to mix and knead the dough.

Make the dough: In a large bowl, combine the water, yeast, and sugar. Mix with a fork until integrated, then cover with a damp paper towel and let it rest until it bubbles and foams, about 10 minutes.

Add the flour, oil, powdered milk, salt, and baking powder to the yeast mixture. Oil your hands and use your fingers to stir the ingredients into a rough mixture. Once everything is integrated, squeeze the dough to bring it together. Don't worry if it seems a bit loose and sticky. Your goal at this stage is to have a rough, sticky dough ball but without any visible patches of flour. If your dough feels dry, you can add more water, 1 tablespoon at a time, up to 4 tablespoons.

Transfer the dough to a clean, lightly floured work surface. With lightly floured or oiled hands, knead the dough for 10 to 15 minutes until it's smooth and passes the Poke Test (see page 169).

Lightly oil the bowl, place the dough back inside, cover with plastic wrap, and let it rise until doubled in size, about 1½ hours.

Gently punch any air bubbles out of the dough. Use your hands to pinch off the dough into twelve equal portions and then gently roll them into smooth balls (see page 169). Place the dough balls on a lightly floured work surface, cover them with a dry cloth, and let them rest until they're about one and one-half times their original size, 15 to 30 minutes.

Preheat the oven to 400°F. Line several sheet pans with parchment paper or spray them lightly with cooking spray.

recipe continues →

BREADS & SAVORY BAKED GOODS

ka'ak al-quds, *continued*

Make the pomegranate wash: In a small bowl, stir together the milk, molasses, and honey. Place the sesame seeds in a rimmed pan (a half-sheet pan works well).

Shape the dough into ring shapes (see page 169), then stretch the dough into ring shapes that are 8 to 10 inches long. Place the shaped dough rings on the lined sheet pans—depending on the size of your pan, you can fit two to four.

Brush both sides of the dough with the pomegranate wash, then dip both sides into the sesame seeds. Return the dough to the lined pans, cover with plastic wrap, and let rest for 10 to 15 minutes.

Remove the plastic wrap and bake until the bottoms are slightly browned, about 15 minutes.

Serve immediately or store in an airtight container at room temperature for a couple days, in the refrigerator for up to 1 week, or in the freezer for up to 3 months.

fluffy japanese milk bread

Makes 1 loaf

Tangzhong
3 tablespoons / 35g bread flour
½ cup / 120g whole milk
¼ cup / 55g heavy cream

Dough
½ cup / 120g whole milk, warmed to 110°F
2 teaspoons active dry yeast
1 tablespoon sugar
2½ cups / 315g bread flour, plus more for dusting
⅓ cup / 65g sugar
1 heaping teaspoon Diamond Crystal kosher salt
3 tablespoons powdered milk
1 large egg, whisked
2½ tablespoons unsalted European or other high-quality butter, softened, plus more for the pan
Egg wash: 1 egg, whisked with 2 tablespoons milk or water (optional)

This is one of my favorite breads, ever. If you've never had milk bread before, it's impossibly soft, pillowy, and springy. I encourage you to use it to make a perfect egg salad or chicken salad sandwich. The bread is melt-in-your-mouth tender and doesn't have a crunchy crust, making it great for mayonnaise-y sandwiches. Very lightly toast it, and it becomes the ideal vehicle for a fried cutlet sandwich. Or you can eat it lightly toasted with butter and jam for a simple breakfast. I even like eating it plain—like brioche, it is rich and flavorful on its own.

Make the tangzhong: In a small saucepan, whisk together the flour, milk, and cream until no lumps remain. Cook over low heat, stirring constantly, until it thickens to a paste, 3 to 5 minutes. The mixture should reach a temperature of 150°F on an instant-read thermometer. Remove the pan from the heat and let cool to room temperature.

Make the dough: In a measuring cup or small bowl, combine the milk, yeast, and sugar. Mix with a fork until integrated, then cover with a damp paper towel and let it rest until it bubbles and foams, about 10 minutes.

In a stand mixer fitted with the dough hook attachment (or in a large bowl by hand), combine the flour, sugar, salt, and powdered milk. Add the tangzhong, the yeast mixture, and egg. (If mixing by hand, see Working Brioche by Hand, page 192, for the rest of the instructions.) Mix on low speed until the ingredients are roughly combined, then increase to medium speed and knead until the dough is fairly smooth, about 5 minutes.

With the mixer on medium speed, add the butter to the dough in two or three additions, ensuring each addition is incorporated before adding the next. Continue to knead the dough for another 10 minutes or until it becomes silky and pulls away from the sides of the bowl.

Shape the dough into a ball and place it in a large bowl lightly greased with butter. Cover with a damp

recipe continues →

BREADS & SAVORY BAKED GOODS

fluffy japanese milk bread, *continued*

towel or plastic wrap and let the dough rise in a warm place until it has doubled in size, 1 to 1½ hours.

Gently punch any air bubbles out of the dough. Divide the dough into three equal portions. Shape each portion into a smooth ball. Place the dough balls on a clean work surface, cover them with a damp towel, and let rest for 15 minutes. This resting period makes the dough easier to shape.

On a lightly floured work surface, use a rolling pin to flatten one of the dough balls so it's about 16 inches long and 3 inches wide. Starting with a short end, tightly roll the rectangle into a log. Press down on the seam with your fingers to ensure it's sealed well. Place the log, seam-side down, on the work surface while you repeat with the remaining two dough balls.

Butter a 1-pound loaf pan (ideally a milk bread pan; see Milk Bread Notes at right). Arrange the logs, crosswise and seam-sides down, in the pan. Cover the pan with plastic wrap or, if your pan comes with a lid, use that. Let the dough rise until it has taken up most of the pan, 1 to 2 hours, depending on the humidity of your environment (see Milk Bread Notes at right).

Preheat the oven to 325°F (but make sure to remove your loaf first, if you did your final rise there!).

Remove the plastic from the pan and brush the top of the loaf with the egg wash, if desired. If your pan comes with a lid and if you'd like a loaf with a traditional rectangular shape, omit the egg wash and leave the lid on during baking.

Bake until the crust is a nice burnished brown and the sides of the loaf begin to pull away from the pan, 40 to 45 minutes.

Remove the pan from the oven and let the bread cool in the pan for 10 minutes, then transfer to a wire rack to cool completely, usually about 1 hour. Slicing into your bread too early can lead to a gummy-doughy interior and edges, and we don't want that!

When cool, slice and serve the bread or store in an airtight container for up to 5 days at room temperature to maintain its softness.

Milk Bread Notes

• **The technique of making milk bread is a little different from that of the other breads in this book.** First, you make a tangzhong, which is like a sponge or roux. It involves lightly cooking some flour in milk and cream, then adding that starter to the rest of the dough. If you've ever made a roux before, you should have no trouble with this step.

• **When I bake this bread, I use a nonstandard loaf pan designed specifically for milk bread.** Its interior dimensions are 7½ × 4 × 4½ inches. If you use a smaller pan, your loaf will dome up differently from what's pictured.

• **For the bread's final rise, I like to fill up a heatproof bowl with boiling water and place it in the bottom of my oven.** Then I place the shaped loaf in the oven for its final rise, as the steam will create the ideal environment for the dough to rise.

BREADS & SAVORY BAKED GOODS

sourdough loaf

Makes 1 large loaf or 2 medium loaves

- 95 grams active Sourdough Starter (page 188)
- 1¾ teaspoons / 13g honey
- 1⅔ cups / 390g lukewarm water
- 4 cups / 540g unbleached bread flour, plus more for dusting
- 2 teaspoons / 15g fine sea salt
- Rice flour, for dusting

Sourdough Saturdays are my favorite day of the week. I'm relatively new to baking sourdough, but now I'm completely hooked. There's something so pleasing about baking bread with a little sourdough starter that you birthed from practically nothing—just some flour and water—and kept alive by feeding, almost as if it's your little carbohydrate pet.

My tradition is to make two or three loaves every week—one I slice and eat for my daily breakfast, and one or two I experiment with. I might carve designs or paint a loaf with food-safe food coloring, then give it away to friends and neighbors. They've almost come to expect it!

Some people are intimidated by baking sourdough from scratch, but please, just try it once, and you'll realize it's the opposite of anxiety-inducing. It's calming, almost meditative, to feed your starter and stretch and fold your dough. It does take some time, but almost all of it is inactive. Take a look at the sample schedule (see Sourdough 101, page 187) to see how I fit it into my week.

tip This recipe calls for a large Dutch oven, which I find is the best and most consistent way to bake sourdough. But if you do not have a Dutch oven, you can bake the bread on a baking stone instead. Your bread won't be covered during baking, so you'll have to carefully transfer the loaf to the preheated baking stone.

In a large bowl, combine the starter, honey, and water. Stir with a dough whisk or spoon until the starter is fully dissolved and frothy.

Gradually add the bread flour and salt and stir with a wooden spoon or your hands until a shaggy dough forms and no dry flour remains.

Cover the bowl with plastic wrap and let it rest for 1 hour. This rest period allows the flour to fully hydrate and the gluten to develop.

Stretch and fold the dough: Perform a total of three stretches and folds (see Hands-On Bread Basics, page 189).

Re-cover the dough with plastic and allow it to rest in a warm, draft-free area for its bulk fermentation, 5 to 8 hours, or until it has doubled in size, has visible bubbles on the surface, and has a bit of a jiggle to it. If your dough doesn't have visible bubbles on top and is still stiff when you try to jiggle your bowl, your bulk fermentation is not complete.

To gently turn the dough out onto a lightly floured surface, tilt the bowl so that the dough slowly falls out by itself rather than ripping it from the bowl. The goal is to retain the dough's airiness.

Shape it into a round or oval loaf by pushing the dough away with your palm, then bringing it back in with your fingers, creating surface tension on the top of the loaf. Handle the dough carefully to retain its airiness.

Place the shaped dough into a proofing basket generously dusted with rice flour, or a bowl lined with a cloth (also dusted with rice flour), seam-side up. Cover with plastic or a towel and let it cold proof in the refrigerator for 8 to 12 hours.

recipe continues →

sourdough loaf, *continued*

Place a 5½-quart Dutch oven in the oven and preheat to 450°F for at least 45 minutes, ideally an hour, to ensure it is thoroughly heated.

Gently turn the dough out onto a piece of parchment paper. If desired, you can dust the surface with more rice flour, so that the pattern of your scoring is quite visible after baking. Using a sharp knife or razor blade, score the top of the dough with a few deep slashes to allow for expansion during baking.

Hold onto the sides of the parchment paper and carefully transfer the dough and parchment into the preheated Dutch oven. Cover with the lid.

Bake for 20 minutes. Remove the lid and bake for an additional 20 to 25 minutes, or until the loaf is deep golden brown and sounds hollow when tapped on the bottom.

Remove the pan from the oven and place the loaf on a wire rack to cool completely—at least 1 full hour—before slicing.

note: This recipe's high hydration makes for a stickier dough. Use flour sparingly on your hands and work surface to manage the dough without compromising its structure when shaping. During stretch-and-fold, use only water on your hands.

variation

Sourdough Bread Bowls: Divide the dough into four equal portions. Then, you can shape, proof, and bake each of these dough portions exactly as directed in the recipe. (Depending on the size of your oven and how many Dutch ovens you have, you'll probably have to bake in batches.)

Once the bread loaves have cooled completely, using a serrated knife, slice off the top of the bread to create a circle. Then, using a spoon, carefully hollow out the interior, leaving a 1-inch-thick shell to hold the contents without collapsing. (Save the filling in a resealable plastic bag in the freezer to use for bread crumbs or croutons.)

I SLEEP IN MY KITCHEN

sourdough 101

If you're anything like me, you'll try your first bite of homemade sourdough and decide you're hooked. So this section is for anyone who wants to geek out on bread science even more!

Using temperature to gauge bulk fermentation time

The colder your dough is when you start, the longer it will need for bulk fermentation. Use an instant-read thermometer to measure the temperature of the dough after the last stretch-and-fold and then reference this guide:

65°F dough = 16-hour bulk fermentation
70°F dough = 12-hour bulk fermentation
75°F dough = 7-hour bulk fermentation
80°F dough = 5½-hour bulk fermentation

Longer fermentation

You can experiment with taking the cold fermentation step even further, leaving the dough in the fridge for as long as thirty-six hours. The bread might become assertively sour, and it might not rise as much, but I've taken the cold proof up to thirty-six hours and enjoyed the result.

Designs

You can have fun and also get creative with designs once you start to get the hang of sourdough! I love to cover the top of my loaf with rice flour before scoring. Rice flour allows the design to show more prominently once baked in the oven.

Expanding the score

This is an optional step for more experienced bakers. Six minutes into my loaf's initial bake time, I like to reinforce my expansion score to ensure that the loaf bakes properly. Carefully remove the lid and retrace the score, then cover the loaf again with the lid and allow it to finish baking with the lid on for the remaining 14 minutes before uncovering and continuing to bake, lid off.

My schedule for Sourdough Saturdays

I like to bake on Saturdays, which means I pull my sourdough starter from the fridge on **Thursday** before I go to bed. I feed the starter, which takes two seconds—just put flour and water in the jar and leave it out at room temperature.

When I wake up on **Friday morning**, I start to mix my dough. If you read about baking sourdough online, you'll see a lot of people saying scary things like, "YOU HAVE TO USE YOUR STARTER WHEN IT'S AT ITS PEAK!" So this might lead you to believe that you have to mix your dough the second you wake up, or even wake up early. I completely disagree. So long as your starter is still a little risen and not *completely* deflated, it's fine. If it's a little deflated, I like to tell myself that it's hungry . . . and hungry starter often makes the best bread!

Anyway, at some point on Friday morning, I mix the starter with the other ingredients. **One hour later**, I do my first stretch-and-fold. **Thirty minutes after that**, I do my second. **Thirty minutes after that**, I do my last stretch-and-fold. Since I typically start around 6:00 a.m. (I know, I'm crazy), I'm usually done by 8:30 a.m.

Bulk fermentation usually takes 6 to 8 hours, depending on how hot or cold your house is. My home is 72°F, so my bread is usually ready by **2:00 p.m.** If your house is 80°F or super humid, bulk fermentation might take as little as 4½ hours.

I shape my bread, transfer it to the fridge for its cold proof, and leave it there for anywhere from eight to thirty-six hours. This means I can bake my bread **whenever I want on Saturday** and have fresh loaves to last the week!

sourdough starter

Whole wheat flour
Bread flour
Lukewarm filtered tap water

Day 1: Starting the Starter
In a clean small jar, combine ½ cup / 60g whole wheat flour and ¼ cup / 60g water. Stir until no dry flour remains and the mixture resembles thick pancake batter.

Loosely cover the jar with a breathable cover (such as a cloth jar cover or a cloth secured with a rubber band), or loosely screw on the lid. Let the jar sit at room temperature, 70° to 75°F, for 24 hours.

Day 2: Feeding the Starter
To the same jar, add another ½ cup / 60g whole wheat flour and ¼ cup / 60g water. Stir until smooth.

Loosely cover and let sit at room temperature for another 24 hours.

Day 3: Beginning the Discards
Transfer a scant 2 tablespoons / 30g of your starter to a clean small jar (discard the remaining starter in the previous jar).

Add ¼ cup / 60g water and stir to combine. Add ¼ cup / 30g bread flour and ¼ cup / 30g whole wheat flour. Stir until smooth.

Loosely cover and let sit at room temperature for 24 hours.

Day 4: Continuing the Process
In a clean small jar, combine a scant 2 tablespoons / 30g of your starter (discard the remaining starter in the previous jar).

Add ¼ cup / 60g water, ¼ cup / 30g bread flour, and ¼ cup / 30g whole wheat flour. Stir until smooth.

Loosely cover and let sit at room temperature for 24 hours.

Day 5: Strengthening the Starter
In a clean small jar, combine a scant 2 tablespoons / 30g of your starter (discard the remaining starter in the previous jar).

Add ¼ cup / 60g water, ¼ cup / 30g bread flour, and ¼ cup / 30g whole wheat flour. Stir until smooth.

Loosely cover and let sit at room temperature for 24 hours.

Day 6: Increasing the Bread Flour
In a clean small jar, combine a scant 2 tablespoons / 30g of your starter (discard the remaining starter in the previous jar).

Add ¼ cup / 60g water and ½ cup / 60g bread flour. Stir until smooth.

Loosely cover and let sit at room temperature for 24 hours.

Day 7: Final Feeding
In a clean small jar, combine a scant 2 tablespoons / 30g of your starter (discard the remaining starter in the previous jar).

Add ¼ cup / 60g water and ½ cup / 60g bread flour. Stir until smooth.

Loosely cover and let sit at room temperature for 24 hours.

Maintaining Your Starter

Once your starter consistently doubles in size, within six to eight hours of feeding, it is considered "active" and ready to use for baking.

If you bake frequently (daily or every other day), keep your starter at room temperature and feed it daily. For less frequent baking, store the starter in the refrigerator and feed it once a week.

If you're not planning on baking immediately and just want to maintain your starter, feed it with a ratio of 1:1:1—starter to water to flour. The quantity is up to you—you could do as little as 10 grams starter, 10 grams water, and 10 grams flour. But when you know you want to bake with it, feed it in a ratio of 1:2:2 and increase the quantities: 60 grams starter, 120 grams water, 120 grams flour.

tip If you prefer a strong wheat flavor, continue feeding your starter with half whole wheat flour and half bread flour. If you prefer a milder flavor, feed your starter only bread flour after Day 5.

brioche buns

Makes 12 small or 8 large buns

1 cup / 240g lukewarm water
1 tablespoon sugar
2 teaspoons active dry yeast
5 cups / 625g all-purpose flour, plus more as needed
1 large egg plus 1 large egg yolk, whisked
2 teaspoons fine sea salt
½ cup unsalted butter, at room temperature
Egg wash: 1 egg, whisked with 2 tablespoons water

I'm a huge fan of making homemade buns to use for both burgers and sandwiches. Once you try homemade brioche buns, you'll never want to go back to store-bought. Not only do you get the satisfaction of knowing you made them yourself (which makes every bite taste better), you can also splurge on nice, fancy butter to make these truly decadent.

Speaking of butter: Because of the high butter content of this recipe, it can be tricky and quite messy to mix it by hand. A stand mixer, if you have one, is going to be your best friend.

In the bowl of a stand mixer (or in a large bowl by hand), combine the water, sugar, and yeast. Mix with a fork until integrated, then cover with a damp paper towel and let it rest until it bubbles and foams, about 10 minutes.

Add the flour, eggs, and salt to the yeast mixture. Snap on the dough hook attachment and mix on medium-low speed just until the ingredients come together, 3 to 5 minutes. (If you'd rather work by hand, see Working Brioche by Hand, page 192.) With the mixer running, gradually add the butter, 1 tablespoon at a time, waiting until each piece is starting to get incorporated into the dough before adding the next. Once the butter is fully incorporated, mix the dough on medium-low speed for 10 to 15 minutes, or until it becomes smooth and starts to pull away from the sides of the bowl.

Add a bit of flour to the sides of the mixer bowl so that the dough doesn't stick while it rises. (If working by hand, place the dough in a lightly floured or oiled bowl.) Cover the bowl with a damp towel and let it rest in a warm, draft-free place until doubled in size, about 1 hour.

Line two sheet pans with parchment paper.

Gently punch down the dough to release the gas. Use your hands to pinch off the dough into equal portions—twelve for smaller, slider-size buns and eight for larger buns—and roll gently into balls. Place the dough balls on the lined sheets and cover them with a damp towel. Let them rest for an additional 30 minutes to allow the gluten to relax.

recipe continues →

BREADS & SAVORY BAKED GOODS

brioche buns, *continued*

Preheat the oven to 350°F.

Brush the dough balls with the egg wash. Bake until they turn golden on the tops and bottoms, 30 to 45 minutes.

Remove the pans from the oven and transfer the buns to a wire rack, then let cool completely before slicing in half to use for sandwiches, burgers, and more! Store any leftovers in an airtight container at room temperature for 2 days or in the refrigerator for up to 5 days.

variation
Brioche Loaf: Use this dough but follow the shaping and baking instructions for Fluffy Japanese Milk Bread (page 181).

Working Brioche by Hand

I love encouraging people to knead dough by hand, but I'll admit brioche dough is a bit harder because of the butter. So here's how to do it:

1. Mix the dry ingredients together in a bowl, then add the wet ingredients and stir to combine. Transfer the dough mass to a clean work surface.

2. When it comes time to add the butter to the dough, add it all to the center of the dough mass.

3. Fold the dough over on top of the butter to enclose it.

4. Knead it by hand for 10 to 15 minutes: With lightly floured or oiled hands, use the palm of your hand to push the dough away from you, then bring it back to the center of the dough mass and repeat. Give the dough mass a quarter-turn every four stretches or so.

fluffy browned butter rolls *with* flaky sea salt

Makes 12 rolls

- 1 cup / 240g lukewarm water
- ⅓ cup / 65g plus 1 tablespoon sugar
- 2¼ teaspoons active dry yeast
- 4 cups / 540g bread flour, plus more for dusting
- 1 large egg, whisked
- 2 teaspoons Diamond Crystal kosher salt
- 4 tablespoons / 60g Browned Butter (recipe follows), at room temperature, plus more for finishing
- Extra-virgin olive oil, for greasing
- Egg wash: 1 egg, beaten with 1 tablespoon milk
- Flaky sea salt, for sprinkling
- Butter, for serving (optional)

These are my homemade take on the classic crescent rolls you find in a tube in the refrigerated section of any grocery store. But I promise you, these rolls are so much more beautiful, tasty, and special than anything you can buy—your friends won't believe you when you tell them you made them from scratch. The secret ingredient is browned butter, which adds a nutty richness. These rolls are so flaky and tender, and if you want to try your hand at homemade bread and only have two hours rather than the twenty-four you need for homemade croissants, this is the recipe for you.

In a measuring cup or small bowl, combine the water with the 1 tablespoon sugar and the yeast. Mix with a fork until integrated, then cover with a damp paper towel and let it rest until it bubbles and foams, about 10 minutes.

In a stand mixer fitted with the dough hook attachment, combine the flour, egg, kosher salt, and remaining ⅓ cup / 65g sugar. Mix well. Add the yeast mixture and mix on medium-low speed until just combined.

With the mixer on medium-low speed, add the browned butter 1 tablespoon at a time, waiting until each addition is incorporated before adding the next.

Continue mixing the dough on medium speed for 10 minutes or until it becomes smooth and elastic. The dough should be soft but not sticky.

Transfer the dough to a lightly oiled bowl and cover with a clean kitchen towel or plastic wrap. Let the dough rise in a warm, draft-free place (for example, inside your oven while it is turned off) until it has doubled in size, about 1½ hours.

Gently punch down the dough to release any air bubbles and gently turn it out onto a lightly floured surface. Using a lightly floured rolling pin, roll out the dough into a 14 × 18-inch rectangle. Use a pizza cutter to trim the edges if you need to.

With a long side facing you, cut the dough vertically into six rectangular strips measuring 3 × 14 inches. Then cut each rectangle on the diagonal into triangles for a total of twelve.

Starting at the flat end of a triangle and rolling toward the point, roll each triangle into a croissant shape.

recipe continues →

BREADS & SAVORY BAKED GOODS

fluffy browned butter rolls with flaky sea salt, *continued*

Arrange the rolls on a sheet pan with some space in between them to allow for expansion during the second rise. Make sure the point (or "tail," as I like to think of it) of the roll is facing down and in contact with the sheet pan—this will prevent the rolls from unraveling during baking. Cover with a clean kitchen towel and let rise until they have puffed up, about 30 minutes.

Meanwhile, preheat the oven to 375°F.

Brush the rolls with the egg wash and sprinkle with the flaky salt.

Bake until they are golden brown, 15 to 20 minutes.

Remove the pan from the oven and brush the rolls with more browned butter or plain butter, if desired. Enjoy warm!

browned butter

Makes about ½ cup / 120g

½ cup / 115g unsalted butter, cut into even pieces

In a light-colored medium skillet (see Tip), melt the butter over medium heat. Swirl and stir occasionally to make sure the butter is cooking evenly. The butter will begin to foam, and then the color will begin to darken. When it reaches a nice toasty brown color and smells nutty, immediately take the pan off the heat. Pour the butter into a heatproof bowl.

When the butter has cooled slightly, transfer it to a glass container. It can be stored, covered, in the fridge for up to 2 weeks.

tip I recommend using a pan with a light-colored bottom so you can immediately tell when the butter is the correct color; browned butter can turn into burned butter quite quickly.

honey-butter cast-iron cornbread

Makes one 12-inch round cornbread

Butter, for the pan
1½ cups / 270g fine cornmeal
1½ cups / 190g all-purpose flour
1 tablespoon baking powder
½ teaspoon baking soda
½ teaspoon fine sea salt
1 cup / 225g buttermilk
½ cup / 100g granulated sugar
⅓ cup / 75g (packed) brown sugar
⅓ cup / 80g sour cream
⅓ cup / 65g vegetable oil
6 tablespoons / 85g unsalted butter, melted
2 large eggs, whisked

Honey Butter
½ cup / 115g unsalted butter, melted
¼ cup / 85g honey
¼ teaspoon fine sea salt
¼ teaspoon ground cinnamon

When my mom's family immigrated to America from Palestine, they went to Cleveland, Ohio. Like me, my mom comes from a big family—there were seven siblings, total. They never had very much money, but one of the things they could afford was Jiffy cornbread mix, which is ubiquitous in the Midwest and South. My mom's mom would make the kids Jiffy cornbread and then slather it with butter and jam, and it was their favorite thing . . . until they realized it had lard in it.

I inherited my mom's love of cornbread, so, of course, I had to develop my own halal version. This one is pretty traditional, and you can serve it with butter and jam if you'd like, but I recommend making a delicious whipped honey butter, spiked with a bit of cinnamon.

Preheat the oven to 375°F. Butter a 12-inch cast-iron skillet and place it in the oven while the oven preheats.

In a large bowl, whisk together the cornmeal, flour, baking powder, baking soda, and kosher salt.

In a separate large bowl, whisk together the buttermilk, granulated sugar, brown sugar, sour cream, vegetable oil, butter, and eggs until well combined.

Slowly add the cornmeal mixture to the wet ingredients, folding gently with a spatula until just combined. Be careful not to overmix; a few lumps are okay.

Pour the batter into the preheated skillet, using the spatula to spread it evenly. Bake until a toothpick inserted into the center comes out clean or with only a few moist crumbs attached, 20 to 35 minutes.

Meanwhile, make the honey butter: In a small bowl, stir to combine the butter, honey, fine salt, and cinnamon.

When the cornbread comes out of the oven, use a toothpick to poke it all over the surface about 20 times. Brush the top of the warm cornbread with the honey butter and serve immediately. (Alternatively, you can store it at room temperature and reheat it before serving.)

BREADS & SAVORY BAKED GOODS

feta-chive buttermilk biscuits *with* roasted garlic butter

Makes 6 large or 9 small biscuits

Roasted Garlic Butter
- 1 garlic bulb
- Extra-virgin olive oil, for drizzling
- ½ cup / 115g unsalted butter, at room temperature
- ¼ teaspoon red pepper flakes
- 1 tablespoon chopped fresh parsley
- Pinch of fine sea salt

Biscuits
- 1 cup / 225g salted butter, cold
- 3 cups / 375g all-purpose flour, plus more for dusting
- 1 tablespoon baking powder
- 1½ teaspoons Diamond Crystal kosher salt
- 1½ teaspoons sugar
- 1 (8-ounce) block feta cheese, sliced into thin strips
- ⅓ cup / 15g chopped fresh chives
- 1 cup / 225g plus 1½ tablespoons buttermilk

If you ask me, everyone needs a staple buttermilk biscuit recipe. My twist on the classic is to incorporate feta and chives into the dough, two ingredients that pair together so well. I slather the biscuits with a roasted garlic butter because garlic makes *everything* taste better (although that might be my Middle Eastern-ness talking). Feel free to experiment with other herbs in the butter; parsley is classic, but let your creativity shine.

Make the roasted garlic butter: Preheat the oven to 400°F.

Cut off the top of the garlic bulb to expose the cloves, then drizzle with a bit of oil and wrap tightly in aluminum foil. Roast until the cloves are soft and caramelized, 30 to 35 minutes.

When the garlic is cool enough to handle, squeeze the cloves into a small bowl. Add the softened butter, pepper flakes, and parsley and use a fork to mash them together. Season with the fine salt.

Make the biscuits: Place the butter in the freezer for 10 minutes before beginning the baking prep.

Using the large holes of a box grater, grate the butter into a small bowl. If the butter begins to soften, place the grated butter back in the freezer while you weigh and prepare the rest of the ingredients.

Preheat the oven to 425°F. Line a sheet pan with parchment paper or a silicone baking mat.

In a large bowl, whisk together the flour, baking powder, kosher salt, and sugar.

Add the chilled grated butter to the flour mixture. Using your fingertips or a pastry cutter, quickly and gently work the butter into the flour mixture until it resembles coarse crumbs with pea-size pieces of butter throughout. Use a wooden spoon to gently fold in the feta and chives.

Pour the buttermilk into the bowl and stir until the dough just comes together. Be careful not to overmix; the dough should be slightly shaggy and sticky.

Turn the dough out onto a lightly floured surface. Pat it into a rectangle about 6 × 9 inches and 1 inch thick. Fold the dough over itself two or three times to create layers, then pat it back into a 1-inch-thick rectangle. Cut the rectangle in half, then stack the two halves on top of each other and pat it down to a rectangle about 5 × 8 inches and 1½ inches thick.

Using a floured knife, cut the dough into six large or nine small biscuits. Generously spread some roasted garlic butter on top of each, then transfer them to the lined sheet pan and refrigerate for 15 minutes to firm up the butter again.

Bake until golden brown and cooked through, 20 to 25 minutes.

Remove the pan from the oven and let the biscuits cool slightly on a wire rack. Serve warm with a generous dollop of any remaining roasted garlic butter.

homemade garlic knots

Makes 12 garlic knots

Dough
- ¾ cup / 180g lukewarm water
- 1 tablespoon sugar
- 2 teaspoons active dry yeast
- 2⅓ cups / 300g all-purpose flour, plus more as needed
- 3 tablespoons powdered milk
- 2 teaspoons fine sea salt
- 2 tablespoons extra-virgin olive oil
- Egg wash: 1 egg, mixed with 1 tablespoon water

Garlic Butter
- 6 tablespoons / 85g unsalted butter
- 3 garlic cloves, grated or very finely minced
- ½ teaspoon red pepper flakes (optional)
- 1 tablespoon chopped fresh parsley
- ¼ teaspoon fine sea salt

When it comes to bread recipes, I consider this one pretty foolproof—which means it's a nice one to start with if you're new to baking. These aren't delicate or finicky, so you can be a little rough when you handle them. For example, if they don't have a perfectly smooth top, it's fine! And you get to practice your knotting action, which is always fun. I love to make these when I'm having friends over for delivery pizza . . . that way, there's one tasty homemade element that everyone can enjoy!

Make the dough: In a measuring cup or small bowl, combine the water, sugar, and yeast. Mix with a fork until integrated, then cover with a damp paper towel and let it rest until it bubbles and foams, about 10 minutes.

In a stand mixer fitted with a dough hook (or in a large bowl by hand), combine the flour, powdered milk, and salt. Stir to distribute evenly, then add the activated yeast mixture and oil. Mix until a shaggy dough forms.

Mix on medium-low speed for 8 to 10 minutes, until the dough is smooth and elastic. If it feels too sticky, add more flour, 1 tablespoon at a time, until it's manageable. (To knead by hand, see Hands-On Bread Basics, page 169.)

Transfer the dough to a lightly oiled bowl, turning it to coat. Cover with a damp cloth or plastic wrap and let it rise in a warm place until doubled in size, 1 to 1½ hours.

Line a sheet pan with parchment paper.

Punch down the dough and transfer it to a floured surface. Divide it into twelve equal portions and roll each piece into a rope about 8 inches long. Tie the rope into a knot, tucking the ends underneath the knot. Place the knots on the lined sheet pan, leaving space for them to proof and expand in size.

Cover the shaped knots with a damp cloth and let them rise until puffy, about 30 minutes.

Meanwhile, preheat the oven to 375°F.

Brush the knots with egg wash and bake until golden brown on top, 12 to 15 minutes.

Meanwhile, make the garlic butter: In a small pan, combine the butter and garlic and melt over low heat until fragrant, 30 seconds to 1 minute. This is just to infuse the butter with garlic flavor; you don't want the garlic to develop color, only flavor! In the last 15 seconds or so, stir in the pepper flakes (if using). Stir in the parsley and salt.

When the knots come out of the oven, brush them generously with garlic butter. Serve immediately for best results.

fan fave

mozzarella-stuffed pull-apart bread

Makes 12 rolls

Dough Balls

2½ cups / 315g all-purpose flour, plus more as needed

1 cup / 240g lukewarm water

2 tablespoons sugar

1 tablespoon active dry or instant yeast

⅓ cup / 65g extra-virgin olive oil

2 teaspoons Diamond Crystal kosher salt

1 pound / 455g freshly shredded mozzarella cheese or small fresh mozzarella balls (such as ciliegine)

Egg wash: 1 egg, whisked with 2 tablespoons water

Garlic Butter

¼ cup / 55g unsalted butter, melted

1½ teaspoons garlic powder

1 teaspoon chopped fresh or dried parsley

½ teaspoon red pepper flakes

¼ teaspoon Diamond Crystal kosher salt

I've been making variations of this recipe ever since I started testing and posting recipes online, but this version is the best. It's basically a warm, comforting bread roll with a cheesy center—and since warm bread and cheese are my two favorite things, you could call this a Mxriyum classic. I just feel like it's hard to go wrong with anything that involves a cheese pull.

Make the dough balls: In a stand mixer (or in a large bowl by hand), combine 1 cup / 125g of the flour, the water, sugar, and yeast. Mix with a fork until integrated, then cover with a damp paper towel and let it rest until it bubbles and foams, about 10 minutes.

Snap on the dough hook attachment and add the remaining 1½ cups / 190g flour, the oil, and salt and use a large wooden spoon to stir until you have a rough dough.

Mix on medium-low speed for 8 to 10 minutes, until the dough is smooth and elastic and passes the Poke Test (see page 169). If needed, you can add up to ½ cup / 63g of additional flour, but you might not need it. (To knead by hand, see Hands-On Bread Basics, page 169.)

Cover the dough with a kitchen towel and let it rest for 15 minutes, or until the gluten relaxes.

Preheat the oven to 375°F. Line two 5-inch cast-iron skillets or one 9 × 13-inch baking dish with parchment paper.

With a knife or bench scraper, divide the dough into twelve equal portions (about 60g each) and roll into smooth balls. To stuff each ball with mozzarella, start by making a small divot in the center of a ball and then place 2 to 3 tablespoons cheese inside the divot. Pinch and pull the dough so that it encloses the cheese, making sure your dough is tightly closed so the cheese doesn't leak out during baking.

If you're using the skillets for this recipe, arrange six of the balls in each of the lined pans, with one ball in the center of the pan and the remaining five arranged around the circumference. If you're using the baking dish, arrange the balls so they're evenly spaced. Either way, you want to leave a bit of space—maybe ½ inch—between the dough balls since they will rise while baking.

Cover with a damp cloth and allow to rest for 10 minutes or until slightly increased in size.

Brush with the egg wash and bake until the bottoms and tops of your bread are beautifully golden, 25 to 30 minutes.

Meanwhile, make the garlic butter: In a small bowl, mix together the butter, garlic powder, parsley, pepper flakes, and salt and set aside.

As soon as you pull your bread out of the oven, generously brush the tops with the garlic butter. Serve warm!

fan fave

everything bagels

Makes 8 bagels

- 1½ cups / 360g lukewarm water
- 1 tablespoon active dry or instant yeast
- 1 tablespoon granulated sugar
- 5 cups / 625g all-purpose flour, plus more as needed
- ¼ cup / 60g plus 3 tablespoons (packed) light brown sugar
- 2 teaspoons Diamond Crystal kosher salt
- Cooking spray, for the parchment (optional)
- Egg wash: 1 egg, whisked with 2 tablespoons water (optional)
- Everything bagel seasoning, for sprinkling

Bagels are one of the first "intimidating" baking projects I ever tackled. I put *intimidating* in quotation marks because I think a lot of people assume that bagels are difficult to make and best left to the professionals. But when I made them, they turned out perfectly the first time, and now I love making them as a Sunday project. That way I'm stocked for the rest of the week.

In a measuring cup or small bowl, combine the water, yeast, and granulated sugar. Mix with a fork until integrated, then cover with a damp paper towel and let it rest until it bubbles and foams, about 10 minutes.

In a large bowl, combine the flour, the 3 tablespoons brown sugar, and salt and whisk to combine. Add the yeast mixture and stir to combine. If the dough is too sticky to handle with your hands, add 1 tablespoon of flour at a time until it comes together into a rough ball, then transfer it to a lightly floured work surface.

With lightly floured or oiled hands, knead the dough for 10 to 15 minutes until it becomes smooth and passes the Poke Test (see page 169). (If you have a stand mixer, mix the dough with the dough hook attachment on low speed until the flour is incorporated, then gradually work your way up to medium speed.)

Use your hands to pinch off the dough into eight equal portions and gently roll them into smooth balls (see page 169). Set the balls on a lightly floured surface, cover with a damp towel, and let rest until the dough balls are one and one-half times their original size, about 15 minutes.

After 15 minutes, take your index finger and press a hole through the center of each dough ball. Lightly flour your hands and thread your pointer finger and thumb through the hole of the bagel, bringing those two fingers together to make an O-shape. Use your other hand to rotate the bagel 360 degrees—as you turn it, your O-shaped fingers should help the bagel maintain its shape. Your goal is to slightly stretch the dough without ruining the overall shape of your bagels.

recipe continues →

BREADS & SAVORY BAKED GOODS

everything bagels, *continued*

Cut eight squares of parchment paper slightly larger than the proofed bagels. Spray them lightly with cooking spray or dust them lightly with flour. Add a parchment paper square under each bagel as you finish shaping them. This step will be extremely helpful once you begin boiling the bagels. Cover the bagels once again with a clean damp towel. Allow to rest for 30 minutes.

Preheat the oven to 350°F. Line a sheet pan with parchment paper.

Fill a large pot with about 2 quarts water. Whisk in the remaining ¼ cup / 60g brown sugar and bring to a boil.

Working in batches of two or three bagels at a time so as not to crowd the pot, grab the bagels (holding them by the parchment sheet) and tip them into the boiling water (don't put the parchment into the water). Boil the bagels for 1 minute on each side. Use a wooden spoon or flat spatula to transfer the boiled bagels to the lined sheet pan.

If desired, brush the top and sides of each bagel with the egg wash. This creates an extra chewy and slightly more golden crust. Sprinkle the everything bagel seasoning on top (the amount is up to you).

Bake until the bagels are beautifully golden, 25 to 35 minutes.

Remove from the oven. Let the bagels cool on the sheet pan for 10 to 15 minutes, then transfer them to a wire rack to cool completely. Toast before serving!

For longer storage, cover any leftover bagels tightly with plastic wrap or store them in an airtight container for a few days at room temperature or up to 5 days in the refrigerator.

za'atar soft pretzels

Makes 8 pretzels

Roasted Garlic and Herb Dipping Oil
1 garlic bulb
½ cup extra-virgin olive oil, plus more for drizzling
¼ teaspoon red pepper flakes
1 teaspoon dried oregano
¼ cup freshly grated Parmesan cheese
1 tablespoon chopped fresh parsley
Fine sea salt and black pepper

Za'atar Soft Pretzels
1¼ cups / 300g lukewarm water
1 tablespoon active dry yeast
1 tablespoon granulated sugar
2½ cups / 340g bread flour
1 cup / 125g all-purpose flour, plus more as needed
¼ cup / 55g (packed) brown sugar
Diamond Crystal kosher salt
6 tablespoons / 25g za'atar
¼ cup / 50g extra-virgin olive oil, plus more for greasing
¼ cup / 45g baking soda

Before I fell in love with making bread, there were these pretzels. I tweaked the recipe again and again, trying to find the perfect version—it became an obsession. My inspiration was humble: the big black box of frozen soft pretzels my mom would buy at Sam's Club. But by making my own version from scratch, I was able to add a bit of Palestinian flair in the form of za'atar, a delicious, earthy spice that makes everything better. With a side of roasted garlic dipping oil, this becomes a beautiful snack to impress your guests.

Make the roasted garlic and herb dipping oil: Preheat the oven to 400°F.

Cut off the top of the garlic bulb to expose the cloves, then drizzle with a bit of oil and wrap tightly in aluminum foil. Roast until the cloves are soft and caramelized, 30 to 35 minutes.

In a small bowl, combine the oil, pepper flakes, and oregano. Squeeze in the roasted garlic cloves and mash to combine. Stir in the Parmesan and parsley, then season with fine salt and black pepper to taste. Set aside.

Make the za'atar soft pretzels: In a measuring cup or small bowl, combine the water, yeast, and granulated sugar. Mix with a fork until integrated, then cover with a damp paper towel and let it rest until it bubbles and foams, about 10 minutes.

In a large bowl, combine the bread flour, all-purpose flour, brown sugar, and 2 tablespoons of the za'atar and whisk to combine. Add the yeast mixture and oil and stir to combine. If the dough is too sticky to handle with your hands, add 1 tablespoon of all-purpose flour at a time until it comes together into a rough ball, then transfer it to a lightly floured work surface.

With lightly floured or oiled hands, knead the dough for 8 to 10 minutes until the dough is smooth and elastic and passes the Poke Test (page 169). (If you have a stand mixer, mix the dough with the dough hook attachment on low speed until the flour is incorporated, then gradually work your way up to medium speed.)

recipe continues →

BREADS & SAVORY BAKED GOODS

za'atar soft pretzels, *continued*

Place the dough in a lightly oiled large bowl, cover with a damp cloth, and let rise in a warm place for 30 minutes.

Gently punch down the dough and use your hands to pinch off eight equal portions, then roll into smooth balls and let them rest, covered with a damp cloth, for 30 minutes.

Preheat the oven to 400°F. Line a sheet pan with parchment paper.

Roll each ball into a 22- to 26-inch rope. To shape the ropes into pretzels, form a U-shape, twist the ends together twice, then fold and firmly press the twisted ends down onto the bottom of the U. Make sure those seams are secure, or your pretzels will lose their shape during boiling. (If desired, you can reinforce the seams with a flour paste made from one part all-purpose flour and one part warm water.)

Let the shaped pretzels rest, covered, for another 30 minutes while you bring a large pot of water to a boil.

Add the baking soda to the boiling water. Working in batches of two pretzels (they need enough room in the pot to bounce around without touching), carefully drop them one at a time into the boiling water and cook for 30 seconds per side. Remove with a slotted spoon and place on the lined sheet pan.

Sprinkle kosher salt followed by 1½ teaspoons za'atar on each pretzel, lightly patting it into the surface so it adheres.

Bake until golden brown, about 12 minutes.

Serve immediately with the dipping oil or store in an airtight container at room temperature for 3 days.

fan fave

za'atar manakeesh

za'atar flatbread

Makes 7 flatbreads

Dough
- 1½ cups / 360g lukewarm water
- 1½ teaspoons active dry yeast
- 1½ teaspoons sugar
- 3½ cups / 440g all-purpose flour, plus more for dusting
- 2 tablespoons powdered milk
- 1 tablespoon extra-virgin olive oil, plus more as needed
- 1½ teaspoons fine sea salt

Za'atar Topping
- ½ cup extra-virgin olive oil
- ¾ cup za'atar
- Pinch of fine sea salt

Popular throughout the Levant, manakeesh is a type of flatbread with origins in Lebanon. The dough is the same one we use for our Khubiz Taboon (page 172), and after it is stretched into a thin round, you can add all sorts of toppings. Shredded mozzarella is a classic (you could also use the cheese topping from the fatayer on page 217); some people use ground meat similar to that found on Sfeeha (page 213). I love it topped with my nicest olive oil and a healthy amount of za'atar. This was a classic in our household for breakfast and breakfast-for-dinner. Here, I am having you bake it on stones, like the Khubiz Taboon; this results in a delicious crispy bottom and a soft, pillowy top. That textural contrast is what makes this bread so special, in my opinion.

Make the dough: In a measuring cup or small bowl, combine ½ cup / 120g of the water, the yeast, and sugar. Mix with a fork until integrated, then cover with a damp paper towel and let it rest until it bubbles and foams, about 10 minutes.

In a large bowl, combine the flour, powdered milk, oil, and salt. Add the yeast mixture to the flour mixture, along with the remaining 1 cup / 240g water.

Oil your hands, then use them to start mixing the dough; it will feel sticky and tough to start, but trust the process. Using both hands, stretch some of the dough away from you, then fold it down into the center of the dough mass. Then, use one hand to stretch a corner of the dough and fold and punch it down into the center. Alternate this stretching, folding, and punching process until the dough becomes smoother, 3 to 4 minutes. Once it's somewhat smoother, add a bit more oil (around 1 tablespoon) and keep folding until the dough is completely smooth, about 10 minutes more. Test the dough readiness with the Poke Test (see page 169). Cover the dough with a damp cloth and let it rest until it doubles in size, 1½ to 2 hours.

Place baking stones in a round baking pan (see How to Bake on Stones, page 175) and place the pan directly on the floor of your oven. Either remove the oven racks or position them in the highest position so you have room to work. Preheat the oven to 550°F or as high as it will go to superheat the stones.

recipe continues →

BREADS & SAVORY BAKED GOODS

za'atar manakeesh, *continued*

Gently punch any air bubbles out of the dough. Use your hands to pinch off the dough into seven equal portions and then gently roll them into smooth balls (see page 169). Place the balls on a lightly floured surface, cover them with a damp cloth, and let them rest for an additional 15 minutes to allow the gluten to relax.

Lightly flour a work surface and your hands. Flatten a ball with your hands to about ¼ inch—thin, but not so thin that it's see-through. (I prefer a flatbread with a slightly poofy rim, so I don't make it uniform; I leave a rim.) Keep the remaining dough covered with the damp cloth as you work.

Make the za'atar topping: In a small bowl, combine the oil, za'atar, and salt and stir with a fork until combined. Spread a thin, even layer of the za'atar mixture over each piece of manakeesh, leaving a ½- to 1-inch border around the rim. Sprinkle za'atar over top to fill in any holes, if desired.

Working with one piece at a time, use your hands to transfer a dough round onto the preheated baking stones. You might have to stretch the dough a bit once it hits the rocks to help it maintain its circular shape, but you're not looking to stretch it any thinner.

Bake until the pockets of the bread that are in contact with the stones turn a lovely golden brown, 5 to 7 minutes. Keep an eye on the bread, as every oven performs differently and your cooking time will vary. Using your hands, *very* carefully remove the baked flatbread, transfer it to a bread basket or serving plate, and loosely cover it with a towel to keep it soft and warm. Repeat the process with the remaining dough pieces.

The manakeesh are best served fresh, but they'll hold at room temperature for 1 to 2 days. For even longer storage, you can do what my mama does and store them in an airtight plastic bag in the freezer for up to 3 months. Thaw at room temperature, then warm in the oven before serving.

sfeeha

open-faced meat and pine nut pies

Makes 8 pies

Dough
- 1 cup / 240g lukewarm water
- 1½ tablespoons sugar
- 1 tablespoon active dry yeast
- 3 cups / 375g all-purpose flour, plus more for dusting
- ½ cup / 110g vegetable oil
- ¼ cup / 30g powdered milk
- 1 teaspoon fine sea salt
- ½ teaspoon baking powder

Filling
- 2 whole tomatoes, plus 1 tomato, coarsely chopped
- 1 large yellow onion, peeled but whole
- 2 pounds ground beef (80/20)
- 1 green bell pepper, minced
- 1 jalapeño, seeded and minced
- 8 garlic cloves, minced
- 1 cup chopped fresh curly parsley
- ⅓ cup toasted pine nuts, plus more for garnish
- 1 heaping tablespoon tomato paste
- 1 tablespoon fresh lemon juice
- 1 tablespoon sfeeha spice or seven spice
- 2½ teaspoons fine sea salt
- 2 teaspoons black pepper
- 1½ teaspoons paprika
- Egg wash: 1 egg yolk, whisked with 1 tablespoon water

Every country in the Levant has its version of sfeeha, a delicious open-faced meat pie studded with pine nuts and fragrant with spices. I remember waking up on Saturday mornings and smelling the nutty, meaty aroma as soon as I opened my bedroom door . . . that's when I knew Mom had made us something special. There is a similar savory pastry called kross, which some of you might be familiar with: There, the dough is folded to enclose the filling. But I like sfeeha because you can see the tantalizing filling, and it's a smidge easier to make because there is no folding. This is a recipe you can certainly make in a stand mixer, but you don't have to—so it's a great recipe to make if you don't have that piece of equipment.

Make the dough: In a large bowl, combine the water, sugar, and yeast. Mix with a fork until integrated, then cover with a damp paper towel and let it rest until it bubbles and foams, about 10 minutes.

Add the flour, oil, powdered milk, salt, and baking powder and gently mix with your hands until a rough dough forms.

Transfer the dough to a floured surface. Lightly flour or oil your hands and knead for 10 minutes or until the dough is smooth and passes the Poke Test (see page 169).

Return the dough to the bowl, cover with a damp towel, and let it rest in a warm place until doubled in size, about 1 hour.

Make the filling: Grate the 2 whole tomatoes and onion on the large holes of a box grater. Gather the grated tomato and onion in a clean towel and squeeze to remove any excess liquid. Transfer to a large bowl, then add the chopped tomato, beef, bell pepper, jalapeño, garlic, parsley, pine nuts, tomato paste, lemon juice, sfeeha spice, salt, black pepper, and paprika. Mix with your hands or a spoon until well incorporated. Cover and set aside until ready to use.

Preheat the oven to 375°F. Line a sheet pan with parchment paper.

Gently punch down the dough to release the gas. Use your hands to pinch off twelve equal portions and roll each piece into a smooth ball. Cover with a clean towel and let rest for about 15 minutes so the gluten can relax.

recipe continues →

sfeeha, *continued*

Roll out each ball into a round ¼ to ½ inch thick and 4 inches in diameter. In the center of each dough round, place 3 to 4 heaping tablespoons (65 to 90g) of filling. Use your hands to spread the filling into a thick, even layer that stops about ½ inch from the edge of the dough. Use your fingers to pack the filling firmly; this will minimize shrinkage during baking. Sprinkle a few more toasted pine nuts on top of the meat mixture. Brush the exposed edges of the dough with the egg wash. Place the assembled meat pies on the lined sheet pan.

Bake until the bottoms are golden brown and the meat filling is cooked through, 20 to 25 minutes.

These are best served warm, but you can also refrigerate for a day or store them in an airtight plastic bag in the freezer for up to 3 months.

cheese fatayer

Makes 10 pastries

Dough
- 2½ cups / 315g all-purpose flour, plus more for dusting
- 1 cup / 240g lukewarm water
- 2 tablespoons sugar
- 1 tablespoon active dry or instant yeast
- 2 teaspoons Diamond Crystal kosher salt
- ⅓ cup / 65g extra-virgin olive oil

Assembly
- 1 pound / 455g (about 4 cups loosely packed) freshly grated mozzarella cheese
- 1¼ cups crumbled feta cheese
- Handful of chopped fresh parsley
- ¼ cup / 55g unsalted butter, melted
- 1½ teaspoons garlic powder
- ¼ teaspoon Diamond Crystal kosher salt
- Egg wash: 1 large egg, whisked with 2 tablespoons water

This savory pastry was a major staple in my household growing up. I swear, I woke up almost every weekend to the smell of fresh, cheesy bread seeping through the cracks of my bedroom from the kitchen downstairs. My mom has hands of magic, and my heart always felt so full when I'd walk downstairs to join her doing what she loves most—making bread for the family. Whenever I see, smell, or hear someone talk about cheese bread, I always think of my mom and those cherished childhood memories.

Make the dough: In a stand mixer (or in a large bowl by hand), combine 1 cup / 125g of the flour, the water, sugar, and yeast. Mix with a fork until integrated, then cover with a damp paper towel and let rest until it bubbles and foams, about 10 minutes.

Snap on the dough hook attachment and add the remaining 1½ cups / 190g flour, the salt, and oil and mix until you have a rough dough.

Mix on medium-low speed for 10 to 12 minutes, until the dough is smooth and elastic and passes the Poke Test (see page 169). Don't add any extra flour to this recipe. The dough will start off quite sticky, but after several minutes of kneading, it will come together beautifully. (To knead by hand, see Hands-On Bread Basics, page 169.)

Use your hands to separate the dough into ten equal portions (about 65g each) and roll into smooth balls. Cover with a damp towel and allow to rest until one and one-half times their original size, about 10 minutes.

Preheat the oven to 425°F. Line a sheet pan with parchment paper.

Assemble the pastries: In a medium bowl, combine 3 cups of the mozzarella, the feta, and parsley.

In a separate small bowl, combine the butter, garlic powder, and salt.

Lightly flour a work surface. Roll out each dough ball into a round about ¼ inch thick. With the remaining 1 cup mozzarella, sprinkle a small handful of the cheese around the edge of each dough round. Start folding the edge of the dough over the mozzarella, pressing down to seal the edges, then shape the round into a diamond, pinching two opposite corners to reinforce the shape even more. Use your hands to transfer the shaped crusts to the lined sheet pan.

Brush the egg wash on the edges of the dough and brush garlic butter in the center. Generously spread the mozzarella-feta filling on top of the garlic butter.

Bake until the bottoms of the pies and the crust are beautifully golden, 20 to 30 minutes.

Remove the pan from the oven and let the pastries cool on a wire rack for a couple minutes before serving with a nice cup of tea. Store any leftover fatayer in an airtight container at room temperature for a couple days or in the refrigerator for up to 1 week.

sweets & desserts

tahini and browned butter banana bread

Makes one 9 × 5-inch loaf

- Softened butter and flour, for the pan
- ¾ cup / 150g granulated sugar
- ½ cup / 110g (packed) brown sugar
- ½ cup / 120g Browned Butter (page 194), at room temperature
- 2 cups / 420g mashed ripe bananas (about 3 large bananas)
- 2 large eggs
- 2 teaspoons vanilla extract
- ¼ cup / 60g sour cream
- ¼ cup / 60g tahini
- 1½ cups / 190g all-purpose flour
- 1 teaspoon baking soda
- 1 teaspoon baking powder
- 1½ teaspoons Diamond Crystal kosher salt
- ¼ teaspoon ground cinnamon
- ⅛ teaspoon ground cloves
- 6 ounces / 170g chocolate chips (optional)

I have a classic banana bread recipe on my website, and it's always been a fan favorite. But for this cookbook, my starting point was browned butter. That's because I feel as if its nutty richness makes all desserts taste better. Tahini is a classic Arab ingredient made from ground sesame seeds. It adds a complex, almost savory flavor that complements the toasty nuttiness of browned butter perfectly. When you taste this, it doesn't scream "TAHINI!" Rather, there's a subtle warmth and dialed-down sweetness that I find irresistible.

Preheat the oven to 325°F. Grease and flour a loaf pan. (Alternatively, you can line the bottom and sides of the pan with parchment paper.)

In a stand mixer fitted with the paddle attachment (or in a large bowl using a whisk), combine the granulated sugar, brown sugar, and cooled browned butter. Beat on medium speed for 1 to 2 minutes.

Add the bananas and mix on medium speed until incorporated. Add one egg at a time, mixing well after each addition and scraping down the sides of the bowl as needed. Add the vanilla, mixing until fully incorporated. Mix in the sour cream and tahini until the mixture is smooth and creamy.

In a small bowl, whisk together the flour, baking soda, baking powder, salt, cinnamon, and cloves.

With the mixer on medium-low speed (or mixing by hand), gradually add the dry ingredients to the wet, stirring until just combined. Be careful not to overmix—this can cause your bread to sink in the center. Once the majority of the flour has been folded in, stop mixing. (It's okay if there are a few lumps.) If desired, fold in the chocolate chips with a rubber spatula.

Pour the batter into the prepared pan, smoothing the top with a spatula.

Bake until a toothpick inserted into the center comes out clean, 55 to 65 minutes.

Remove the pan from the oven and let the bread cool in the pan for 10 minutes, then transfer the bread to a wire rack to cool completely.

fan fave

cinnamon rolls

Makes 6 large or 8 to 12 smaller rolls

Dough
- ¾ cup / 180g lukewarm water
- 2¼ teaspoons active dry yeast
- ⅓ cup / 65g plus 1 tablespoon granulated sugar
- 3 cups / 375g all-purpose flour, plus more as needed
- ¼ cup / 55g unsalted butter, melted
- 1 large egg, whisked
- 1 large egg yolk, whisked
- 1 teaspoon Diamond Crystal kosher salt

Filling
- 1 cup / 220g (packed) light brown sugar
- ⅓ cup / 75g unsalted butter, at room temperature
- 2 tablespoons ground cinnamon
- ⅛ teaspoon ground cloves
- ⅛ teaspoon ground nutmeg

Frosting
- ¾ cup / 75g confectioners' sugar, sifted
- 4 ounces cream cheese, at room temperature
- 3 tablespoons unsalted butter, at room temperature
- 1 teaspoon vanilla extract
- ⅛ teaspoon fine sea salt (optional)
- ½ cup coffee creamer (I use French vanilla, but you can use any flavor you love!) or heavy cream, plus more as needed

Assembly
- All-purpose flour, for dusting
- Heavy cream, as needed

Cinnamon rolls are definitely one of my favorite desserts. Note that I said *dessert*, not breakfast food, because I love to eat them after dinner, too. I don't believe they should be limited to the morning, even if they *are* delicious with a cup of coffee.

After obsessively testing this recipe, I realized that with cinnamon rolls, less is more, which is why this is probably the simplest route I've ever gone with a dough recipe. I prioritized staple ingredients like flour, butter, eggs, and sugar, and called it a day. After three years of tinkering, I was finally satisfied with the result—and I hope you'll agree that this truly is the perfect cinnamon roll.

notes:
- If you have a stand mixer, you can knead the dough with the dough hook attachment. Mix on low speed until the flour is incorporated, then gradually work your way up to medium speed and mix for about 8 minutes.
- When mixing the dough, remember that climate and altitude play a large part in how much flour you will need—in cooler, dryer regions you might need less flour than recommended, and in hot, humid regions you might need more.

Make the dough: In a measuring cup or small bowl, combine the water, yeast, and the 1 tablespoon granulated sugar. Mix with a fork until integrated, then let it rest until it bubbles and foams, about 10 minutes.

In a large bowl, combine the remaining ⅓ cup granulated sugar, the flour, melted butter, whole egg, egg yolk, and salt. Add the yeast mixture and mix with a wooden spoon until a rough dough forms. If it is too sticky, add 1 tablespoon of flour at a time until it is still sticky but workable.

Lightly flour a work surface and your hands, then transfer the dough to the surface and knead for 8 to 10 minutes until it becomes smooth and elastic and passes the Poke Test (see page 169).

Place the dough in a lightly floured bowl and cover it with a damp cloth. Let it rest in a warm place until it doubles in size, 1½ to 2 hours.

Make the filling: In a medium bowl, combine the brown sugar, softened butter, cinnamon, cloves, and nutmeg and stir with a wooden spoon until spreadable.

recipe continues →

SWEETS & DESSERTS

cinnamon rolls, *continued*

Make the frosting: In a separate medium bowl, combine the confectioners' sugar, cream cheese, butter, vanilla, and fine salt, if desired. Stir with a wooden spoon until incorporated, then add the coffee creamer. The consistency should be pourable but not so thin that it rushes out over the cinnamon rolls when you pour it; it should pour in ribbons. If necessary, add more creamer, a teaspoon at a time, until you're happy with the consistency.

Assemble the rolls: Punch the dough down gently and place on a floured surface, smooth side down (this way, the smooth side becomes the outer layer when rolling the log). Roll it out into a rectangle about 12 × 14 inches and ¼ inch thick. The thickness is more important than the exact size of the rectangle. Use an offset spatula to spread the filling over the dough, all the way to the edges of the rectangle.

With a short side of the rectangle facing you, roll the dough into a log. Your goal is to roll it up as tightly as possible without stretching or tearing the dough. I like to start at the center of the edge I'm rolling and work my hands outward; this ensures that there are tight, even layers in the finished roll.

Cut the log crosswise (see Cutting Cinnamon Rolls at right) into either 2-inch sections for a batch of six rolls or 1- to 1½-inch sections for eight to twelve rolls.

Line a 9 × 13-inch baking dish with parchment paper, leaving a bit of overhang so you can easily remove the rolls later. Arrange the rolls in the baking dish, cover with a damp cloth, and let rest until they're about one and one-half times their original size, about 30 minutes.

Meanwhile, preheat the oven to 350°F.

Spoon about 1 tablespoon of the cream on top of each roll.

Bake until nicely puffed in the center and some of the rolls have taken on a golden color, 25 to 30 minutes.

Remove the pan from the oven and let the rolls cool in the pan for a few minutes before topping them with the frosting. I use a spoon to attractively dollop and drizzle the frosting, but you can just pour the frosting from the bowl. Cinnamon rolls are at their best when they're fresh from the oven.

Cutting Cinnamon Rolls

To cut these rolls, I recommend using dental floss (make sure it's plain, unflavored floss!) instead of a knife because it creates a much cleaner cut and prevents the cinnamon rolls from getting smushed down while cutting.

1. When I want to be *very* precise, I use a bench scraper with a ruler as my guide, then score the log to mark where I want to cut.

2. I cut a length of floss, then wiggle it underneath the dough log and position it where I want to cut.

3. I pull the ends of the floss length up and cross them over the log, as if I were about to tie my shoelaces.

4. Finally, I close the loop and tug up to cut the roll and then repeat with the remaining rolls.

old-fashioned sour cream donuts

Makes 24 donuts

Donuts

2 cups / 250g all-purpose flour, plus more for dusting
⅔ cup / 85g cake flour
1½ teaspoons baking powder
1½ teaspoons Diamond Crystal kosher salt
½ teaspoon ground cinnamon
¼ teaspoon ground nutmeg
½ cup / 100g granulated sugar
¼ cup / 55g unsalted butter, at room temperature
1 large egg
1 large egg yolk
½ cup / 125g sour cream
Vegetable oil, for frying

Vanilla Glaze

3 cups / 300g confectioners' sugar
1½ teaspoons vanilla extract
½ cup half-and-half

When I was younger, you would never have caught me with any donut besides a Boston cream. (If you don't know what I'm talking about, then I feel sad for you, and you need to get one of those yellow custard-filled, chocolate-glazed donuts in your life immediately.) In those days, the sweeter and more sugary the dessert, the better. I'd actually judge people who said things like, "Oh, that's too sweet for me." Too sweet? There's no such thing!

I also didn't believe people who said your taste buds change dramatically as you get older. Turns out, they were right. These days, I am less sugar-crazy, and when it comes to donuts, I crave the simplicity of an old-fashioned cake donut.

tip It's important that you adjust the heat to maintain the oil temperature. If it drops too low, you risk your donuts becoming very oil-heavy, and if you fry them at too high a temperature, the outside of the donuts will burn before the inside gets a chance to fully cook, leaving you with burned and raw donuts.

Make the donuts: In a medium bowl, sift together the all-purpose flour, cake flour, baking powder, salt, cinnamon, and nutmeg. Set aside.

In a stand mixer fitted with the paddle attachment (or in a bowl with a hand mixer), beat the granulated sugar and butter on medium-low speed until smooth and creamy, 1 to 2 minutes. Add the whole egg and egg yolk, increase the speed to medium, and continue to beat until well combined, about 1 minute. Scrape down the sides and bottom of the bowl as needed. Add the sour cream and mix on low speed just until combined.

On low speed, gradually add the flour mixture in three additions, mixing until just combined. Be careful not to overmix. Stop the mixer to scrape down the sides and bottom of the bowl as needed.

Lightly flour a countertop. The dough will be slightly sticky but firm. Scrape the dough onto the floured surface and gently form into a disk. Cover with plastic wrap and refrigerate for 1 hour.

Cut out twenty-four 3-inch squares of parchment paper. On a floured work surface with a lightly floured rolling pin, roll out the dough to a ¾-inch thickness. Using a 2½-inch donut cutter, cut out the donuts, reflouring the cutter between the cuts so the dough doesn't stick. Use a spatula or bench scraper to carefully move the donuts onto the squares of parchment paper. Gently brush off any excess flour with a pastry brush. Gather the scraps, gently knead into a ball, roll it out, and repeat the process.

recipe continues →

SWEETS & DESSERTS

old-fashioned sour cream donuts, *continued*

Place a wire rack over a baking sheet lined with paper towels and set near the stove. Pour 2 inches oil into a 2-quart saucepan and heat over medium-low heat until temperature reaches 325°F on an instant-read thermometer.

Working in batches of two (the donuts need a bit of room to move around), add them one at a time to the oil. They will sink initially and then rise to the surface. Fry, flipping gently after about 2 minutes, until golden brown, 2 to 3 minutes per side. You might notice a bit of foam form while frying. Don't worry, this is just because of some remaining flour on your dough, and it won't affect the outcome at all. Transfer to the wire rack to drain. Continue to fry more donuts, maintaining the oil temperature between 325° and 330°F (see Tip).

Meanwhile, make the vanilla glaze: While the first two donuts are cooling just slightly, in a medium bowl, whisk together the confectioners' sugar, vanilla, and half-and-half until smooth.

Set a wire rack in a sheet pan lined with parchment paper. While the donuts are still warm, submerge the ridged top side of each donut into the glaze. Set them on the wire rack glaze-side up and allow the excess glaze to drip off.

Serve fresh!

choose-your-own-adventure brioche donuts

Makes 12 to 14 donuts

¼ cup / 60g lukewarm water
¼ cup / 50g plus 1 teaspoon sugar
2½ teaspoons active dry yeast
4 cups / 500g all-purpose flour, plus more as needed
6 large eggs, at room temperature, whisked
2 teaspoons salt
3 tablespoons powdered milk
1 cup / 225g unsalted butter, chopped, at room temperature
Olive oil, for greasing
2 cups / 480g vegetable oil
Filling of your choice (see Tip)
Confectioners' sugar, for dusting (optional)

Remember how, on page 225, I was talking about the virtues of a not-too-sweet donut? Well, now I want you to forget everything you just read. This recipe is for the kid in you—the kid who wants an ooey, gooey, luscious, and sweet-filled donut. The best part is, you can fill it with whatever your heart desires.

In a measuring cup or small bowl, combine the water, the 1 teaspoon sugar, and the yeast. Mix with a fork until integrated, then cover with a damp paper towel and let it rest until it bubbles and foams, about 10 minutes.

In a stand mixer fitted with the dough hook (or in a large bowl by hand), combine the yeast mixture, flour, eggs, salt, powdered milk, and the remaining ¼ cup sugar. Mix on medium-low speed until smooth, about 10 minutes. If, after 5 minutes, the dough isn't pulling away from the sides, add 1 to 3 tablespoons of flour. (Alternatively, see Working Brioche by Hand, page 192.)

With the mixer on medium-low, add the butter, one piece at a time, until fully incorporated. Mix for an additional 10 minutes, until smooth and elastic.

tip **Donut filling options:** What can you fill the donuts with? Fruit jam? Absolutely. White chocolate ganache? Oh, yes. Leftover apple pie filling? It sounds crazy, but I swear, it all works! Just make sure to use a wide-enough tip on your piping bag to get any larger pieces of fruit into the donut (or, alternatively, chop everything finely before adding to the piping bag).

Place the dough in a lightly oiled bowl. Cover with plastic wrap and let it rise in a warm place until it has doubled in size, about 1½ hours.

Cut out fourteen 4-inch squares of parchment paper (FYI, you might not need them all). Transfer the dough to a lightly floured surface. Roll it out to a thickness of ½ inch, then use a 2½-inch round cutter to cut out the donuts. Do not reroll the dough to cut more donuts—they will be dense and unpleasant—but you can cut the leftover dough into small donut holes.

Transfer the donuts to the parchment paper squares, cover with plastic, and let rest for 30 minutes.

Line a large plate or tray with paper towels and set near the stove.

Pour 2 inches vegetable oil into a 2-quart saucepan and heat over medium-low heat until the temperature reads 350°F on an instant-read thermometer.

Working in batches (the donuts need a bit of room to move around), add them to the oil. They will sink initially and then rise to the surface. Fry, flipping gently after about 2 minutes, until golden brown, 2 to 3 minutes per side. Transfer to the paper towels to drain. Continue to fry more donuts, maintaining the oil temperature between 345° and 350°F.

To fill the donuts, fill a pastry bag with the filling of your choice. If you don't have a pastry bag, fill a resealable plastic bag with the filling, then twist it to seal. Grab scissors and snip off a tiny corner of the bag. Hold a donut in your nondominant hand and gently poke the side with the tip of the pastry bag or a knife. Now, give the bag a squeeze to fill the donut. You'll feel the magic as it fills up—aim for plump but not bursting. Sprinkle with a dusting of confectioners' sugar, if desired. Serve fresh!

SWEETS & DESSERTS

apple fritters

Makes about 15 fritters

Apple Filling
- 2 large apples (such as Granny Smith or Honeycrisp), peeled, cored, and diced
- 1 tablespoon granulated sugar
- 1½ teaspoons ground cinnamon

Batter
- 2 cups / 250g all-purpose flour
- ¼ cup plus 2 tablespoons / 75g granulated sugar
- 2 teaspoons baking powder
- 1 teaspoon cornstarch
- 1 teaspoon fine sea salt
- ½ teaspoon ground cinnamon
- ¼ teaspoon ground nutmeg
- ¼ teaspoon ground cloves
- ⅔ cup / 160g whole milk
- 2 large eggs
- 2 tablespoons unsalted butter, melted
- 1½ teaspoons vanilla extract

To Finish
- Neutral oil, for frying
- 1½ cups / 150g confectioners' sugar
- 2 tablespoons milk, plus more as needed
- ½ teaspoon vanilla extract
- Pinch of fine sea salt

By now you've probably figured out that I *love* donuts. But some mornings, I want that classic donut flavor and am feeling too lazy to carefully shape and proof them. That's where these easy apple fritters come in. Typically, donut and pastry shops make apple fritters with leftover scraps of donut or brioche dough (you're welcome to do that if you have scraps on hand). But I decided to make a quick and easy batter, and I fold the apple filling directly into it. Then all you have to do is ladle big spoonfuls into your frying oil, and you're done!

Make the apple filling: In a medium bowl, toss the apples with the granulated sugar and cinnamon. Set aside.

Make the batter: In a large bowl, whisk together the flour, granulated sugar, baking powder, cornstarch, salt, cinnamon, nutmeg, and cloves.

In a separate small bowl, whisk together the milk, eggs, melted butter, and vanilla. Gradually add the wet ingredients to the dry ingredients, stirring just until combined. Gently fold in the spiced apples, taking care not to overmix (this would over-activate the gluten and make the fritters tough).

To finish: Line a wire rack with paper towels and set near the stove. Pour 2 inches oil into a deep heavy-bottomed pot and heat over medium heat until the temperature reaches 350°F on an instant-read thermometer.

Working in batches so as not to crowd the pot, use a large spoon or ice cream scoop to drop heaping spoonfuls—if you want to be precise, they should be about ⅓ cup / 60g—of batter into the hot oil. Fry until the fritters are golden brown and cooked through, 2 to 3 minutes per side. Use a slotted spoon to transfer the fritters to the paper towels to drain. Make sure to give the oil time to return to temperature in between batches.

In a small bowl, whisk together the confectioners' sugar, milk, vanilla, and salt until smooth. Adjust the consistency with more milk, if needed; you're looking for a fairly thick, smooth glaze.

While the fritters are still warm, dip them into the glaze or drizzle it over the top. Let the glaze set for a few minutes before serving.

"generational" chocolate chip cookies

Makes 18 cookies

- 1 cup / 225g unsalted butter (such as Kerrygold), chopped, at room temperature
- 1 cup / 220g (packed) dark brown sugar
- ¼ cup / 50g plus 2 teaspoons granulated sugar
- 1 large egg
- 2 large egg yolks
- 2 teaspoons vanilla extract
- 2 cups plus 2 tablespoons / 270g all-purpose flour
- ¾ cup plus 2 tablespoons / 115g cake flour
- 1 teaspoon baking powder
- ¾ teaspoon Diamond Crystal kosher salt
- ½ teaspoon baking soda
- 1 cup / 175g milk chocolate chips
- 1 cup / 175g semisweet chocolate chips
- Flaky sea salt, for finishing

I call this recipe "generational," because I think it's the perfect cookie, and one you'll want to pass down for generations. I know that's a big claim, but you have no idea how long I spent developing this recipe and how many different versions of chocolate chip cookies I went through. This one has everything I'm looking for: a beautifully golden, crisp exterior and a soft, decadent interior.

One thing I will say is that the quality of the butter does make a difference. I like using creamy Irish Kerrygold butter, but any high-quality European-style butter will do. If these are going to become the cookies you end up baking for your grandchildren, don't you think it's worth the small splurge?

Arrange oven racks in the upper and lower thirds of your oven. Preheat the oven to 350°F. Line two or three sheet pans with parchment paper or silicone baking mats.

In a stand mixer fitted with the paddle attachment (or in a large bowl with a hand mixer), combine the butter, brown sugar, and granulated sugar. Cream on medium speed until light and fluffy, about 5 minutes.

Add the whole egg, beat until combined, then add the egg yolks and vanilla and beat until combined, about 1 minute, pausing to scrape down the sides of the bowl to ensure everything is well incorporated. Avoid overmixing.

In a separate large bowl, sift together the flour, baking powder, kosher salt, and baking soda.

On low speed, gradually add the flour mixture to the wet ingredients, mixing just until combined. Stop mixing when there are only a few streaks of flour mixture left, being careful not to overmix.

Use a spatula to gently fold in the milk chocolate chips and semisweet chocolate chips until evenly distributed throughout the dough.

Use a scoop or your hands to roll the dough into 2-tablespoon balls (70g each). You should end up with eighteen. Arrange them on the sheet pans about 3 inches apart. Sprinkle flaky salt on top of each.

Working with two sheet pans at a time, bake until the edges are lightly golden brown and the centers are mostly set, 12 to 15 minutes. Rotate the pans if you feel like one sheet of cookies is browning more quickly than the other. The cookies may look slightly underbaked in the center, but they will continue to set as they cool on the sheet pans.

Remove the pans from the oven and let the cookies cool on the sheet pans for 5 minutes, then transfer them to a wire rack to cool completely.

ma'amoul
date-stuffed butter cookies

Makes about 60 mini cookies

- 5 cups / 900g fine semolina flour, plus more as needed
- 1 cup / 130g cake flour
- 1 cup / 225g unsalted butter, melted and cooled
- 1 cup / 225g ghee
- 26 ounces (about 2½ cups) date paste
- 3 teaspoons ground anise seed
- ¼ teaspoon ground cinnamon
- ¼ cup / 30g powdered milk
- 2 tablespoons orange blossom water
- 1 tablespoon plus 1 teaspoon mahlab powder
- 1 tablespoon granulated sugar
- 2 teaspoons instant yeast
- 1 teaspoon baking powder
- 1 teaspoon ma'amoul spice (optional; see Tip)
- ½ teaspoon mastic powder
- ¾ cup heavy cream
- ½ cup / 50g confectioners' sugar

Ma'moul is an iconic Arab dessert that we most often eat for Eid, to celebrate the end of Ramadan. Every year, my mom used to make a batch of *one thousand* (have I mentioned that she is extra?) to split among the ten of us kids. This recipe isn't for one thousand, but it does make quite a few—that's because I want you to wrap some up in pretty packages to give away to your friends!

I like to describe the flavor of ma'moul as Middle Eastern shortbread, because it has a buttery crumb that falls apart when you bite into it, plus those classic Arab flavors of semolina, orange blossom water, and earthy dates. The cookie itself isn't terribly sweet, because we love to dust it with confectioners' sugar. But if you're someone who's watching their sugar intake (or just doesn't like overly sweet things), this is the cookie for you (just omit the confectioners' sugar garnish).

In a large bowl, combine the semolina, cake flour, butter, and ghee. Using your hands, mix until the flours are evenly coated with the fats. Cover the bowl with plastic wrap and set aside at room temperature for 24 to 36 hours.

The next day, in a separate bowl, use your hands to mix together the date paste, 1 teaspoon of the anise, and the cinnamon until well combined. Use your hands to roll the mixture into sixty balls (about 1 tablespoon / 12g each) and set aside.

To the semolina mixture, add the powdered milk, orange blossom water, mahlab, granulated sugar, instant yeast, baking powder, ma'amoul spice (if using), mastic, and the remaining 2 teaspoons ground anise. Mix with your hands until all ingredients are fully incorporated. Set aside.

In a small saucepan, warm the heavy cream over medium-low heat until the temperature reaches 100°F on an instant-read thermometer (don't let it boil). Gradually add the warmed cream, ¼ cup at a time, to the semolina mixture while kneading with your hands until the dough starts to come together. You may not need the whole quantity of cream; the dough should be soft and workable, not crumbly or falling apart when shaped. Test the dough consistency by shaping a cookie with a cookie mold (see How to Shape Ma'amoul, page 236). If it holds its shape well, the dough is ready. If it's too dry, add more cream. You'll know you added too much liquid if the dough is too soft to shape (in that case, add semolina flour, a tablespoon at a time, until you've reached the correct consistency).

recipe continues →

I SLEEP IN MY KITCHEN

ma'amoul, *continued*

Line several sheet pans with parchment paper.

Divide the dough into sixty portions (about 2 tablespoons / 26g each) and flatten them down gently. Place a date ball in the center of the flattened dough and wrap the dough around it, shaping and rolling it into a ball. Shape the cookies using one of the techniques described at right and place the cookies on the lined sheet pans as you go.

Arrange oven racks in the upper and lower thirds of your oven. Preheat the oven to 350°F.

Bake the cookies, two sheet pans at a time, until the tops and bottoms are beautifully golden, 15 to 20 minutes, switching racks and rotating the pans front to back halfway through.

Remove the pans from the oven and let the ma'amoul cool on the pans for at least 5 minutes, then transfer the ma'amoul to a wire rack to cool completely.

Once cool, dust with an even layer of confectioners' sugar. Serve with tea or package up to give to your loved ones. Stored in an airtight container, the ma'amoul will stay fresh for a few days at room temperature or a week in the fridge. My mom would always store extras in the freezer so we could have them year-round.

tip Look for ma'amoul spice, also known as ka'ak spice, at your local Middle Eastern grocery store. It's very warm and comforting, with notes of cinnamon, ground anise, cardamom, and cloves.

How to Shape Ma'amoul

To shape these cookies, we typically use ma'amoul molds, which are widely available at Arab markets and online. They are similar to the molds used to make Chinese mooncakes, which you can absolutely use instead. Keep in mind that if you have a small ma'amoul mold, you might need to roll small dough balls.

You can also shape the cookies with decorative tongs instead of wooden molds; my mom used to make them both ways.

Here are several different ways to shape them:

- **Ma'amoul mold:** Spray the mold lightly with cooking spray. Place the dough in the mold and press gently. If you press too hard, the cookie might stick or the date filling might poke through your design. Lay a kitchen towel on a flat surface. Flip the mold over and tap it gently onto the towel. The cookies should pop right out, and the design should be beautifully defined on one side and flat on the other.

- **Tongs:** Use pastry decorating tongs to gently pinch and decorate the sides and tops of the cookies—we don't want to show too much of the filling.

- **Donut shape:** Use your pointer finger to gently poke the middle of each filled ball of dough, all the way down through the date filling, to create a "donut" shape.

I SLEEP IN MY KITCHEN

katayef
fried stuffed "pancakes"

Makes 24 "pancakes"

Batter
- 2 cups / 360g fine semolina flour
- 1 cup / 125g all-purpose flour
- 3 tablespoons sugar
- 3 tablespoons powdered milk
- 1 tablespoon orange blossom water
- 1 tablespoon instant yeast
- 1 teaspoon baking powder
- ½ teaspoon baking soda
- ½ teaspoon fine sea salt
- 4 cups / 945g warm water

Walnut Filling
- 2 cups crushed walnuts
- 1 cup unsweetened shredded coconut
- 2 tablespoons sugar
- 2 tablespoons ground cinnamon
- Dash of ground nutmeg

Cheese Filling
- 1 cup Middle Eastern sweet (unsalted) cheese (see Note)
- ½ cup freshly grated mozzarella cheese
- ¼ cup unsweetened shredded coconut
- 1 tablespoon sugar

To Finish
- Cooking spray or butter, for the pan (optional)
- Vegetable oil, for frying
- 1½ cups Orange Blossom Simple Syrup (page 22), at room temperature, or honey
- Chopped pistachios (optional)

This Middle Eastern recipe is traditionally made for Ramadan, and it's something my siblings and I would look forward to all year long. I have such vivid memories of my mom spreading a tablecloth over our kitchen island, and then my sisters and I eagerly gathering around. She would pipe the filling onto our electric griddle, cook as many pancakes as would fit onto its surface, then flip them onto the tablecloth to cool slightly. That's when my sisters' and my work began: Half the pancakes would be filled with a walnut mixture; the other half with a cheese mixture. Then we'd fold and seal the pancakes and set them on a tray.

However, if you don't feel like going to the trouble of making the fillings and stuffing the pancakes, they are also delicious on their own, drizzled with the orange blossom syrup or honey. This is how they are often served in Morocco, where they are called *baghrir*.

tip I have an electric griddle at home, which is the best way to cook katayef as well as American-style pancakes because you can monitor the temperature and keep it very consistent. This ensures that your katayef cook uniformly on the bottom. Nonstick skillets are your second-best option. Cast iron is not ideal here because it encourages browning and bits of caramelization; that is actually *not* what you are looking for. The goal is an evenly browned bottom.

Make the batter: In a blender, combine the semolina, all-purpose flour, sugar, powdered milk, orange blossom water, yeast, baking powder, baking soda, salt, and water. Blend on high speed until smooth. The batter will have a thin, pourable consistency.

Let rest, covered, for 15 minutes.

Make the walnut filling: In a small bowl, mix together the walnuts, coconut, sugar, cinnamon, and nutmeg.

Make the cheese filling: In a medium bowl, mix together the sweet cheese, mozzarella, coconut, and sugar.

To finish: Heat an electric griddle to 375°F or heat your largest nonstick skillet over medium-high heat (see Tip). If you don't have a nonstick pan, lightly grease the pan with a small amount of butter or cooking spray. Spread out a large tablecloth on your countertop.

Working in batches, pour ¼ to ⅓ cup batter onto the griddle to create medium-sized pancakes. Cook on one side until the top bubbles, the batter sets, and the bottom is golden brown, 30 seconds to 1 minute. Do not flip the pancakes. If the bottom of your pancake is dark brown before the top sets, reduce the heat. If the bottom is still pale by the time your batter sets, increase the heat.

recipe continues →

SWEETS & DESSERTS

katayef, *continued*

Toss the pancakes onto the tablecloth to cool while you work on the remaining batches.

Once the pancakes have cooled, it's time to fill them. Add a heaping teaspoon of either the walnut or cheese filling to the bubbly side (i.e., the side that wasn't in contact with the griddle) of each pancake, being careful not to overfill (you may end up with some extra filling at the end of the process). Fold the pancakes in half to make semicircles, then pinch the edges closed tightly—you don't want them to open up while they are being fried.

Pour 2 to 3 inches oil into a deep heavy-bottomed pot and heat over medium heat until the temperature reaches 350°F on an instant-read thermometer.

Pour the orange blossom syrup into a medium bowl and set near the stove. Working in batches so as not to crowd the pan, fry the filled pancakes until they develop a beautiful golden color and are a bit crisp, 2 to 4 minutes. Using a slotted spoon, remove the katayef from the oil and immediately place them into the syrup. Let the katayef soak for about 30 seconds, then transfer to a platter. Sprinkle with pistachios, if desired, and serve immediately, while the cheese is still gooey!

note: "Sweet cheese" is the most common translation for *jibnah hilwah* جبنة حلوة. It is unsalted, which is important for this recipe. Look for it in 16-ounce vacuum-sealed packages in the refrigerated section of a Middle Eastern grocer. You can substitute ricotta if you cannot find it.

I SLEEP IN MY KITCHEN

fan fave

perfect fudge brownies

Makes sixteen (2-inch) brownies

- 1½ cups / 300g semisweet chocolate chips
- ¾ cup / 170g unsalted butter, chopped
- ⅓ cup / 40g unsweetened cocoa powder
- 1 teaspoon espresso powder
- ¼ teaspoon ground cinnamon (optional but highly recommended!)
- 3 large eggs
- 1½ cups / 300g granulated sugar
- 2 tablespoons light brown sugar
- 1½ teaspoons vanilla extract
- 1 cup / 125g all-purpose flour
- 2 tablespoons powdered milk (optional)
- 1 teaspoon fine sea salt
- Confectioners' sugar, for dusting (optional)

I am a huge fudge brownie lover, so I was definitely my own harshest critic while developing this recipe. I believe I went through almost five rounds of recipe testing before I was content (elated, really!) with how they came out. These are decadent brownies, perfectly balanced between a fudgy, moist interior and a crackly, shiny top. It's important to let the brownies cool completely in the pan before you slice into them, meaning this is a wonderful recipe to make a day in advance—bring them to a potluck or picnic!

Preheat the oven to 350°F. Line an 8-inch square pan with parchment paper, leaving enough of an overhang to make it easy to pull out the brownies after they bake.

In a medium saucepan, combine the chocolate chips and butter and slow-melt over medium-low heat, stirring frequently with a silicone spatula.

Meanwhile, in a small bowl, mix together the cocoa, espresso powder, and cinnamon (if using).

Once the chocolate and butter have melted, turn off the heat and immediately whisk in the cocoa mixture.

In a stand mixer fitted with the paddle attachment (or in a large bowl using a hand mixer), beat together the eggs, granulated sugar, brown sugar, and vanilla on medium speed until light, fluffy, and slightly thickened, about 4 minutes. You'll know it's done if you can rub the mixture between your fingers and there are almost no detectable granules of sugar.

On low speed, slowly mix the melted chocolate mixture into the egg-sugar mixture, scraping down the bowl as needed to ensure they are thoroughly combined.

In a medium bowl, whisk together the flour, powdered milk (if using), and salt. On low speed, add the dry ingredients to the wet ingredients and mix just until there are no visible streaks of flour remaining. Avoid overmixing. This is also where you can throw in any add-ins (extra chocolate chips, for example)!

Pour the batter into the lined pan, using a rubber spatula to spread it evenly.

Bake until the edges are set and the center of the brownies slightly jiggles when gently shaken, about 30 minutes.

Remove the pan from the oven and let the brownies cool completely in the pan, about 1 hour. This cooling process will help them set properly and develop their fudgy texture.

Once cooled, carefully lift the brownies out of the pan and cut into sixteen pieces. Dust confectioners' sugar over top, if desired. Store any leftovers in an airtight container at room temperature for up to 3 days.

knafeh kishna
sweet cheese pie

Makes 12 squares

- 1 pound / 455g frozen knafeh dough
- ½ cup / 115g salted butter, at room temperature
- ½ cup / 110g ghee
- ⅛ teaspoon knafeh food coloring
- ½ cup / 120g ricotta cheese
- 1 cup / 120g freshly shredded mozzarella cheese
- ¾ cup / 85g freshly shredded Akkawi cheese or sweet cheese (see Note, page 238)
- Orange Blossom Simple Syrup (page 22), for drizzling
- Chopped raw pistachios (salted or unsalted—your choice!), for garnish

Knafeh is a classic dessert in the Arab world, and many countries have their own regional version. What they all have in common is a beautiful pastry layer, melty cheese, and a sugar syrup topping. The way you can quickly identify a Palestinian knafeh is if there is red or orange food coloring in the dough. (Lebanese knafeh, by contrast, keeps it natural with a pale gold dough.)

You can buy knafeh dough (often labeled kataifi dough) frozen at Arab groceries; it is essentially shredded phyllo pastry. You pack the crumbs into a pan, then layer cheese on top. Traditionally, this would be cooked over an open flame, and you would rotate the tray frequently until all the cheese was melted. In my version, you bake it in the oven because it makes it a little easier and more hands-off. At the end, you flip the whole thing onto a tray and drizzle it with orange blossom syrup, which I make in bulk and always have on hand in my pantry.

Cut the knafeh dough into large chunks so it fits into your food processor. Add it to the processor and pulse until ground into ¼- to ½-inch-long threads.

In a large bowl, combine the butter, ghee, and food coloring and use your hands to mix together. Add the shredded dough and massage between the palms of your hands until it is fully coated in the butter mixture.

Preheat the oven to 350°F.

In a 9 × 13-inch baking pan, pack down the dough mixture into an even layer that comes slightly up the sides. Use a flat-bottomed cup to press the dough firmly—this part is important to ensure it holds its shape when you flip it later. Pop the pan into the oven for 5 minutes, just to help it set a little.

Remove the pan from the oven and dollop the ricotta evenly over the surface of the dough. Use your fingertips to gently spread the ricotta into an even layer—but be careful, since the dough is very tender. Sprinkle the mozzarella and Akkawi cheeses evenly over the ricotta.

If the edges of the dough are higher than the cheese layer, gently press them down to be level with the cheese.

Bake until the cheese is melted but not browned, about 15 minutes.

Remove the pan from the oven, then immediately place a platter larger than the pan over top and quickly flip the knafeh onto the platter. Carefully lift the baking pan, using a table knife, if needed, to reveal the knafeh. Drizzle as much orange blossom syrup on top as you want—some people like it sweet; others, less so—then garnish with the pistachios either strewn all over the surface or arranged in a cute design of your choice around the perimeter. Cut into squares immediately and serve warm.

SWEETS & DESSERTS

awamah
fried dough balls in orange blossom simple syrup

Makes about 35 fritters

- 2 cups / 250g all-purpose flour
- ¼ cup / 30g cornstarch
- 2 tablespoons powdered milk
- 2 teaspoons sugar
- 1½ teaspoons instant yeast
- ½ teaspoon fine sea salt
- 1½ cups / 360g lukewarm water, plus more as needed
- Neutral oil, for frying
- Orange Blossom Simple Syrup (page 22), warmed, for coating the fritters
- Chopped pistachios, for garnish (optional)

The best way I can describe these is Middle Eastern donut holes. During Ramadan, I always look forward to eating these fried little fritters, which we dunk in the orange blossom simple syrup I always have in my pantry. These aren't traditional donuts we're shaping—it's more of a thicker funnel cake situation where we're scooping dollops of dough into the oil. The batter is quite wet, so it might take a few tries to really get the shaping process down—but stick with it and by the end you'll be a pro.

In a large bowl, whisk together the flour, cornstarch, powdered milk, sugar, instant yeast, and salt. Add ½ cup of water to start, then gradually add up to 1 cup more water, mixing until you have a loose, sticky, but smooth dough. It should resemble a thick pancake batter. Cover the bowl with a damp towel and let the dough rest for 1½ hours.

Line a sheet pan with paper towels and set near the stove. Pour about 2 inches oil into a deep heavy-bottomed pot and heat over medium heat until the temperature reaches 350°F on an instant-read thermometer. The oil should be deep enough for the dough balls to float. Test the oil by dropping a small piece of dough into it; the dough should sizzle immediately and float to the surface.

When the oil is ready, pour the orange blossom syrup into a pot or deep bowl and set near the stove. Place a bowl of water near your work surface. Dip your dominant hand into the bowl of water and shake off the excess. Your hand should be damp, not dripping wet, to prevent the sticky dough from clinging to your fingers (see Tip). With your damp hand, scoop some dough into your palm. Squeeze the dough gently so it forms a small ball, roughly the size of a quarter, that pops out between your thumb and forefinger.

Dip a small spoon in the bowl of water and allow any excess to drip back into the bowl. Now use the spoon to scoop the dough ball from your hand and lower it directly into the hot oil. Lower the dough gently to avoid splashing. Working in batches so as not to crowd the pot, continue forming and dropping dough balls into the oil, rewetting your hand and the spoon as needed.

Fry the dough balls, stirring occasionally with a slotted spoon, to cook them on all sides, until golden brown and crisp, 3 to 4 minutes. Make sure to maintain the oil temperature, especially between batches (see Tip, page 225)—the oil should not drop below 335°F. Transfer the fried dough balls to the paper towels to drain. While still hot and fresh, transfer the awamah to the orange blossom syrup and toss gently to coat. Let them soak for a minute or two, then serve immediately, dusted with pistachios, if desired.

tip The traditional way to shape these is by hand, but if you're struggling with shaping the balls of wet batter in this way, you can always shape them with two spoons dipped in water, like you're shaping quenelles of ice cream.

SWEETS & DESSERTS

riz bi haleeb

rich and creamy rice pudding

Serves 12 to 14

- 2 cups medium-grain white rice
- 12¼ cups whole milk
- 2 to 3 cups sugar
- 1 (8-ounce) can table cream (aka media crema; optional)
- 2 teaspoons vanilla extract
- 1 capful (about ¼ teaspoon) orange blossom water
- 1 heaping tablespoon cornstarch
- ½ teaspoon Diamond Crystal kosher salt
- Ground cinnamon, for garnish
- Shredded unsweetened coconut, for garnish
- Dried rose buds, for garnish (optional)

Okay, I'll be honest with you—this makes a LOT of rice pudding. If you don't want to make that much, cut the recipe in half. But if I wrote the recipe to make less, the Palestinians in my life would come for me, asking, "Who makes so little riz bi haleeb?" This is a classic Arab dessert, one that you can customize to make as sweet (or not) as you'd like. My dad preferred his less sweet, so we'd use two cups of sugar. The consistency you're looking for is like stovetop oatmeal. It will look very loose when it has just finished cooking, but keep in mind it will stiffen once you pour it into your serving bowl. Enjoy it in the morning for breakfast or in the evening for dessert; you really can't go wrong.

Rinse the rice until the water runs clear. Place the rice in a large pot with 5 cups of water. Bring to a boil over medium-high heat. Once boiling, reduce the heat to low, cover, and simmer for 7 minutes—the rice will be about halfway cooked at this point.

Add 12 cups of the milk, the sugar (as much or as little as you want), table cream (if using), vanilla, and orange blossom water and stir to combine. Increase the heat to medium until the mixture reaches a boil, then reduce the heat to low. Cover the pot and simmer for 40 minutes, stirring every 5 minutes to prevent sticking and to ensure even cooking.

In a small bowl, use a fork to mix the cornstarch with the remaining ¼ cup milk until smooth. Add the cornstarch slurry to the pot of rice pudding along with the salt. Stir well to incorporate.

Uncover and continue to simmer over low heat until the mixture has thickened to your desired consistency, about 10 minutes. Remember that the pudding will thicken as it cools.

Allow the pudding to cool a bit before transferring to serving bowls, then garnish with a light dusting of cinnamon, a bit of shredded coconut, and dried rose buds, if desired. Serve warm. (Alternatively, you can cover the pudding with plastic wrap, refrigerate, and serve chilled.) Store the pudding in an airtight container in the refrigerator for up to 1 week.

apple and apricot galette *with* maple crème fraîche

Makes one 10-inch galette

Galette Dough (page 38), chilled

Apricot Compote
1 pound fresh apricots (about 5), pitted and quartered
¼ cup granulated sugar
1 tablespoon fresh lemon juice
1 teaspoon vanilla extract
Pinch of Diamond Crystal kosher salt
¼ teaspoon ground cinnamon

Apple Filling
4 medium apples (such as Granny Smith or Honeycrisp), cored and sliced about ¼ inch thick
¼ cup granulated sugar
1 tablespoon brown sugar
1 teaspoon ground cinnamon
¼ teaspoon ground nutmeg
¼ teaspoon ground ginger
⅛ teaspoon ground cloves
⅛ teaspoon Diamond Crystal kosher salt
1 tablespoon fresh lemon juice
1 tablespoon cornstarch
¼ cup maple syrup

Assembly and Serving
All-purpose flour, for dusting
Egg wash: 1 egg, whisked with 1 tablespoon milk
1 cup crème fraîche
2 tablespoons maple syrup
Vanilla ice cream
1 tablespoon chopped toasted pecans (optional)

A galette is basically a free-form pie. It's a classic French dessert, and it's one you should definitely have in your repertoire because you can fill it with any seasonal fruit you like. For this recipe, I decided to fuse two of my favorite flavor profiles, apple pie and apricot jam, into one perfect dessert. Apples and maple syrup are also a beautiful pairing that gave me the idea of infusing crème fraîche with maple syrup for a tangy, creamy topping.

But wait, there's more! I firmly believe that any warm dessert tastes better when it's contrasted with something cold. So in addition to the maple crème fraîche, I top each slice of galette with a scoop of vanilla ice cream. Honestly, I think I could eat this for my sweet treat every single night.

Make and chill the galette dough as directed.

Make the apricot compote: In a medium saucepan, stir together the apricots, granulated sugar, lemon juice, and ¼ cup water. Bring to a simmer over medium heat. Reduce the heat to low and simmer gently, stirring occasionally, until the apricots are soft and the liquid has thickened to a jammy consistency, about 30 minutes.

Remove the pan from the heat and stir in the vanilla, salt, and cinnamon. Set aside to cool completely.

Make the apple filling: In a large bowl, combine the apples, granulated sugar, brown sugar, cinnamon, nutmeg, ginger, cloves, salt, lemon juice, cornstarch, and maple syrup. Toss to coat the apples evenly. Let sit for 15 minutes.

Assemble and serve the galette: Preheat the oven to 400°F. Line a sheet pan with parchment paper.

On a lightly floured surface, using a lightly floured rolling pin, roll out the chilled dough into a 12-inch round. Transfer the dough to the lined sheet pan.

Spread the apricot compote into the center of the dough, leaving a 2-inch border around the edge. You might not use all of the compote; use more or less depending on your preference and how jammy you want the base. Arrange the apple slices on top of the compote. You might not use all of them—don't try to overfill the crust.

Fold the edges of the dough over the apples, pleating as you go to create a rustic look. Brush the dough edges with the egg wash.

Bake the galette until the crust is golden brown and the apples are tender, 30 to 35 minutes.

Meanwhile, in a medium bowl, whisk together the crème fraîche and maple syrup. Keep chilled until ready to serve.

Remove the pan from the oven and let the galette cool slightly in the pan before moving to a serving platter. Serve warm, topping each slice with the maple crème fraîche, a dollop of ice cream, and the pecans (if using).

mtabouk

sweet layered pastry

Makes 8 pastries

4 cups / 500g all-purpose flour
1 tablespoon powdered milk
1 teaspoon granulated sugar
½ teaspoon fine sea salt
½ teaspoon baking powder
½ teaspoon distilled white vinegar
½ cup / 110g plus ½ teaspoon vegetable oil, plus more for coating the dough balls
1 cup / 225g ghee

Optional Toppings
Kishta Topping (page 252)
Honey
Confectioners' sugar or equal parts cinnamon and granulated sugar
Orange Blossom Simple Syrup (page 22)

The direct translation for *mtabouk*, sometimes spelled *m'tabbak*, is "folded." There are all sorts of different mtabouk throughout the Muslim world (there's even a popular version in Indonesia); some are sweet, others are savory. But what they all share is that thin pieces of tasty pastry are folded like an envelope to create crisp, flaky layers. You can make mtabouk with phyllo pastry, but my mom always made her own dough from scratch—a relatively straightforward process. Usually, the dough layers would be folded over a filling to enclose it like a parcel. In this version, I have you fold and cook the dough without filling it; this means you can top it with whatever you'd like: honey, a dusting of confectioners' sugar, cinnamon sugar, orange blossom syrup, kishta (essentially Arab clotted cream), chocolate spread, or whatever your guilty pleasure is! You could even keep it super simple and just drizzle with olive oil.

In a large bowl, combine the flour, powdered milk, granulated sugar, salt, and baking powder.

In a liquid measuring cup, combine 1¼ cups / 300g water with the vinegar and the ½ teaspoon oil. Gradually add to the dry ingredients (you may not use all of it), stirring until a soft dough forms.

Knead the dough for 8 to 10 minutes until mostly smooth. This dough is going to be rougher than a lot of the others in this book—that's how it should be! Cover the dough with a dry cloth and let it rest for 1 hour at room temperature. (Alternatively, you can cover it with plastic wrap and let it rest overnight in the fridge, in which case you should let it come to room temperature for 1 to 2 hours before continuing with the recipe.)

Preheat the oven to 350°F.

Use your hands to divide the dough into sixteen equal portions, then roll them into smooth balls. Lightly coat each ball with oil, place on a sheet pan, cover, and let rest for 1 hour.

In a small bowl, mix the remaining ½ cup oil and the ghee together.

Oil a clean work surface with a bit of the oil-ghee mixture. Take a dough ball and flatten it with your hands. Begin stretching the dough, working from the center outward, until it is paper thin and almost transparent. The good news is, this is a super-stretchy dough, so you can go quite thin with it and it won't rip. Even if it does rip, you can still use your dough—none of the rips will matter once you start folding it in the next steps. Stretch until each dough ball is a round 10 to 12 inches in diameter.

recipe continues →

mtabouk, continued

Brush the surface generously with the oil-ghee mixture. Repeat the process with a second dough ball, then layer it directly on top of the first. Brush the second layer with the oil-ghee mixture.

Imagine the center point of your dough round, then fold the top of the dough so the top edge touches this center point. Use a brush to cover this now-exposed folded-over part with the oil-ghee mixture. Now fold the bottom of your dough round up and all the way over the folded-over part, so it overlaps it. Brush the now-exposed folded-over part with the oil-ghee mixture. Fold the left side the dough round to the center, so its edge touches the imaginary center point. Brush this with the oil-ghee mixture, then fold the right side over so it completely overlaps the left part. Brush the top with the oil-ghee mixture. You should have a nice, layered rectangular package; press it down lightly to secure it.

Repeat this process for the remaining dough until you have eight rectangular packages. Transfer the mtabouk seam-side down onto a sheet pan (lined with parchment if you'd like to make cleanup easier).

Bake until the bottoms are golden brown and cooked through (it's okay if the tops are still a bit pale), 10 to 15 minutes.

Serve immediately, with whichever toppings you'd like: kishta topping, a drizzle of honey, a dusting of confectioners' sugar or cinnamon-sugar, or dipped in orange blossom syrup.

kishta topping

Makes about 2 cups

1 cup / 225g unsalted butter, at room temperature
1 cup Kishta (page 22) or store-bought
1 teaspoon vanilla extract

In a small bowl, use a spatula to mix together the butter, kishta, and vanilla until smooth and creamy.

fan fave

carrot cake loaf *with* cream cheese frosting

Makes one 10 × 5-inch loaf

Butter and flour, for the pan

Cake
- 4 large eggs
- 1¼ cups / 275g (packed) brown sugar
- ¾ cup / 150g granulated sugar
- ½ cup / 120g sour cream
- ½ cup / 110g vegetable or coconut oil
- 1 tablespoon vanilla extract
- 2¼ cups / 280g all-purpose flour
- ¾ teaspoon fine sea salt
- 2 teaspoons baking powder
- 2 teaspoons baking soda
- 1 tablespoon ground cinnamon
- ¼ teaspoon ground nutmeg
- 2 large carrots, shredded on the large holes of a box grater (about 3 cups)
- 1 cup walnuts, coarsely chopped, plus more as needed
- ¾ cup unsweetened shredded coconut
- Grated zest of ½ orange or lemon

Cream Cheese Frosting
- 1 cup / 225g unsalted butter, at room temperature
- 8 ounces / 225g cream cheese at room temperature
- 4½ cups / 450g confectioners' sugar, sifted
- 1 tablespoon vanilla extract
- ¼ teaspoon fine sea salt
- 3 tablespoons heavy cream, plus more as needed
- Crushed walnuts or pistachios, for garnish

Carrot cake is just the perfect dessert, in my opinion. And I love this one in particular because a loaf is easy. But you can still use your creativity to decorate it. Treat it like a little art project—add whatever decorative elements are exciting to you, whether it's piped carrots, sprinkles, or even edible flowers. This cake is all about having fun and expressing yourself! It would be great to serve for a dinner party because it's simple to make but is still eye candy.

Preheat the oven to 350°F. Grease and flour a 10 × 5-inch (1½-pound) loaf pan. (Alternatively, you can line the pan with parchment paper.)

Make the cake: In a stand mixer fitted with the paddle attachment (or in a bowl using a hand mixer), beat together the eggs, brown sugar, and granulated sugar on medium speed until well combined and fluffy, about 4 minutes. Add the sour cream, oil, and vanilla and mix on low speed until fully incorporated, 30 seconds to 1 minute.

In a large bowl, whisk together the flour, salt, baking powder, baking soda, cinnamon, and nutmeg.

On low speed, add the flour mixture to the wet ingredients in three additions, until the ingredients are incorporated. Avoid overmixing.

Use a spatula to fold in the carrots, walnuts, coconut, and citrus zest. Mix until all the ingredients are well incorporated. Pour the batter into the prepared pan and smooth the top with the spatula.

Bake until a toothpick inserted into the center comes out clean, 50 to 60 minutes.

Remove the pan from the oven and let the cake cool in the pan for 10 minutes, then turn out onto a wire rack to cool completely before frosting. (If it's even slightly warm, the frosting WILL slide off!)

recipe continues →

SWEETS & DESSERTS

carrot cake loaf with cream cheese frosting, *continued*

Make the cream cheese frosting: In a stand mixer fitted with the paddle attachment (or in a bowl using a hand mixer), beat the butter on medium-high speed until it is lighter in color and fluffy, about 4 minutes. Add the cream cheese and beat on medium speed until well combined, about 1 minute. Don't overmix, because you don't want the cream cheese to release too much moisture.

Gradually add the confectioners' sugar, about 1 cup at a time, beating well after each addition. Scrape down the sides of the bowl as needed. Add the vanilla and salt and mix on low speed until incorporated. Gradually pour in the cream while continuing to mix on low speed, then increase to medium-high and beat for an additional 2 to 3 minutes, until the frosting is light and fluffy. If the frosting seems too thick, you can add more cream, 1 tablespoon at a time, until you reach your desired consistency.

Spread a generous amount of frosting on top of the cake and, if desired, frost the sides as well. I like to transfer my frosting to a piping bag fitted with a Wilton 8b piping tip and use that to frost my cake, but you can also use an offset spatula. Sprinkle with the crushed nuts.

Store leftover cake in an airtight container in the refrigerator. It will stay fresh for a few days. Bring it to room temperature before serving to enhance the flavors. You can also wrap it tightly in plastic and freeze it for longer storage; just make sure it's cooled completely beforehand.

blueberry, basil, and lemon olive oil loaf cake

Makes one 9 × 5-inch loaf

Butter and flour, for the pan
2 cups / 250g all-purpose flour, plus 1 tablespoon for coating the blueberries

Cake
2 teaspoons baking powder
½ teaspoon fine sea salt
½ cup / 120g extra-virgin olive oil
1½ cups / 300g granulated sugar
2 large eggs
2 teaspoons vanilla extract
½ cup / 125g plain whole milk Greek yogurt
Finely grated zest of 1 lemon
Juice of 1 lemon
1 cup / 140g blueberries
½ cup / 10g fresh basil leaves, finely chopped

Lemon Glaze
1 cup / 100g confectioners' sugar, plus more as needed
2 tablespoons fresh lemon juice
2 teaspoons milk, plus more as needed

The first time I tried olive oil cake, I fell in love. The olive oil makes the crumb impossibly moist and decadent and adds a subtle, irresistible savory note. I've also found that this cake is more forgiving than most: Thanks to the olive oil, it's hard to overbake it.

Using basil in a cake might seem controversial, but I promise, the combo of blueberries, lemon, and basil is out of this world.

Preheat the oven to 350°F. Grease and flour a 9 × 5-inch loaf pan. (Alternatively, you can line the pan with parchment paper.)

Make the cake: In a medium bowl, whisk together the 2 cups / 250g flour, baking powder, and salt. Set aside.

In a large bowl, whisk the oil and granulated sugar until light and fluffy, about 2 minutes. Add the eggs, one at a time, beating well after each addition. Mix in the vanilla, yogurt, lemon zest, and lemon juice until well combined.

Gradually add the flour mixture to the wet mixture, mixing just until combined. Be careful not to overmix.

In a small bowl, toss the blueberries in the remaining 1 tablespoon flour; this will help prevent them from sinking to the bottom of the loaf.

Gently fold the floured blueberries and the basil into the batter until evenly distributed throughout. Pour the batter into the prepared pan and smooth the top with a spatula.

Bake until a toothpick inserted into the center comes out clean, about 1 hour.

Remove the pan from the oven and let the loaf cool in the pan for 10 minutes, then turn out onto a wire rack to cool completely.

Make the lemon glaze: In a small bowl, whisk together the confectioners' sugar, lemon juice, and milk until smooth. If the glaze is too thick, add a little more milk; if it's too thin, add more confectioners' sugar.

Once the loaf is completely cool, drizzle the lemon glaze over the top of the cake, letting it drip down the sides. Allow the glaze to set before slicing and serving.

chocolatey tiramisu cake

Makes one two-layer 8-inch cake

I love tiramisu, which is an Italian dessert made of ladyfingers dipped in coffee and layered with a delicious mascarpone custard. For this cake I took the elements of tiramisu that I love—the sharp bitter notes from coffee and the tangy richness of mascarpone—and transformed them into a luscious chocolate cake. I can't wait for you to try this one.

Cooking spray or butter, for the pan

Cake
2 cups / 400g granulated sugar
2 large eggs
1 cup / 240g whole milk
½ cup / 120g vegetable oil
1 teaspoon instant coffee, dissolved in 1 cup / 240g lukewarm water
2 teaspoons vanilla extract
2 cups / 250g all-purpose flour
1¼ cups / 150g unsweetened cocoa powder
1½ teaspoons baking powder
1½ teaspoons baking soda
¼ teaspoon ground cinnamon

Coffee Syrup
1 cup brewed coffee
½ cup granulated sugar
½ teaspoon orange blossom water (optional)

Mascarpone Cream
2 cups heavy cream
¼ cup mascarpone cheese, at room temperature
¼ cup confectioners' sugar
¼ teaspoon Diamond Crystal kosher salt

Assembly
Unsweetened cocoa powder, for dusting
Chocolate shavings, for garnish (optional)

Preheat the oven to 350°F. Grease two 8-inch round cake pans and line with rounds of parchment paper.

Make the cake: In a stand mixer fitted with the paddle attachment (or in a large bowl with a hand mixer), combine the granulated sugar and eggs. Beat on medium speed until pale and fluffy, about 4 minutes.

Pour in the milk, oil, water with instant coffee, and vanilla. Mix on low speed until everything is well combined, scraping down the sides of the bowl as needed.

Add the flour, cocoa powder, baking powder, baking soda, and cinnamon. Mix on low speed until the dry ingredients are just incorporated. Divide the batter evenly between the lined pans.

Bake until a toothpick inserted in the center comes out clean, 35 to 40 minutes.

Remove the pans from the oven and let the cakes cool in the pans for 20 to 30 minutes, then flip them out onto a wire rack to cool completely.

Make the coffee syrup: In a small saucepan, combine the brewed coffee, granulated sugar, and orange blossom water (if using). Heat over medium heat, stirring until the sugar dissolves. Remove the pan from the heat and let cool.

Make the mascarpone cream: In a stand mixer fitted with the whisk attachment (or in a large bowl using a hand mixer), whip the cream on medium-high speed until soft peaks form, 2 to 3 minutes. Add the mascarpone, confectioners' sugar, and salt. Continue whipping until the mixture reaches stiff peaks, 30 to 60 seconds more. Be careful not to overwhip.

Assemble the cake: Brush both layers of the cake generously with the cooled coffee syrup (you won't use all of it). Alternatively, you can transfer the syrup to a spray bottle and spray it evenly over the surfaces of the cakes. Divide the mascarpone cream in half and spread an even, thick layer on top of each layer, then stack the layers. Dust the top with cocoa powder and garnish with chocolate shavings, if desired. Refrigerate for at least 1 hour or overnight before serving.

SWEETS & DESSERTS

fan fave

raspberry cheesecake

Makes one 7-inch cheesecake

To me, this cake is like a fairy tale—the fluffy cloud of whipped cream, the graham cracker crust climbing all the way up the sides, and the shining pool of fresh raspberry jam at the center. I just wanted all the details to add up to something elegant, like a fantasy version of a cake. That said, I'm never upset about cheesecake; it's probably tied with carrot as my favorite type of cake.

Note that this is a two-day recipe, as I suggest you make the cheesecake crust and filling and let the cake chill overnight before finishing it with jam and whipped cream the following day.

Crust
16 sheets graham crackers
¾ cup / 170g unsalted butter, melted, plus more for the pan
2 tablespoons granulated sugar
½ teaspoon fine sea salt

Filling
20 ounces (from 2½ blocks) cream cheese, at room temperature
½ cup granulated sugar
1 tablespoon cornstarch
¼ teaspoon fine sea salt
¼ cup sour cream
2 teaspoons vanilla extract
2 large eggs, at room temperature

Whipped Cream
1½ cups heavy cream
¼ cup confectioners' sugar
¼ teaspoon fine sea salt

Raspberry Jam
4 cups fresh raspberries
1 cup granulated sugar
2 tablespoons fresh lemon juice

Assembly
Fresh raspberries, for garnish
Fresh mint leaves, for garnish
½ lemon, for zesting

Preheat the oven to 350°F.

Make the crust: In a food processor, combine the graham crackers, butter, granulated sugar, and salt. Pulse until the graham crackers are completely pulverized and evenly hydrated by the butter. Using a spoon, scrape up any bits that get stuck to the bottom.

Grease the inside of a 7-inch springform pan. (Alternatively, you can line the bottom and sides with parchment paper.) Transfer the graham cracker mixture to the pan and, using your hands and the bottom of a measuring cup (or anything with a flat surface), press it evenly into the bottom and all the way up the sides of the pan.

Bake the crust for 10 minutes and remove the pan from the oven. The crust will still be soft at this point, but it will firm up as it cools. Leave the oven on.

Make the filling: In a stand mixer fitted with the whisk attachment (or in a bowl using a hand mixer), beat the cream cheese on medium speed until smooth, about 5 minutes. Add the granulated sugar, cornstarch, and salt and mix until smooth, 30 seconds to 1 minute.

Scrape down the bowl, then add the sour cream and vanilla. Finally, add the eggs, one at a time. Mix just

recipe continues →

SWEETS & DESSERTS

raspberry cheesecake, *continued*

until combined—don't overmix your batter!—then scrape down the bowl once more to make sure everything is well combined. Pour the batter into the cooled crust and use a spatula to spread it evenly.

Bring a kettle or saucepan of water to a boil. Wrap the springform pan in two layers of heavy-duty aluminum foil. Place the pan into a baking dish or roasting pan large enough to hold it. Pull out the oven rack and quickly (but carefully) pour enough boiling water into the larger baking dish to reach halfway up the sides of the pan. Shut the oven door as soon as you add the boiling water to trap as much steam in the oven as possible.

Bake until the cheesecake is slightly puffed and golden and the center has a slight jiggle when you nudge the pan, 60 to 75 minutes. Peel back the foil to peek.

Let the cheesecake cool in the pan at room temperature for 2 hours, then wrap it in plastic wrap and pop it in the fridge overnight.

Make the whipped cream: In a stand mixer fitted with the whisk attachment (or in a bowl using a hand mixer), whip the cream, confectioners' sugar, and salt on medium speed until soft peaks form, 4 to 6 minutes.

Make the raspberry jam: In a medium saucepan, combine the raspberries, granulated sugar, and lemon juice. Bring to a boil over medium-high heat while constantly mixing with a wooden spoon. Reduce to a steady simmer and cook until it has a jellylike texture and runs slowly off a spoon, about 20 minutes, stirring constantly so the jam doesn't burn. Allow to cool completely.

Assemble the cheesecake: Remove the cheesecake from the fridge. Uncover and release the sides of the pan, then use a spatula to gently lift the cheesecake from the pan (if the bottom sticks at all, wiggle a knife underneath to loosen the crust from the pan).

Use a spoon or offset spatula to spread the whipped cream across the top of the cheesecake. Use a large spoon to spread the raspberry jam in the center, leaving an attractive border of whipped cream. Decorate with some fresh raspberries and mint on top of the jam, then grate lemon zest over the top. Store in an airtight container in the fridge for up to 5 days, or in the freezer for up to 3 months.

fan fave

chocoflan

Makes one 10-inch chocoflan

This lovely three-layer dessert combines some of my favorite things: creamy, cheesy flan (to me, Mexican cuisine is top-tier); rich chocolate; and sweet, golden caramel. If you're a beginning baker, I highly encourage you to read the Tip about caramel. Caramel can seem intimidating, but I promise it's worth the effort for this beautiful, crowd-pleasing dessert.

tip **Making caramel:** I highly encourage you to stir the sugar constantly while making the caramel to prevent it from burning, especially if you haven't made caramel before. While some recipes may suggest melting sugar without stirring, it's better to err on the side of caution and keep stirring until you gain more experience. The last thing I would want is for you to have to deal with hot, burned caramel.

Cooking spray or olive oil, for the pan

Caramel
1 cup sugar

Queso Flan Layer
1½ cups whole milk
1 (14-ounce) can sweetened condensed milk
5 large eggs
4 ounces cream cheese
2 teaspoons vanilla extract
¼ teaspoon fine sea salt

Chocolate Cake Layer
2 cups / 400g sugar
2 large eggs
1 cup / 240g whole milk
1 teaspoon instant coffee, dissolved in 1 cup / 240g warm water
½ cup / 110g vegetable oil
2 teaspoons vanilla extract
2½ cups / 315g all-purpose flour
1¼ cups / 150g unsweetened cocoa powder
1½ teaspoons baking powder
1½ teaspoons baking soda
¾ teaspoon fine sea salt
¼ teaspoon ground cinnamon

Spray a 12-cup Bundt pan with cooking spray or rub it generously with olive oil.

Make the caramel: Pour the sugar into a medium saucepan, using a silicone spatula to spread it out evenly. Cook the sugar over medium heat, stirring constantly to prevent burning. You're going to notice the sugar start to clump and crystallize. As the sugar melts, it will start to turn into a golden syrup. If you notice any areas where the sugar is not melting, be patient, reduce the heat to low, and continue to stir until you reach a smooth consistency.

As soon as the sugar has completely melted and reached a deep amber color, about 6 minutes, immediately remove the pan from the heat. The residual heat in the pan will continue to darken the caramel, so it's important to act quickly.

Slowly and carefully pour the hot caramel into the bottom of the prepared Bundt pan, tilting it to coat the bottom evenly. Work quickly—the caramel will harden quite fast—but also cautiously, as the caramel is extremely hot and can cause burns.

Set the caramel-coated Bundt pan aside and allow

recipe continues →

SWEETS & DESSERTS

chocoflan, *continued*

the caramel to cool and harden into a solid layer.

Preheat the oven to 350°F.

Make the queso flan layer: In a blender, combine the whole milk, condensed milk, eggs, cream cheese, vanilla, and salt. Start on low speed, then gradually increase the speed to medium or high, depending on how powerful your blender is. Blend for 1 to 2 minutes or until the mixture is smooth and the ingredients are well incorporated. Pause partway through and use a spatula to scrape down the sides of the blender jar, ensuring all the ingredients are fully mixed.

Spray the sides of the Bundt pan or rub it generously with oil again (it's fine—and a good idea, actually—to get some on the caramel layer, too). Pour in the queso flan mixture into the Bundt pan.

Place the filled Bundt pan into a baking dish or roasting pan large enough to hold it. Pour enough hot water into the larger baking dish to reach halfway up the sides of the Bundt pan. Cover the Bundt pan with aluminum foil.

Carefully transfer the water bath with the flan to the oven and bake until the flan layer is firm, with just a slight jiggle to it, about 50 minutes. Carefully remove the Bundt pan from the water bath and allow it to sit at room temperature. Leave the oven on and keep the water bath handy.

Meanwhile, make the chocolate cake layer: About 10 minutes before the flan is done baking, In a stand mixer fitted with the paddle attachment (or in a bowl using a hand mixer), beat together the sugar and eggs on medium speed until pale and fluffy, about 4 minutes.

Pour in the milk, water with instant coffee, vegetable oil, and vanilla and continue mixing on low speed until all the ingredients are well incorporated, scraping down the sides of the bowl as needed. Be careful not to overmix.

In a large bowl, whisk together the flour, cocoa powder, baking powder, baking soda, salt, and cinnamon. On low speed, add the flour mixture to the wet ingredients and mix until incorporated. Be careful not to overmix.

Pour the batter over the baked flan, then re-cover the Bundt pan with foil. Return the Bundt pan to the water bath (add more warm water to come halfway up the sides of the Bundt pan, if needed) and pop the pan back into the oven.

Bake until a toothpick inserted into the center of the cake layer comes out clean, 65 to 75 minutes.

Remove the pan from the oven and let the chocoflan cool in the pan at room temperature for 1 hour. After 1 hour, cover the chocoflan and refrigerate for at least 2 hours before serving—overnight is even better!

To loosen the cake from the Bundt pan, carefully dunk the bottom of the pan in a large bowl of hot water, allowing the warmth to release the cake from the pan. Next, position a platter upside down on top of the cake pan, then confidently flip the pan to unmold the cake. Finally, drizzle any remaining caramel from the pan over the top of the cake. You can make chocoflan up to 3 days in advance. Simply store it in an airtight container in the refrigerator until ready to serve.

Acknowledgments

As always, I want to thank God. What started as a quiet dream tucked in the back of my mind is now something I can hold in my hands. None of this would have happened without Him. Alhamdulilah.

To my parents, thank you for every sacrifice you made to give us the kind of life you never got to have, one full of safety and opportunity. This book is yours as much as it is mine. I hope I continue making you proud.

To my husband, who was there for every recipe (the wins and the fails), who'd find me in the kitchen at 3 a.m. testing and testing again, and who showed me nothing but support and love, thank you for being my backbone—and making me feel less crazy.

To Nicole Tourtelot, the best agent a girl could ask for! Thank you for all the support you have poured into me—this book would not have been possible without you

To my editor Susan Roxborough and designer Marysarah Quinn, thank you for believing in my voice and for helping shape it into a book, something that was in my heart for years. You gave these pages room to breathe, and I'll always be grateful we got to do this together.

To everyone else at Clarkson Potter, including Elaine Hennig, marketer Emily Hotaling, publicist Jina Stanfill, Ashley Pierce, Bridget Sweet, and Philip Leung, thank you for all your efforts on behalf of my book.

To Emily Timberlake, thank you for all the hours you spent listening to me ramble about recipes, life, and everything in between, and for helping me shape it all into words. It's a bond we'll share forever.

To Jim Henkens, thank you for the beauty on every page, and for bringing my vision to life in more ways than I can count. I truly couldn't have asked for a better photographer. To food stylist Kate Buckens and assistants Jami Chiarella-Kopec and Alyse Dufour, thank you for making every dish in the book look so delicious.

To Julie Bishop, thank you for testing every recipe with so much love and attention to detail. I'm endlessly thankful for that.

To Gaza, your pain and your power live within me. You are in my heart, in my prayers, and in every part of this book. I carry you with me.

To every Palestinian hand that has passed down a recipe. Each time a dish is taught or remembered, it becomes a way to hold on to our culture. It's how we stay connected to our ancestors, and how they stay connected to us.

To the whole @Mxriyum family, thank you for making space for these recipes in your kitchen. I hope they bring you comfort and remind you that care can live in the smallest things, even something as simple as food.

And to everyone who showed up for me in ways that are big or small while I worked on this book, thank you. I couldn't possibly name you all, but please know how much your support, kindness, and encouragement carried me through.

Index

Note: Page references in *italics* indicate photographs.

A

Addas (Creamy Lentil Soup), *78*, 79
Aioli, Lemon, 128
Alfredo Sauce, 148
apples
    Apple and Apricot Galette with Maple Crème Fraîche, *248*, 249
    Apple Fritters, 230, *231*
apricots
    Apple and Apricot Galette with Maple Crème Fraîche, *248*, 249
arugula
    Burrata Salad with Steak and Labneh Chimichurri, 74, *75*
    Crispy Potato Salad with Greens, *64*, 65
avocados
    Crispy Potato Salad with Greens, *64*, 65
Awamah (Fried Dough Balls in Orange Blossom Simple Syrup), *244*, 245

B

Baba Ghanoush–Stuffed Eggplant, 50, *51*
bacon
    Croissant Breakfast Sandwiches, 28, *29*
Bagels, Everything, *204*, 205–6
Bamia (Okra Stewed in Tomato Sauce with Lamb), *98*, 99
bananas
    Banana Pastry Cream, 23
    Caramelized Bananas, 24
    Sweet Banana Cream Pudding Crepes, 23–24, *25*
    Tahini and Browned Butter Banana Bread, 220, *221*
Bang Bang Shrimp Tacos with Cabbage Slaw, *126*, 127
Batata o Baid (Eggs with Curry-Spiced Potatoes), *30*, 31
beans. *See* chickpeas; favas
Béchamel, 106
beef
    Burrata Salad with Steak and Labneh Chimichurri, 74, *75*
    Kibbeh (Beef and Bulgur–Stuffed Shells), 57, *58*, 59
    Macarona Béchamel (Egyptian-Style Pasta Bake), 106, *107*
    Marinated Brisket with Olive and Fig Tapenade, *164*, 165
    Oozi (Spiced Rice with Beef, Peas, and Carrots), *112*, 113
    Sambosas, 54, *55*, 56
    Saniyeh Kofta (Beef Patties in Tomato Sauce), *160*, 161
    Sfeeha (Open-Faced Meat and Pine Nut Pies), 213–14, *215*
    Shishbarak (Beef Dumplings in Yogurt Sauce), 93–94, *95*
    Surf and Turf with Filet Mignon and Crab-Stuffed Lobster, 157–58, *159*
    Triple-Stack Smash Burgers, 162, *163*
    Warak Dawali (Stuffed Grape Leaves with Beef Ribs), 120–21, *122*–23
Biscuits, Feta-Chive Buttermilk, with Roasted Garlic Butter, 198, *199*
Blueberry, Basil, and Lemon Olive Oil Loaf Cake, 256, *257*
bouillon cubes, 14
bread
    baking tips, 169
    Brioche Buns, *190*, 191–92
    Cast-Iron Sourdough Focaccia, 176, *177*
    Everything Bagels, *204*, 205–6
    Fattoush (Fried Bread Salad), 66, *67*
    Feta-Chive Buttermilk Biscuits with Roasted Garlic Butter, 198, *199*
    Fluffy Japanese Milk Bread, 181, *182*, 183
    French Onion Soup, *82*, 83
    French Toast Bake with Walnut Filling, *26*, 27
    Homemade Garlic Knots, *200*, 201
    Honey-Butter Cast-Iron Cornbread, *196*, 197
    Ka'ak al-Quds (Jerusalem Bread), *178*, 179–80
    Khubiz Taboon (Traditional Palestinian Flatbread), 172, *173*, 174–75
    Kishta and Pistachio–Stuffed French Toast, *20*, 21–22
    The Middle Eastern Charcuterie Board, 60–61, *61*
    Mozzarella-Stuffed Pull-Apart Bread, *202*, 203
    Msakhan (Flatbread with Chicken, Sumac, and Caramelized Onions), 139, *140*, 141
    Pita Bread, 168–69, *170*–71
    Sourdough Bread Bowls, 186
    Sourdough Loaf, 184, *185*, 186
    Sourdough Starter, 188
    sourdough tips, 187
    Tahini and Browned Butter Banana Bread, 220, *221*
    Za'atar Manakeesh (Za'atar Flatbread), *173*, 210, 211–12
    See also rolls; sandwiches
Brioche Buns, *190*, 191–92
Brownies, Perfect Fudge, 240, *241*
bulgur
    about, 14
    Kibbeh (Beef and Bulgur–Stuffed Shells), 57, *58*, 59
    Loaded Chickpea Salad with Lemon-Garlic Shrimp, *72*, 73
Buns, Brioche, *190*, 191–92
Burgers, Triple-Stack Smash, 162, *163*
Burrata Salad with Steak and Labneh Chimichurri, 74, *75*
butter
    Browned Butter, 194
    Garlic Butter, 201, 202
    Honey Butter, 144, 197
    Roasted Garlic Butter, 198, *199*
    Seasoned Butter, 151
buttermilk
    Buttermilk-Brined Chicken and Waffle Sliders, 144, *145*
    Buttermilk Dressing, 65
    Buttermilk Pancakes, 18, *19*

C

cabbage
    Bang Bang Shrimp Tacos with Cabbage Slaw, *126*, 127
    Coleslaw, 142
cakes
    Blueberry, Basil, and Lemon Olive Oil Loaf Cake, 256, *257*
    Chocolatey Tiramisu Cake, *258*, 259
    Lemon Olive Oil Cake with Mascarpone Cream, 256
    Raspberry Cheesecake, *260*, 261–62
caramel, making, 263
carrots
    Carrot Cake Loaf with Cream Cheese Frosting, 253–54, *255*
    Coleslaw, 142
    Oozi (Spiced Rice with Beef, Peas, and Carrots), *112*, 113
cauliflower
    Maklouba (Upside-Down Rice with Chicken Legs), 114, *115*, 116
Charcuterie Board, The Middle Eastern, 60–61, *61*
cheese
    Alfredo Sauce, 148
    Burrata Salad with Steak and Labneh Chimichurri, 74, *75*
    Buttermilk Dressing, 65

267

Caramelized Onion Ratatouille Tart, 39–40, *41*
Cheese Fatayer, *216*, 217
Chocoflan, 263, *264*, 265
Chocolatey Tiramisu Cake, *258*, 259
Cinnamon Rolls, *222*, 223–24
Coleslaw, 142
Cream Cheese Frosting, 253–54
Croissant Breakfast Sandwiches, 28, *29*
Feta-Chive Buttermilk Biscuits with Roasted Garlic Butter, 198, *199*
French Onion Soup, *82*, 83
Garlic-Bread Grilled Cheese, *90*, 91–92
Garlic-Parmesan Fried Chicken Sandwiches, 142–43, *143*
Katayef (Fried Stuffed "Pancakes"), 237–38, *239*
Knafeh Kishna (Sweet Cheese Pie), *242*, 243
Lemon Olive Oil Cake with Mascarpone Cream, 256
Macarona Béchamel (Egyptian-Style Pasta Bake), 106, *107*
Mediterranean Pasta Salad with Sumac Vinaigrette, *68*, 69
The Middle Eastern Charcuterie Board, 60–61, *61*
Mini Chicken Alfredo Pizzas, 146–47, *148–49*
Mozzarella-Stuffed Pull-Apart Bread, 202, *203*
Pasta with Mussels and Shrimp, *108*, 109
Raspberry Cheesecake, *260*, 261–62
Roasted Garlic and Herb Dipping Oil, 207
Smoked Salmon and Pepper Jelly Pastry, 34, *35*
Three-Cheese Creamy Baked Mac and Cheese, 102, *103*
Triple-Stack Smash Burgers, 162, *163*
chicken
 Buttermilk-Brined Chicken and Waffle Sliders, 144, *145*
 Cast-Iron Chicken with Tarragon, Olives, and Charred Lemon, *152*, 153
 Chicken Noodle Soup, *86*, 87
 Chicken Shawarma Wraps, 136, *137*, 138
 Creamy Chicken Gnocchi Soup, 88, *89*
 Garlic-Parmesan Fried Chicken Sandwiches, 142–43, *143*
 Maklouba (Upside-Down Rice with Chicken Legs), 114, *115*, 116
 Mini Chicken Alfredo Pizzas, 146–47, *148–49*
 Molokhia (Mallow Stew with Chicken), *96*, 97
 Msakhan (Flatbread with Chicken, Sumac, and Caramelized Onions), 139, *140*, 141
 spatchcocking, 151
 Sumac and Lemon Roast Chicken with Tahini Salad, *150*, 151
chickpeas
 about, 14

Falafel, *52*, 53
 Loaded Chickpea Salad with Lemon-Garlic Shrimp, *72*, 73
 Mama's Homemade Hummus, *44*, 45
chiles
 Ful Medames with Tatbila (Favas with Jalapeño Sauce), 46, *47*
 Slow-Roasted Jalapeño Salmon with Citrus Chimichurri, 132, *133*
 Tomatillo Salsa Verde, 135
chimichurri
 Citrus Chimichurri, 132, *133*
 Labneh Chimichurri, 74
chocolate
 Chocoflan, 263, *264*, 265
 Chocolatey Tiramisu Cake, *258*, 259
 "Generational" Chocolate Chip Cookies, *232*, 233
 Perfect Fudge Brownies, 240, *241*
 Tahini and Browned Butter Banana Bread, 220, *221*
Choose-Your-Own-Adventure Brioche Donuts, 228, *229*
cilantro
 Citrus Chimichurri, 132, *133*
 Labneh Chimichurri, 74
Cinnamon Rolls, *222*, 223–24
Citrus Chimichurri, 132, *133*
Clam Chowder, 84, *85*
coconut
 Carrot Cake Loaf with Cream Cheese Frosting, 253–54, *255*
 Katayef (Fried Stuffed "Pancakes"), 237–38, *239*
coconut milk
 Spiced Butternut Squash Soup, 80, *81*
coffee
 Chocolatey Tiramisu Cake, *258*, 259
 Coffee Syrup, 257
Coleslaw, 142
cookies
 "Generational" Chocolate Chip Cookies, *232*, 233
 Ma'amoul (Date-Stuffed Butter Cookies), 234, *235*, 236
corn
 Honey-Butter Cast-Iron Cornbread, *196*, 197
 Loaded Chickpea Salad with Lemon-Garlic Shrimp, *72*, 73
crab
 Spiced Jumbo Crab Cakes with Lemon Aioli, 128, *129*
 Surf and Turf with Filet Mignon and Crab-Stuffed Lobster, 157–58, *159*
crackers
 The Middle Eastern Charcuterie Board, 60–61, *61*
Cream, Whipped, 18, 261–62
crepes
 Sweet Banana Cream Pudding Crepes, 23–24, *25*
 tips for, 24
Croissant Breakfast Sandwiches, 28, *29*
cucumbers
 Crispy Potato Salad with Greens, 64, 65

Fattoush (Fried Bread Salad), 66, *67*
Khiyar bi Laban (Cucumber Yogurt Dip), *48*, 49
Mediterranean Pasta Salad with Sumac Vinaigrette, *68*, 69
Smoked Salmon and Pepper Jelly Pastry, 34, *35*
Tahini Salad, *150*, 151

D
Date-Stuffed Butter Cookies (Ma'amoul), 234, *235*, 236
desserts and sweets
 Apple and Apricot Galette with Maple Crème Fraîche, *248*, 249
 Apple Fritters, 230, *231*
 Awamah (Fried Dough Balls in Orange Blossom Simple Syrup), *244*, 245
 Blueberry, Basil, and Lemon Olive Oil Loaf Cake, 256, *257*
 Carrot Cake Loaf with Cream Cheese Frosting, 253–54, *255*
 Chocoflan, 263, *264*, 265
 Chocolatey Tiramisu Cake, *258*, 259
 Choose-Your-Own-Adventure Brioche Donuts, 228, *229*
 "Generational" Chocolate Chip Cookies, *232*, 233
 Katayef (Fried Stuffed "Pancakes"), 237–38, *239*
 Knafeh Kishna (Sweet Cheese Pie), *242*, 243
 Ma'amoul (Date-Stuffed Butter Cookies), 234, *235*, 236
 Mtabouk (Sweet Layered Pastry), 250, *251*, 252
 Old-Fashioned Sour Cream Donuts, 225–26, *227*
 Perfect Fudge Brownies, 240, *241*
 Raspberry Cheesecake, *260*, 261–62
 Riz bi Haleeb (Rich and Creamy Rice Pudding), 246, *247*
 Tahini and Browned Butter Banana Bread, 220, *221*
dips
 Khiyar bi Laban (Cucumber Yogurt Dip), *48*, 49
 Mama's Homemade Hummus, *44*, 45
 Tatbila (Jalapeño Sauce), 46, *47*
donuts
 Choose-Your-Own-Adventure Brioche Donuts, 228, *229*
 Old-Fashioned Sour Cream Donuts, 225–26, *227*

E
eggplant
 Baba Ghanoush–Stuffed Eggplant, 50, *51*
 Caramelized Onion Ratatouille Tart, 39–40, *41*
 Maklouba (Upside-Down Rice with Chicken Legs), 114, *115*, 116
eggs
 Batata o Baid (Eggs with Curry-Spiced Potatoes), 30, *31*
 Croissant Breakfast Sandwiches, 28, *29*

eggs, *continued*
   Shakshuka, 32, *33*
equipment, 15
Everything Bagels, *204*, 205–6

F
Falafel, *52*, 53
   Falafel Sandwich, 53
fan faves
   Carrot Cake Loaf with Cream Cheese Frosting, 253–54, *255*
   Cheese Fatayer, *216*, 217
   Chocoflan, 263, *264*, 265
   Cinnamon Rolls, *222*, 223–24
   Everything Bagels, *204*, 205–6
   Ka'ak al-Quds (Jerusalem Bread), *178*, 179–80
   Khubiz Taboon (Traditional Palestinian Flatbread), 172, *173*, 174–75
   Macarona Béchamel (Egyptian-Style Pasta Bake), 106, *107*
   Mama's Homemade Hummus, *44*, 45
   Mini Chicken Alfredo Pizzas, 146–47, 148–49
   Mozzarella-Stuffed Pull-Apart Bread, 202, *203*
   Msakhan (Flatbread with Chicken, Sumac, and Caramelized Onions), 139, *140*, 141
   Perfect Fudge Brownies, 240, *241*
   Pita Bread, 168–69, *170–71*
   Raspberry Cheesecake, *260*, 261–62
   Three-Cheese Creamy Baked Mac and Cheese, 102, *103*
   Tomato Soup with Garlic-Bread Grilled Cheese, *90*, 91–92
   Triple-Stack Smash Burgers, 162, *163*
   Za'atar Manakeesh (Za'atar Flatbread), *173*, *210*, 211–12
Fatayer, Cheese, *216*, 217
Fattoush (Fried Bread Salad), 66, *67*
favas
   about, 14
   Ful Medames with Tatbila (Favas with Jalapeño Sauce), 46, *47*
fennel
   Fennel-Radish Salad, 135
   Lamb Shoulder with Labneh and Fennel-Orange Glaze, *154*, 155–56
Fig Tapenade, Marinated Brisket with Olive and, *164*, 165
fish
   Pan-Seared Lemon-Caper Sea Bass, *134*, 135
   Slow-Roasted Jalapeño Salmon with Citrus Chimichurri, *132*, 133
   Smoked Salmon and Pepper Jelly Pastry, 34, *35*
   Teriyaki Salmon with Mango Salsa and Quinoa, *130*, 131
Focaccia, Cast-Iron Sourdough, 176, *177*
French Onion Soup, *82*, 83
French toast
   French Toast Bake with Walnut Filling, *26*, 27
   Kishta and Pistachio-Stuffed French Toast, *20*, 21–22

fritters
   Apple Fritters, 230, *231*
   Awamah (Fried Dough Balls in Orange Blossom Simple Syrup), *244*, 245
   Ful Medames with Tatbila (Favas with Jalapeño Sauce), 46, *47*

G
galettes
   Apple and Apricot Galette with Maple Crème Fraîche, *248*, 249
   Galette Dough, 38
   Tomato Galette with Za'atar, *36*, 37–38
garlic
   Creamy Garlic Sauce, *137*, 138
   Garlic-Bread Grilled Cheese, *90*, 91–92
   Garlic Butter, 201, *202*
   Garlic-Parmesan Fried Chicken Sandwiches, 142–43, *143*
   Garlic Sauce, 142–43
   Homemade Garlic Knots, *200*, 201
   powder, 14
   Roasted Garlic and Herb Dipping Oil, 207
   Roasted Garlic Butter, 198, *199*
"Generational" Chocolate Chip Cookies, *232*, 233
Gnocchi Soup, Creamy Chicken, *88*, 89
graham crackers
   Raspberry Cheesecake, *260*, 261–62
grapefruit
   Burrata Salad with Steak and Labneh Chimichurri, 74, *75*
grape leaves
   about, 14
   Warak Dawali (Stuffed Grape Leaves with Beef Ribs), *120–21*, 122–23

H
Honey Butter, *144*, 197
Hummus, Mama's Homemade, *44*, 45

J
jameed
   about, 13
   Mansaf (Rice with Lamb and Fermented Yogurt Sauce), 117, *118*, 119
   soup starter, 117, 119
Jerusalem Bread (Ka'ak al-Quds), *178*, 179–80

K
Ka'ak al-Quds (Jerusalem Bread), *178*, 179–80
Katayef (Fried Stuffed "Pancakes"), 237–38, *239*
Khiyar bi Laban (Cucumber Yogurt Dip), *48*, 49
Khubiz Taboon (Traditional Palestinian Flatbread), 172, *173*, 174–75
Kibbeh (Beef and Bulgur–Stuffed Shells), *57*, *58*, 59
kishta
   about, 13
   Kishta and Pistachio-Stuffed French Toast, *20*, 21–22

   Kishta Topping, 252
   making, 22
Knafeh Kishna (Sweet Cheese Pie), *242*, 243

L
laban, 13, 119
labneh
   about, 13
   Labneh Chimichurri, 74
   Lamb Shoulder with Labneh and Fennel-Orange Glaze, *154*, 155–56
   Tomato Galette with Za'atar, *36*, 37–38
lamb
   Bamia (Okra Stewed in Tomato Sauce with Lamb), *98*, 99
   Lamb Shoulder with Labneh and Fennel-Orange Glaze, *154*, 155–56
   Mansaf (Rice with Lamb and Fermented Yogurt Sauce), 117, *118*, 119
   Sambosas, 54, *55*, 56
lemons
   Cast-Iron Chicken with Tarragon, Olives, and Charred Lemon, *152*, 153
   Citrus Chimichurri, *132*, 133
   Lemon Aioli, 128
   Lemon Glaze, 256
   Lemon Olive Oil Cake with Mascarpone Cream, 256
   Loaded Chickpea Salad with Lemon-Garlic Shrimp, *72*, 73
   Pan-Seared Lemon-Caper Sea Bass, *134*, 135
   Sumac and Lemon Roast Chicken with Tahini Salad, *150*, 151
lentils
   Addas (Creamy Lentil Soup), *78*, 79
lettuce
   Coleslaw, 142
   Crispy Potato Salad with Greens, *64*, 65
   Fattoush (Fried Bread Salad), 66, *67*
limes
   Citrus Chimichurri, *132*, 133
Lobster, Crab-Stuffed, Surf and Turf with Filet Mignon and, 157–58, *159*

M
Ma'amoul (Date-Stuffed Butter Cookies), 234, *235*, 236
Mac and Cheese, Three-Cheese Creamy Baked, 102, *103*
Macarona Béchamel (Egyptian-Style Pasta Bake), 106, *107*
Maklouba (Upside-Down Rice with Chicken Legs), 114, *115*, 116
Mama's Homemade Hummus, *44*, 45
Manakeesh, Za'atar (Za'atar Flatbread), *173*, *210*, 211–12
Mango Salsa, 131
Mansaf (Rice with Lamb and Fermented Yogurt Sauce), 117, *118*, 119
Mediterranean Pasta Salad with Sumac Vinaigrette, *68*, 69
The Middle Eastern Charcuterie Board, 60–61, *61*

INDEX

milk
    Fluffy Japanese Milk Bread, 181, *182*, 183
    powdered, 14
Molokhia (Mallow Stew with Chicken), *96*, 97
Msakhan (Flatbread with Chicken, Sumac, and Caramelized Onions), 139, *140*, 141
Mtabouk (Sweet Layered Pastry), 250, *251*, 252
Mussels, Pasta with Shrimp and, *108*, 109

N
noodles. *See* pasta and noodles

O
oils
    neutral, 13
    olive, 13
    Roasted Garlic and Herb Dipping Oil, 207
Okra Stewed in Tomato Sauce with Lamb (Bamia), *98*, 99
olives
    Cast-Iron Chicken with Tarragon, Olives, and Charred Lemon, *152*, 153
    Marinated Brisket with Olive and Fig Tapenade, *164*, 165
    Mediterranean Pasta Salad with Sumac Vinaigrette, *68*, 69
    oil, 13
onions
    Caramelized Onion Ratatouille Tart, 39–40, *41*
    Caramelized Onions, 40
    French Onion Soup, *82*, 83
    Msakhan (Flatbread with Chicken, Sumac, and Caramelized Onions), 139, *140*, 141
    powder, 14
Oozi (Spiced Rice with Beef, Peas, and Carrots), *112*, 113
orange blossom water
    about, 14
    Orange Blossom Simple Syrup, 22
oranges
    Burrata Salad with Steak and Labneh Chimichurri, 74, *75*
    Citrus Chimichurri, 132, *133*
    Lamb Shoulder with Labneh and Fennel-Orange Glaze, *154*, 155–56

P
pancakes
    Buttermilk Pancakes, 18, *19*
    Katayef (Fried Stuffed "Pancakes"), 237–38, *239*
parsley
    Citrus Chimichurri, 132, *133*
    Labneh Chimichurri, 74
pasta and noodles
    about, 14
    Chicken Noodle Soup, *86*, 87
    Creamy Chicken Gnocchi Soup, 88, *89*
    Macarona Béchamel (Egyptian-Style Pasta Bake), 106, *107*
    Maklouba (Upside-Down Rice with Chicken Legs), 114, *115*, 116
    Mediterranean Pasta Salad with Sumac Vinaigrette, *68*, 69
    Pasta with Mussels and Shrimp, *108*, 109
    Roasted Yellow Pepper Pasta, *104*, 105
    Three-Cheese Creamy Baked Mac and Cheese, 102, *103*
    Vermicelli Rice, 110, *111*
pastries
    Cheese Fatayer, *216*, 217
    Mtabouk (Sweet Layered Pastry), 250, *251*, 252
    Smoked Salmon and Pepper Jelly Pastry, 34, *35*
peas
    Oozi (Spiced Rice with Beef, Peas, and Carrots), *112*, 113
    Sambosas, 54, *55*, 56
peppers
    Bamia (Okra Stewed in Tomato Sauce with Lamb), *98*, 99
    Caramelized Onion Ratatouille Tart, 39–40, *41*
    Fattoush (Fried Bread Salad), 66, *67*
    Kibbeh (Beef and Bulgur-Stuffed Shells), 57, *58*, 59
    Loaded Chickpea Salad with Lemon-Garlic Shrimp, *72*, 73
    Mediterranean Pasta Salad with Sumac Vinaigrette, *68*, 69
    Roasted Tomato-Pepper Sauce, 39–40
    Roasted Yellow Pepper Pasta, *104*, 105
    Saniyeh Kofta (Beef Patties in Tomato Sauce), *160*, 161
    Sfeeha (Open-Faced Meat and Pine Nut Pies), 213–14, *215*
    Shakshuka, 32, *33*
    Smoked Salmon and Pepper Jelly Pastry, 34, *35*
    Tomato Soup with Garlic-Bread Grilled Cheese, 90, *91*–92
    See also chiles
pies
    Knafeh Kishna (Sweet Cheese Pie), *242*, 243
    Sfeeha (Open-Faced Meat and Pine Nut Pies), 213–14, *215*
pine nuts
    Roasted Squash with Pine Nuts and Tahini, 70, *71*
    Sfeeha (Open-Faced Meat and Pine Nut Pies), 213–14, *215*
    toasting, 141
Pistachio-Stuffed French Toast, Kishta and, *20*, 21–22
Pita Bread, 168–69, *170–71*
pizzas
    Mini Chicken Alfredo Pizzas, *146–47*, 148–49
    Pizza Dough, 148–49
potatoes
    Batata o Baid (Eggs with Curry-Spiced Potatoes), *30*, 31
    Clam Chowder, 84, *85*
    Crispy Potato Salad with Greens, *64*, 65
    Maklouba (Upside-Down Rice with Chicken Legs), 114, *115*, 116
    Sambosas, 54, *55*, 56
    Saniyeh Kofta (Beef Patties in Tomato Sauce), *160*, 161
Pretzels, Za'atar Soft, 207–8, *209*
Pudding, Creamy Rice (Riz bi Haleeb), 246, *247*
puff pastry
    Smoked Salmon and Pepper Jelly Pastry, 34, *35*

Q
Quinoa, Teriyaki Salmon with Mango Salsa and, *130*, 131

R
radishes
    Crispy Potato Salad with Greens, *64*, 65
    Fattoush (Fried Bread Salad), 66, *67*
    Fennel-Radish Salad, 135
Raspberry Cheesecake, *260*, 261–62
rice
    about, 14
    Maklouba (Upside-Down Rice with Chicken Legs), 114, *115*, 116
    Mansaf (Rice with Lamb and Fermented Yogurt Sauce), 117, *118*, 119
    Oozi (Spiced Rice with Beef, Peas, and Carrots), *112*, 113
    Riz bi Haleeb (Rich and Creamy Rice Pudding), 246, *247*
    Vermicelli Rice, 110, *111*
    Warak Dawali (Stuffed Grape Leaves with Beef Ribs), *120–21*, 122–23
Riz bi Haleeb (Rich and Creamy Rice Pudding), 246, *247*
rolls
    Cinnamon Rolls, *222*, 223–24
    Fluffy Browned Butter Rolls with Flaky Sea Salt, 193–94, *195*

S
salad dressings
    Buttermilk Dressing, 65
    Sumac Dressing, 69
salads
    Burrata Salad with Steak and Labneh Chimichurri, 74, *75*
    Coleslaw, 142
    Crispy Potato Salad with Greens, *64*, 65
    Fattoush (Fried Bread Salad), 66, *67*
    Fennel-Radish Salad, 135
    Loaded Chickpea Salad with Lemon-Garlic Shrimp, *72*, 73
    Mediterranean Pasta Salad with Sumac Vinaigrette, *68*, 69
    Tahini Salad, *150*, 151
salmon
    Slow-Roasted Jalapeño Salmon with Citrus Chimichurri, 132, *133*
    Smoked Salmon and Pepper Jelly Pastry, 34, *35*

salmon, *continued*
    Teriyaki Salmon with Mango Salsa and Quinoa, *130,* 131
salsas. *See* sauces and salsas
salt, 14
Sambosas, 54, *55,* 56
sandwiches
    Buttermilk-Brined Chicken and Waffle Sliders, 144, *145*
    Croissant Breakfast Sandwiches, 28, *29*
    Falafel Sandwich, 53
    Garlic-Bread Grilled Cheese, *90,* 91–92
    Garlic-Parmesan Fried Chicken Sandwiches, 142–43, *143*
    Triple-Stack Smash Burgers, 162, *163*
Saniyeh Kofta (Beef Patties in Tomato Sauce), *160,* 161
sauces and salsas
    Alfredo Sauce, 148
    Bang Bang Sauce, 127
    Béchamel, 106
    Citrus Chimichurri, 132, *133*
    Creamy Garlic Sauce, *137,* 138
    Garlic Sauce, 142–43
    Labneh Chimichurri, 74
    Lemon Aioli, 128
    Mango Salsa, 131
    Roasted Tomato-Pepper Sauce, 39–40
    Tahini Sauce, 70
    Tatbila (Jalapeño Sauce), 46, *47*
    Tomatillo Salsa Verde, 135
    Yogurt Sauce, 93–94, 117
Sea Bass, Pan-Seared Lemon-Caper, *134,* 135
sesame seeds
    Ka'ak al-Quds (Jerusalem Bread), *178,* 179–80
seven spice, 14
Sfeeha (Open-Faced Meat and Pine Nut Pies), 213–14, *215*
Shakshuka, 32, *33*
Shishbarak (Beef Dumplings in Yogurt Sauce), 93–94, *95*
shrimp
    Bang Bang Shrimp Tacos with Cabbage Slaw, *126,* 127
    Loaded Chickpea Salad with Lemon-Garlic Shrimp, *72,* 73
    Pasta with Mussels and Shrimp, *108,* 109
Sliders, Buttermilk-Brined Chicken and Waffle, 144, *145*
soups
    Addas (Creamy Lentil Soup), *78,* 79
    Chicken Noodle Soup, *86,* 87
    Clam Chowder, 84, *85*
    Creamy Chicken Gnocchi Soup, 88, *89*
    French Onion Soup, *82,* 83
    Shishbarak (Beef Dumplings in Yogurt Sauce), 93–94, *95*
    Spiced Butternut Squash Soup, 80, *81*
    Tomato Soup with Garlic-Bread Grilled Cheese, *90,* 91–92
sourdough
    Cast-Iron Sourdough Focaccia, 176, *177*
    Sourdough Bread Bowls, 186
    Sourdough Loaf, 184, *185,* 186
    Sourdough Starter, 188
    tips for, 187
spices, 14
spinach
    Creamy Chicken Gnocchi Soup, 88, *89*
squash
    Caramelized Onion Ratatouille Tart, 39–40, *41*
    Roasted Squash with Pine Nuts and Tahini, 70, *71*
    Spiced Butternut Squash Soup, 80, *81*
Starter, Sourdough, 188
stones, baking on, 175
sumac
    Msakhan (Flatbread with Chicken, Sumac, and Caramelized Onions), 139, *140,* 141
    Sumac and Lemon Roast Chicken with Tahini Salad, *150,* 151
    Sumac Dressing, 69
Surf and Turf with Filet Mignon and Crab-Stuffed Lobster, 157–58, *159*
syrups
    Coffee Syrup, 257
    Orange Blossom Simple Syrup, 22

T

Tacos, Bang Bang Shrimp, with Cabbage Slaw, *126,* 127
tahini
    Baba Ghanoush-Stuffed Eggplant, 50, *51*
    Mama's Homemade Hummus, *44,* 45
    Roasted Squash with Pine Nuts and Tahini, 70, *71*
    Tahini and Browned Butter Banana Bread, 220, *221*
    Tahini Salad, *150,* 151
    Tahini Sauce, 70
Tapenade, Fig, 165
tarts
    Caramelized Onion Ratatouille Tart, 39–40, *41*
    Tart Dough, 39
Tatbila (Jalapeño Sauce), 46, *47*
Teriyaki Salmon with Mango Salsa and Quinoa, *130,* 131
Tiramisu Cake, Chocolatey, *258,* 259
Tomatillo Salsa Verde, 135
tomatoes
    Bamia (Okra Stewed in Tomato Sauce with Lamb), *98,* 99
    Burrata Salad with Steak and Labneh Chimichurri, 74, *75*
    Caramelized Onion Ratatouille Tart, 39–40, *41*
    Chicken Shawarma Wraps, 136, *137,* 138
    Fattoush (Fried Bread Salad), 66, *67*
    Macarona Béchamel (Egyptian-Style Pasta Bake), 106, *107*
    Mediterranean Pasta Salad with Sumac Vinaigrette, *68,* 69
    Molokhia (Mallow Stew with Chicken), *96,* 97
    Pasta with Mussels and Shrimp, *108,* 109
    Roasted Tomato-Pepper Sauce, 39–40
    Saniyeh Kofta (Beef Patties in Tomato Sauce), *160,* 161
    Sfeeha (Open-Faced Meat and Pine Nut Pies), 213–14, *215*
    Shakshuka, 32, *33*
    Tahini Salad, *150,* 151
    Tomato Galette with Za'atar, *36,* 37–38
    Tomato Soup with Garlic-Bread Grilled Cheese, *90,* 91–92
    Warak Dawali (Stuffed Grape Leaves with Beef Ribs), *120–21,* 122–23
tortillas
    Bang Bang Shrimp Tacos with Cabbage Slaw, *126,* 127
    Triple-Stack Smash Burgers, 162, *163*

V

Vermicelli Rice, 110, *111*

W

Waffle Sliders, Buttermilk-Brined Chicken and, 144, *145*
walnuts
    Carrot Cake Loaf with Cream Cheese Frosting, 253–54, *255*
    French Toast Bake with Walnut Filling, *26,* 27
    Katayef (Fried Stuffed "Pancakes"), 237–38, *239*
    Warak Dawali (Stuffed Grape Leaves with Beef Ribs), *120–21,* 122–23
Whipped Cream, 18, 261–62
Wraps, Chicken Shawarma, 136, *137,* 138

Y

yogurt
    Khiyar bi Laban (Cucumber Yogurt Dip), *48,* 49
    Labneh Chimichurri, 74
    Mansaf (Rice with Lamb and Fermented Yogurt Sauce), 117, *118,* 119
    Shishbarak (Beef Dumplings in Yogurt Sauce), 93–94, *95*
    Yogurt Sauce, 93–94, 117
    See also jameed; laban; labneh

Z

za'atar
    about, 14
    Za'atar Manakeesh (Za'atar Flatbread), *173, 210,* 211–12
    Za'atar Soft Pretzels, 207–8, *209*
zucchini
    Caramelized Onion Ratatouille Tart, 39–40, *41*

Clarkson Potter/Publishers
An imprint of the Crown Publishing Group
A division of Penguin Random House LLC
1745 Broadway
New York, NY 10019
clarksonpotter.com
penguinrandomhouse.com

Copyright © 2026 by Mariam Daud
Photographs copyright © 2026
  by Jim Henkens
Penguin Random House values and supports copyright. Copyright fuels creativity, encourages diverse voices, promotes free speech, and creates a vibrant culture. Thank you for buying an authorized edition of this book and for complying with copyright laws by not reproducing, scanning, or distributing any part of it in any form without permission. You are supporting writers and allowing Penguin Random House to continue to publish books for every reader. Please note that no part of this book may be used or reproduced in any manner for the purpose of training artificial intelligence technologies or systems.

Clarkson Potter is a trademark and Potter with colophon is a registered trademark of Penguin Random House LLC.

Library of Congress Cataloging-in-Publication Data
Names: Daud, Mariam author | Timberlake, Emily author | Henkens, Jim photographer
Title: I sleep in my kitchen : comfort food recipes from my Palestinian American home / Mariam Daud with Emily Timberlake ; photographs by Jim Henkens.
Description: New York : Clarkson Potter/Publishers, [2026] | Includes index.
Identifiers: LCCN 2025011824 (print) | LCCN 2025011825 (ebook) | ISBN 9780593798416 hardcover | ISBN 9780593798423 ebook
Subjects: LCSH: Comfort food | LCGFT: Cookbooks
Classification: LCC TX714 .D3668 2026 (print) | LCC TX714 (ebook) | DDC 641.59/29274073—dc23/eng/20250327
LC record available at https://lccn.loc.gov/2025011824

LC ebook record available at https://lccn.loc.gov/2025011825
ISBN 978-0-593-79841-6
Ebook ISBN 978-0-593-79842-3

Editor: Susan Roxborough
Editorial assistant: Elaine Hennig
Art director & designer: Marysarah Quinn
Production designer: Christina Self
Production editors: Bridget Sweet and
  Ashley Pierce
Production manager: Philip Leung
Compositors: Merri Ann Morrell and
  Zoe Tokushige
Food stylist: Kate Buckens
Food stylist assistants:
  Jami Chiarella-Kopec and Alyse Dufour
Prop stylist: Jim Henkens
Recipe tester: Julie Bishop
Copyeditor: Dolores York
Proofreaders: Rachel Markowitz and
  Sasha Tropp
Indexer: Ken DellaPenta
Publicist: Jina Stanfill
Marketer: Emily Hotaling

Manufactured in China

10 9 8 7 6 5 4 3 2 1

First Edition

The authorized representative in the EU for product safety and compliance is Penguin Random House Ireland, Morrison Chambers, 32 Nassau Street, Dublin D02 YH68, Ireland, https://eu-contact.penguin.ie.